Lena Ashwell

Actress, Patriot, Pioneer

The Society for Theatre Research

The Society for Theatre Research, founded in 1948, brings together those interested in the history and technique of the British theatre, and it encourages research into these subjects. Lectures are held in London and members receive the Society's illustrated journal, *Theatre Notebook*, as well as (at least) one book annually. The Society makes substantial Research Awards and in 1998 instituted the Theatre Book Prize. New members are welcome. Details of subscription rates and a list of past publications appear on the Society's website – www.str.org.uk – or may be obtained by writing to: The Society for Theatre Research, PO Box 53971, London SW15 6UL.

Lena Ashwell

Actress, Patriot, Pioneer

Margaret Leask

University of Hertfordshire Press

The Society for Theatre Research

First published in Great Britain in 2012 by

University of Hertfordshire Press College Lane
Hatfield
Hertfordshire
AL10 9AB
UK

British Library Cataloguing in Publication Data
A catalogue record for this book is available from the British Library

ISBN 978-1-907396-64-9 hardback
ISBN 978-1-907396-65-6 paperback

Typesetting and design by Tetragon
Printed in Great Britain by Henry Ling Ltd

Dedicated, with gratitude, to the memory of two
strong women who gave me great support, encouragement and love:

Peggy Leask and June Quentin

Contents

Illustrations

Abbreviations

AFL	Actresses' Franchise League
ENSA	Entertainments National Service Association
LAP	Lena Ashwell Players
LCC	London County Council
MRA	Moral Re-Armament
NUWSS	National Union of Women's Suffrage Societies
WEC	Women's Emergency Corps
WSPU	Women's Social and Political Union
YMCA	Young Men's Christian Association

Acknowledgements

My research and preparation was made possible by support from a University of Sydney postgraduate scholarship and a research award from the Society for Theatre Research, for which I am most grateful. It was also made possible by the support of those who shared my enthusiasm for Ashwell's work, either by seeking out information while on their own journeys or by sharing their related research. My special thanks to UK editors Elizabeth Schafer and Marion O'Connor of the Society for Theatre Research; to colleagues Professors Jim Davis, Penny Gay and Kate Newey; to Jean Cooney in Sydney, whose experienced editor's eye provided focus; and to Larry Collins, Geoff Blackburn (Legion of Frontiersmen), Richard Fotheringham, Christopher Fry, Michael Kilgarriff and the late Godfrey Kenton. My thanks also to staff at the Theatre Museum, London, in the 1990s; the Imperial War Museum, London; the British Newspaper Library, Colindale; Mary Huth of the Rush Rhees collection, University of Rochester, USA, and Aline Faunce, Moral Re-Armament Archives, England. Special thanks to Lena's nephew, Henry Macnicol, who gave me an insight into her later life; to Karl Levett, whose packages of Ashwell postcards and programmes always arrived at the right moment to encourage me; and to Stuart Gough who made his personal collection of Ashwell memorabilia available. I was sustained by memories of colleagues who encouraged me in the pursuit of scholarship, the late Marysia Kreisler, Marlis Thiersch and Philip Parsons. Thanks are also due to my generous family and friends, including Jan Duncan, Brian D. Barnes, Mary Quinton, Christine Roberts and especially Brendon Lunney. I am grateful for his love, patience and quiet determination to help me complete this story.

Siegfried Sassoon, 'The Concert Party', is quoted by kind permission of the Estate of George Sassoon. John Masefield, *Sonnets of Good Cheer to the Lena Ashwell Players*, is quoted by kind permission of the Society of Authors, Literary Representative, Estate of John Masefield.

Preface

Lena Ashwell first entered my life in 1992 when I read Donald Spoto's biography of Laurence Olivier. Although amused to learn she had fired this great actor from her company in 1925, I was more intrigued by the brief mention of her wartime work and her 'Once a Week Players' touring London boroughs in the 1920s. At the time I was Principal Arts Officer for Westminster City Council, talking with many borough-based arts organisations, including the Theatre Museum in Covent Garden, about ways we could work together to engage local residents in arts activities.

I discovered the Theatre Museum's large, untouched collection of Lena Ashwell scrapbooks and my curiosity was aroused – I think by the sense that my career at this time had in some way had its origins in the work of this pioneer. When I realised she had pursued an active dialogue with local authorities to make theatre accessible to residents, I felt a great affinity with her, which grew to awe and respect as I uncovered more of her extraordinary life. Through the Society for Theatre Research, I found further scrapbooks in the Imperial War Museum and realised that not only was her story unusual; it needed to be told.

Although Lena Ashwell published four books including an autobiography in 1936, she provided little detail about or explanation of her work, particularly during the 1920s, choosing rather to convey her strong belief in the value of theatre in society and its importance in the life of the nation.

As my research took me on its journey, I met three people who had known her: actor Godfrey Kenton, playwright Christopher Fry and her nephew, Henry Macnicol. They agreed with G.B. Shaw's view, in his 1933 preface to Lillah McCarthy's *Myself and My Friends*, that she was one of those actresses 'who had awakeningly truthful minds as well as engaging personalities' and concurred that she was an inspiring, formidable woman, totally committed to the important role theatre and its practitioners can play in society.

Yet it seemed she had been largely neglected in theatre histories; even the Peter Lamda bust of her, inscribed 'Lena Ashwell OBE, Actress and Pioneer of a National Theatre', languished out of sight in the Chairman's unused bathroom at the National Theatre. I set about to acknowledge and celebrate her contribution.

My research journey began and ended in Westminster: not far from the Theatre Museum I found a tribute to her at the (now fire-damaged) Westminster Theatre, which eloquently summed up my appreciation of her. Dressing Room 2 was dedicated to 'Lena Ashwell: actress, patriot, pioneer'. This is her story...

1

Actress: early performing career

She was a queer-looking child, handsome, with a face suggesting all manner of possibilities. When she stood up to read the speech from *Richard II* she was nervous, but courageously stood her ground. She began slowly, and with a most 'fetching' voice, to *think* out the words. You saw her think them, heard her speak them. It was so different from the intelligent elocution, the good recitation, but bad impersonation of the others! 'A pathetic face, a passionate voice, a *brain*', I thought to myself. It must have been at this point that the girl flung away the book and began to act, in an undisciplined way … but with such true emotion, such intensity, that the tears came to my eyes … It was an easy victory for her. She was incomparably better than any one. 'She has to work', I wrote in my diary that day. 'Her life must be given to it, and then she will … achieve just as high as she works'. Lena Pocock was the girl's name, but she changed it to Lena Ashwell when she went on the stage.[1]

Thus wrote Ellen Terry, describing the occasion in 1890 when she distributed medals at the Royal Academy of Music while her daughter, Edith Craig, was studying there. Although she didn't know it at the time, Terry's response to Lena Pocock influenced not only this young woman's future, but also future directions in English theatre, which continue to resonate today.

Lena Margaret Pocock was born into a close-knit family of intrepid and determined individualists. Her father, Charles Ashwell Pocock, to whom she was devoted, was a Clerk in Holy Orders and a Royal Navy Commander.[2] His uncle was the sea artist Nicholas Pocock, and there was a seafaring tradition in the family. Lena was born on 28 September 1869[3] on board the *Wellesley* training ship, berthed on the river Tyne and 'commanded' by her father as a home for 'boys "unconvicted of crime" but under suspicion'.[4] Her mother, Sarah Stevens, was also from a seafaring family. Lena, always called Daisy by her family, was the second youngest of seven children, one of whom died when the family was in New Zealand. She was closest in age to Roger, Ethel and Hilda, while her eldest siblings, Francis and Rosalie, left home when she was very young.

Her early schooling was in England, but when she was eight, Lena's father's health broke down and the family moved to Canada, living in a wood cabin near

Brockville, overlooking the St Lawrence River. 'Here was great beauty; but also great discomfort. No water laid on in the house, no drainage, no gas nor electric light, no modern conveniences whatever.' But there was 'a river to swim in, a canoe to sail or paddle, a forest to wander in, and at home, plenty of hard work'.[5] An avid reader, she 'had a passion for words and their sound ... "illegitimate" had a swinging kind of sound, and I liked to sing it'.[6] She attended a government school, but her education was interrupted by expulsion (perhaps because of the above), illness and a family move to Toronto. In 1887 her mother, aged 48, died in a carriage accident. Lena and Hilda became boarders at Bishop Strachan's School for Young Ladies, where Lena established a pattern to be repeated throughout her life. Determined to work hard, she rose before dawn and matriculated at the University of Toronto fourteen months after her mother's death. Devastated by the loss of his wife, Pocock gave up his Treasury of God work and moved to Europe with his three daughters.

Lausanne, Switzerland, was their destination, where Lena attended a French-speaking school and studied music at the Conservatoire. She was preparing to be a governess, but on hearing her sing, an English cathedral organist recommended study at London's Royal Academy of Music. Lena's father disapproved and she 'was torn between my love for my father and my determination to follow my dream and be an opera-singer'.[7] Helped by a wealthy school friend, Belle Hevener, she managed to go to London and stayed with some unwelcoming cousins until, on her acceptance into the Academy, her father, Ethel and Hilda joined her and they set up house together.[8]

Encouraged by Ellen Terry, after graduation Lena Ashwell (taking her name from her father's family) set her sights on a theatrical rather than musical career. She described herself as 'passionate and terribly nervous', in which state she made her professional debut at the Islington Grand Theatre on 30 March 1891.[9] Her role, a servant girl in *The Pharisee*, was notable mainly because, overcome with stage fright, she left the stage without uttering the four words assigned to her.[10]

Between this small debacle and October 1900, Ashwell's career took a similar path to that of many aspiring actresses, although she was based mostly in London and did not learn her trade on tour or with provincial companies. She sought employment from producers such as Frederick Harrison at the Haymarket, who promised not to forget her, should an opportunity arise, after her appearance in *That Dreadful Doctor*.[11] Initially, she did not impress George Alexander and was disappointed when not given a promised role in London following a minor part (at Terry's intervention) in his 1892 touring production of *Lady Windermere's Fan*. As she describes in her autobiography,

> the control of the theatres was in the hands of the actor-managers, most of whom had been through every kind of experience ... in the provinces before they arrived in London. To be engaged in these managements was as if you were permitted to pay a visit to some distinguished house where your host was always present to see that all the fine traditions and accepted laws of hospitality

1.1 Ashwell (Martin) in *The Pharisee*, Islington Grand, 1891
(photographer unknown, author's collection)

were conformed to and where everyone knew his or her position in the general scheme of life.[12]

Ashwell was cast in some noteworthy productions (and some less memorable), making her West End debut in two curtain-raisers, *Through the Fire* and *Two in the Bush* (which preceded the comedy *Gloriana* at the Globe between November 1891 and early February 1892), where she conformed to the practice of playing a small role and understudying. She established friendships with Eva Moore and Gertrude Kingston, and was a member, briefly, of the ill-fated Amy Roselle's company, in *Man and Woman* at the Opera Comique in early 1893.[13] The *Referee* noticed that 'Miss Lena Ashwell, a refined and sympathetic young actress, made a big step forward', but Moore sensed Ashwell was unhappy.[14] It appeared Roselle did not like her and did nothing to make things easier for her. According to Moore, 'Lena, in those days, was a vague person, which was rather extraordinary, as she was a very fine athlete, and the two qualities did not seem to go together.'[15]

Through Terry, Ashwell met producer Joseph William Comyns Carr, who engaged her to understudy Winifred Emery in *Frou-Frou* at the Comedy in June 1893.[16] On signing a two-year contract with him, she had guaranteed work but little choice of roles. While understudying Rosamund in Grundy's *Sowing the Wind*, she played in the curtain-raiser, *In Strict Confidence*, and from mid-December to early February 1894 appeared in daily matinees of *The Piper of Hamelin*.[17] She had a minor break, replacing the indisposed Emery on the third night of *Frou-Frou* and impressing the company and the small audience who remained. Alice Comyns Carr 'plied her with *sal volatile* during the intervals, but I don't think she really needed the stimulant … the minute she was back on the stage all discouragement slipped from her. She was an artist, and enthusiasm and excitement … her best restoratives … Perhaps the greatest tribute … was Emery's rapid recovery … the understudy was only allowed to play the role for one night!'[18] Mrs Comyns Carr described her as 'the gentle girl with the good voice … very adaptable … and though very modest about her own capabilities, took her new vocation with the utmost seriousness, and studied almost night and day to fit herself for the part'.[19] Ashwell, aware of her inexperience, observed later that at the time she might not have been able to repeat the performance, which was 'inspired by a sudden opportunity … Acting is a curious, elusive art and difficult to really learn … it is necessary not only to make an effect but to know exactly in what way the effect has been produced.'[20]

She then played in Buchanan's comedy *Dick Sheridan* and, when *Frou-Frou* returned to the repertoire, played Pauline for the matinees, taking the lead when it went into the evening bill. Like many actresses, she had special admirers, including Reginald Golding Bright, who became an agent and apparently enjoyed talent spotting.[21] His letters, signed 'your sincere admirer' and commenting on her performances, provide insight into the strengths and weaknesses of her acting:

> Your only fault on Saturday was that you spoke your lines too quickly and consequently the audience lost much of what they should have heard … you will of course remedy this defect … the part is a poor one … after all it is only a question of time, for talent and genius such as yours cannot long remain hidden.[22]

Golding Bright sent stamps so that she could send him a telegram if called to play Gilberte Brigard in *Frou-Frou*. He could not resist giving her advice: 'Work it up deliberately until you reach "crescendo" (the meaning of which you as a musician will comprehend).'[23] On 9 April 1894, when Ashwell played Emery's role, Golding Bright wrote with praise tempered with criticism: 'you rose to a height which even I had scarcely expected of you … though I fear the strain rather told upon you'. She was very nervous, had taken some prompts and he felt she hurried her words on occasion. He wrote two notices of her performance, sent to the *Star* and the *Sun*, the latter publishing a shortened version, under his *nom de plume* Leonard Fanfare. He hoped her elevation to the top ranks would mean he could write more detailed praise of her work.

In May, Ashwell was 'lent' by Comyns Carr for a Royal Court revival of *Marriage*, in a season that ran into July. She enjoyed this play, which was reviewed enthusiastically by the *Daily Telegraph*: 'Miss Lena Ashwell is evidently one of the actresses of the future. She has a voice of infinite tenderness and variety, a voice full

MISS LENA ASHWELL

CHANCELLOR
PHOTO·BERLIN?

0270

1.2 Ashwell (Rosamund) in *Sowing the Wind*, Gaiety, 1894
(Chancellor Photo, author's collection)

of expression and charm, and an earnestness that is better than all. Miss Ashwell does not take up acting as a trivial pastime, but a serious undertaking. Her heart is in her work and she shows it in every line of it.'[24]

She returned to Comyns Carr's tour of *Sowing the Wind*, opening at Dublin's Gaiety in mid-August.

This popular love story involved the illegitimate daughter of a gentleman whose adopted son falls in love with her; the drama focused on the resolution of unknown identities and of her mother's reputation before they could be united. The Irish critics were generous and Ashwell was relieved, having struggled to take on the mantle of Rosamund from Evelyn Millard who had toured it with the grand old actor W.H. Vernon playing the father. As she gained confidence, Vernon 'drilled and drilled me in the path of virtue, but at last gave me up in despair and told me to play the part in my own way ... It was in Dublin that I was allowed to act the part without trying to be like someone else.'[25] Her instincts paid off for the *Irish Times*, whose reviewer found it difficult

to fully convey how truthfully Miss Ashwell interprets this difficult role. There are very many temptations to overdo it, to tear passion to tatters. But in all she does there is a perfect naturalness, and reserve of force, which, combined with her intelligent rendering of the dialogue, her tenderness of expression, pathos, youth, charming grace, sympathetic voice, and freshness, render her acting almost perfect. There was something intensely impressive and powerful in her delivery (it was too artistic to be called mere declamation) of the lines in defence of erring woman, or rather in denunciation of that society which shrinks from the stricken sister ... in [this] ... the gifted young actress was sublime.[26]

Others recognised her strong inclination to naturalism. An admirer, John Glover, wrote: 'I have never witnessed or listened to anything that stirred me so deeply, and made me experience so keen enjoyment as your natural acting ... I have no object but to express my deep obligation for a benefit conferred, and for the revelation afforded of what true acting is.'[27] She then experienced the rigours of provincial touring, described with wry humour in *Myself a Player*, and gave promotional interviews to local newspapers, declaring to the *Blackpool Gazette* that she was 'the property of Mr Carr for two years, wailing [*sic*] like a famous character in fiction, for something to turn up'.[28] When asked why she had gone on the stage, when originally educated to be a governess, she responded: 'I think you must see that I would not probably have been much of a success as a governess, and I do like to get on in whatever I take up.'[29]

In 1895 Ashwell had a rare opportunity: to play with Henry Irving and Ellen Terry in Comyns Carr's *King Arthur*, which opened at the Lyceum on 12 January. As the *Queen* pointed out: 'It is always promotion for a young actress to go to the Lyceum, even though it be to take a part smaller than some she may have already played.'[30] As Elaine (she was also Terry's understudy), Ashwell was noticed, attracting favourable reviews: 'The actress spoke from her heart, and when she was not speaking she was showing the workings of her soul; an art that few young actresses understand.'[31] She adored Irving, but her first experience in his company was not easy. Irving's grandson, Laurence, writes that Terry's 'undisguised partiality for Frank Cooper',[32] who was playing Mordred, set tongues wagging and Ashwell was distressed 'to discover an undercurrent of petty rivalries and conspiracies in what she looked upon as a hallowed temple of the art in which she was so earnest an initiate. One night, in the wings, Irving found her in tears. "Is there anything I can do?" he asked, adding by way of kindly consolation, "You know – we were born crying".'[33] Golding Bright wrote with unqualified praise of her performance as Elaine, but sensed tension in her demeanour. He felt she was overworking herself to an alarming extent:

> Ambition in a young actress is highly commendable; but do not, let me implore you, carry it too far. You have done well … since I saw you play the blind girl in *Young Mrs Winthorp* at an amateur entertainment, which first gave me a hint of hidden powers. Be advised and take a good rest … Nature will have its revenge for hours stolen from sleep and given to study, and a breakdown is to be dreaded.[34]

But for Ashwell, despite these tensions, it was a 'golden time … I was in the seventh heaven. The stage-door of the Lyceum is still the same, and I can't pass it now without a thrill.'[35] The run of *King Arthur* was an emotional time: Oscar Wilde was arrested and, she remembered, 'the atmosphere of London was horrible and cruel. His plays were so very brilliant, and I had seen him when I was in *Lady Windermere's Fan*, so I felt that he was a friend in desperate trouble.'[36] She also knew the Terry/Irving partnership was breaking up. There were a number of influences at work, but 'the great difficulty was that there were few leading parts for the mature woman. All the heroines were young. Heroes might be any age, but the older women were merely backgrounds to the drama.'[37] Later, Ashwell was deeply affected by the fact that Terry, for financial reasons, was giving 'one-night stand' American lecture tours at the age of 65: 'Almost all the histories are tragic of those who devote their lives to art.'[38]

King Arthur played for over 100 performances; from the playbills it appears Ashwell last played Elaine on 25 May, and was replaced by Annie Hughes. The Comedy Theatre playbill for *The Prude's Progress*, which opened on 22 May, includes Ashwell in the cast, so it seems she played both roles for a few days. Her 'Nelly Morris is a lovable creation, the loyalty and devotion of the self-sacrificing sister being sweetly delineated. Mr Arthur Playfair makes the egoism of Travers extremely amusing.'[39] Ashwell also played Sybil in *A Practical Joker*, a new comic curtain-raiser, which joined the bill in mid-June.[40] Golding Bright noted 'a growing tendency to allow your voice to be tinged with a note of sadness which is ever present and is apt to become just a wee bit monotonous'.[41] For the *St James's Gazette* she 'revealed a genuine sense of humour and particularly in the semi-tragic passages, played with a mock intensity that at once stamped her as a comedienne of approved ability'.[42] It was during this time she became engaged to Arthur Playfair and they married in late 1895.

No longer under contract to Comyns Carr, in September 1895 she played Blanche in *Her Advocate* at the Duke of York's. Now established in London, Ashwell obtained work on a regular basis without any further long-term contractual agreements. The reviews of *Her Advocate* were mostly positive, and she was grateful for the good notices, especially as

> the part is a difficult one to play, as, speaking as a woman, I think there are few of my sex who would have made such determined efforts to hold a recreant lover or to accept his lukewarm manifestation of second-hand affection. However, it is my duty to work on the lines laid down by the author, and the character certainly meets with appreciation, especially from the men ... I wonder why it is I am always being cast for the love-sick maidens?[43]

Already determined to pursue a career as a serious actress, Ashwell was keen to gain insight into human nature. Her research took her to a Sunday service at Wormwood Scrubs prison and she expressed interest in visiting Bethlem insane asylum, and in being present at a murder trial. She described her ideal part as one in which

> humour and pathos are combined ... when you hardly know whether to laugh or cry – that is, to me, true pathos ... But I am getting almost tired of pathetic parts: I want a change – something lighter ... [but] we [actresses] are always wanting to do the very thing we can't, and we are too apt to forget that the public are far better judges of our capabilities than we are ourselves.[44]

She was thinking about the roles she was best suited to and soon recognised that to have choice, she would have to take more control over her career.

Reviewing her next performance, in *The Fool of the Family* at the Duke of York's, G.B. Shaw was very critical of her vocal ability, wishing 'Miss Ashwell would remember there are short vowels in the dictionary as well as long vowels'.[45] During the summer of 1896 she played in a new comedy, *A Match-maker*, at the Shaftesbury and in *Carmen* at the Gaiety.[46] Neither play was considered worthwhile. 'With positive regret is the name of Miss Ashwell associated with this unfortunate production. Her refined, graceful and sympathetic work only serves to heighten the painfulness of Miss Nethersole's performance [as Carmen].'[47] Then, surprisingly, Irving cast her as Edward, Prince of Wales, in *Richard III*, opening at the Lyceum on 19 December. The *Daily Telegraph* considered her 'pathetic voice and utterances had a world of meaning in them',[48] but Shaw took issue with Irving's casting while recognising Ashwell's recent development as an actress worthy of notice:

1.3 Ashwell (Edward, Prince of Wales) in *Richard III*, Lyceum, 1896
(Theatre Museum, V&A Picture Library)

From the moment she came on the stage all serious historical illusion necessarily vanished ... Probably Sir Henry cast Miss Ashwell ... because he has not followed her career since she played Elaine in *King Arthur*. She was then weak, timid, subordinate, with an insignificant presence and a voice which contrasted as it was with Miss Terry's, could only be described – if one had the heart to do it – as a squall. Since then she has developed precipitously ... She now returns ... as an actress of mark, strong in womanly charm, and not in the least the sort of person whose sex is so little emphasized that it can be hidden by a doublet and hose ... Nothing can be more absurd than the spectacle of Sir Henry elaborately playing the uncle to his little nephew when he is obviously addressing a fine young woman in rational dress, who is very thoroughly her own mistress, and treads the boards with no little authority and assurance as one of the younger generation knocking vigorously at the door. Miss Ashwell makes short work of the sleepiness of the Lyceum, and though I take urgent exception to her latest technical theory ... that the bridge of the nose is the seat of facial expression, I admit she does all that can be done to reconcile us to the burlesque of her appearance in a part that should have been played by a boy.[49]

After the first performance Irving injured his leg and *Richard III* was not performed again until late February, by which time Ashwell had joined Playfair at Terry's Theatre in the curtain-raiser *Delicate Ground*. For a week she started her evening at Terry's, then after a quick costume change would rush to the Lyceum for *Richard III*.[50] In March 1897, Ashwell replaced Julia Arthur as Lady Anne: 'For the first time she was able to play a sustained scene with Irving and to appreciate the precision of movement and timing which characterized his method. In the wooing scene, he told her never to be beyond arm's length from him; when she discovered every time Lady Anne wavered in her hatred of Richard, a bell tolled off-stage, the whole mood and meaning of the scene became clear to her.'[51] Although Laurence Irving implies Arthur became difficult and left the company, from the playbills it appears she had a week away, during which Ashwell played Lady Anne, resuming her Prince Edward role on 27 March.

After the season finished in April, Ashwell was unemployed until mid-August, when she appeared in *The Sleeping Partner* at the Criterion. In this, she was thanked for toning down the 'roughness of the playwright' and suggesting 'the poetry … [in fact she] lifted the play, turned its artifice into nature … [She] is an actress who helps us to think that the English stage is not all trickery and stale affectation.'[52] More successful was Louis N. Parker's *The Vagabond King*, which after a week at the Camberwell Metropole transferred to the Royal Court in late October.[53] Her Stella was 'a conspicuous success – very few young actresses with so little effort could have thrown such energy and earnestness into a part that carried home conviction by the very simplicity of the methods employed, and we doubt if the by-play she associated with the character could have been more intelligently expressed'.[54] In December 1896 Ashwell took part in a matinee performance of *Sweet Nancy*, adapted from Rhoda Broughton's novel. She returned to the role (Barbara Gray) at the Avenue Theatre, in early 1898, with Annie Hughes and Martin Harvey. *The Sea Flower* with Playfair and Eva Moore followed at the Comedy, under Charles Hawtrey's management. The *Saturday Review* stated: 'If Miss Ashwell is not careful, she will play herself off the stage; it is dangerous to act too well under existing conditions.'[55] She had been noticed as a young actress likely to carry on the traditions of 'gifted predecessors' with 'conspicuous talent' by Clement Scott. He thought Ashwell, 'with her pathetic, pleading voice, and her thoughtful, poetic style, [is] bound to win when she gets the chance she so well deserves'.[56] When she played alongside Harvey again in *The Broad Road*, at Terry's in late 1898, she seized the opportunity to reveal 'she is an actress of a high order, who, if the dramatic authors can supply her with true plays, may make for herself a great name'.[57] The *Morning Leader* likened her, with enthusiastic admiration, to Mrs Kendal, but the play was not good and the season was short.[58]

From Christmas Eve, with Laurence Irving (playing an evil sorcerer), she experienced some hair-raising physical perils, including a dramatic escape from a burning house and walking a plank to obtain the globe, in *The Crystal Globe* by Sutton Vane. One night, the Princess Theatre scenery caught fire and her 'double' was injured. There were hazardous props including a dripping oil-lantern and 'locked' doors flying open at the wrong moment. Ashwell's problems were not only those encountered on stage: by this time her short marriage was in trouble. She had thought Playfair

> amusing and a good actor. His imitations of famous people were amazing, and I enjoyed the laughter and the fun. There was no sign of his weakness as he was on the 'water waggon', going through a period of reform. The reformation did not last ... after our marriage, I was plunged into the world of sordid horror and misery which drunkenness creates.[59]

Ashwell's beloved father was very ill and she 'was forced to go through a breaking up of all my illusions and day-dreams; to see life raw. My soul was stripped of its comfortable covering as I fought my way to freedom.'[60] She resumed the role of breadwinner for herself and her ailing sister Ethel. Her personal distress added intensity to her performance in *Grierson's Way*, in a series of experimental matinees at the Haymarket in February 1899. Cast member J.H. Barnes described the play as dealing with a 'somewhat gruesome subject ... a cripple whose nature and temperament were warped by his misfortune'. He doubted Ashwell 'ever played better than in this play ... I have seen and admired much of her work ... but with the advantage of the author's ideas, and in consultation with him, I think she never reached a higher plane in her art than in *Grierson's Way*'.[61] She was already demonstrating her ability to work with contemporary authors and to contribute to the development of new plays. For Max Beerbohm 'no actress could have intensified the character of Pamela's reality better than Miss Ashwell. She did not move gracefully on the stage or use her voice beautifully, but she played with intense sincerity and power. And in a realistic play of this kind grace of movement and diction are of less importance than sincerity and power.'[62] Initially she had refused the role, changing her mind on advice from Elizabeth Robins, and later acknowledged that this performance led to her being cast as Mrs Dane.[63]

Charles Pocock died in late February 1899 during rehearsals for Parker's *The Mayflower*. The playwright was very supportive of a bereft Ashwell, urging her 'not to lose courage. Don't lose faith ... remember that you are surrounded with friends ... We mean to see you get on ... Work is the thing.'[64] This may have emboldened her, in collaboration with actress Henrietta Watson, to what she herself later described as an 'impertinence' during the *Mayflower* tour which opened at the Metropole in early March, playing Manchester and Liverpool in late April:

> The play was in many ways most charming, and the public were intensely interested until the middle of the story, when it seemed to 'flop' and did not recover. We ... decided to reconstruct the script ... and changed the sequence of the scenes. The

1.4 Ashwell (Joan Mallory) in *The Mayflower*, Royal Court, 1899
(J. Beagles & Co, author's collection)

manager was more or less of an amateur ... I ... asked Parker to come and see the improvements we had made. There was a row! He was more than furious at the mess we had made and the play was restored. I was not only surprised and disappointed, but deeply injured that all our hard work and valuable efforts had not been properly appreciated.[65]

Unaware of this fiasco, the *Liverpool Daily Post* considered it 'a beautiful play of original interest' about the Pilgrim Fathers, with Ashwell giving 'a stirring portrayal'.[66] Putting a brave face on her personal distress, she told the *Manchester Evening News* that off stage she enjoyed fencing, sailing, canoeing, swimming and reading, particularly Shakespeare.[67]

Back in London, Ashwell went straight into rehearsals for the reopening, on 23 May, of the Royal Court. In R.C. Carton's *Wheels Within Wheels*, Mrs Onslow Bulmer, attempting to stop her sister-in-law Lady Curtois (Ashwell) from continuing to be unfaithful to her husband, becomes embroiled in the intrigue and comic compromising situations which she seeks to prevent.[68] 'Miss Ashwell is the most seductive, albeit the most heartless, of matrons that ever deceived both her husband and her lover.'[69] The production had a comparatively long run, playing until late September, by which time England was embarking on the Boer War, which would last until 1902.

Ashwell had not alienated Parker completely when she tampered with *The Mayflower*: she returned to the Lyceum and Comyns Carr in *Man and His Makers*, by Parker and Wilson Barrett. In a play of modern life dealing with heredity, Sylvia Faber (Ashwell) and John Radleigh (Wilson Barrett) are thwarted in their love by her father's belief that John is doomed by his antecedents. Sir Henry Faber is proved wrong and hope is restored, but not before the characters experience considerable pain. 'Miss Ashwell was the individual success of the evening. She took hold of the horrible subject and never once flinched, and her realisation of the truth and the real condition of her opium fiend sweetheart was a perfect piece of art.'[70] At the end of this season, feeling acutely her father's loss, she struggled to escape her disastrous marriage. Such was her despair, she might have taken to drink but for the support and advice of friends. Playfair's family dreaded scandal, and it was decided she and Ethel would stay with two former Playfair family governesses in Berlin until he left her house. They spent Christmas with these kindly people before returning to London, where once again she threw herself into work, knowing she had to deal with difficulties through her own determined will.

Work with American actor, Robert Taber, a friend in whom she confided both professionally and personally, came at the right time. His first, albeit unsuccessful, experiment in management, Laurence Irving's historical drama *Bonnie Dundee*, opened at the Adelphi in March 1900. 'Mr Taber and Miss Ashwell, both really good actors, can do nothing in such parts.'[71] *Westminster Gazette* reviewer Malcolm Watson, who had given Ashwell her first professional engagement, thought her 'very well chosen for the part, in which her reticent style, real power, and curious charm, enabled her to present an interesting and pathetic figure', but the play was irritatingly unsatisfactory.[72]

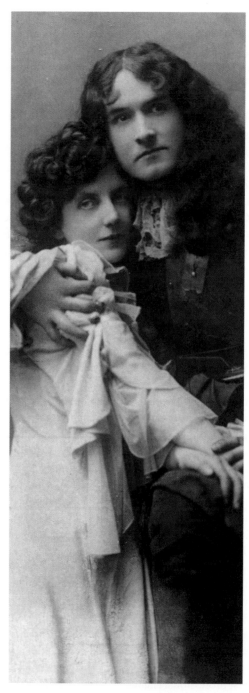

1.5 Ashwell (Lady Jean Cochrane) and Robert Taber (John Graham of Claverhouse)
in *Bonnie Dundee*, Adelphi, 1900
(Rotary Photo, courtesy of Stuart Gough)

They followed *Bonnie Dundee* with *Quo Vadis* on 5 May. It was preceded by controversy over the rights: there were two versions in America as well as Wilson Barrett's *The Sign Of The Cross*. The *St James's Gazette* thought that 'a more thankless role than that of Lygia could hardly be assigned to any actress, and although Miss Ashwell bravely struggled to breathe into it life and meaning, even her efforts could not accomplish the impossible.'[73] Max Beerbohm was compelled to ask: 'Why is her uncompromising intelligence, her almost uncouth sincerity, always chartered for melodrama, which it can but ruin, and so kept out of the serious plays which it would glorify?'[74] For the *Daily Mail*, 'the tawdry and irreverent could no further go; *Quo Vadis* ... is a compound of magnificent scenery and irreverence ... the note is insincerity ... the chief impression is that never before has religion been quite so cynically used ... to fill the shilling gallery and the half-crown pit ... the audience cheered itself hoarse in praise of play, playwright and players. There is possibly a numerous public for such pieces.'[75] But England was at war: *Quo Vadis* ran for four weeks, and Taber's management plans were put on hold.

Except for participating in summer charity events, Ashwell rested in June and July. By early August she was preparing for Beerbohm Tree's revival of his 1898 *Julius Caesar* at Her Majesty's. Tree was again playing Mark Antony and Ashwell replaced Evelyn Millard as Portia. While critics acknowledged her intelligence and sincerity, she was not an obvious choice for Shakespeare's women:

Ashwell's engagement for the part of Portia was an interesting experiment, and the note of sexual passion always evident in this sympathetic actress's voice lends much tenderness to the wife's appeal to Brutus. But it is impossible for so typically modern and neurotic a woman to suggest the classic dignity of a Roman matron, the quiet heroism of Cato's daughter – and there are not a few faults of mistaken emphasis and false intonation in [her] elocution.[76]

For Ashwell's subsequent, rare appearances in Shakespeare's plays, critics continued to observe that her style of acting was not in keeping with accepted interpretation of the time: 'I have already praised her way of seeming like a real person. In some parts – in any Shakespearean part – this very realism, this utter refusal to compromise with beauty, is rather a drawback.'[77] Ashwell left *Julius Caesar* during the season and was replaced by Eleanor Calhoun. Tree had called her in to help out in the short term, as she was already committed to an important next step: *Mrs Dane's Defence*.

'No one believed "Mrs Dane" would be a success. I was a dark horse, and Mrs Dane was a woman with a murky past, and heroines should have virtue on their side. Even if for a time circumstances were against them, they should be proved innocent in the end.'[78] The opening, at Wyndham's on 9 October 1900, of *Mrs Dane's Defence* by Henry Arthur Jones was a significant theatrical occasion. Mrs Dane (Ashwell) almost manages to convince a small community outside London that she is a respectable married woman, instead of Felicia Hindmarsh, whose affair with a married man led to his wife's suicide. As her past catches up with her,

Lionel, adopted son of esteemed judge Sir Daniel Carteret (Charles Wyndham), falls in love with her. Undoubtedly, this was Ashwell's most significant role to date. Her memory of that first night, written thirty-five years later, was vivid:

> The cross-examination scene took three-quarters of an hour to play before Sir Daniel realised Mrs Dane was lying. On the first night the long act held the audience breathless with interest, for they knew she was guilty yet wanted her to escape. The English love a hunt. Wyndham said the applause when the curtain fell was the most tremendous he had ever known. In my dressing-room I was singing with joy and thankfulness ... I was a success; I had got there. I was no longer one of the supports in a play but a star.[79]

The next day, the *Morning Post* described the gamut of emotions she conveyed:

> Her Mrs Dane was from first to last one of the finest, deepest and truest impersonations that one has ever seen. Her assumed indifference at the outset, her apparent sincerity, her growing wretchedness as she finds the ground she thought so firm slipping away from beneath her feet, her hysterical outbursts of defence and refusals to be further questioned and her piteous breakdown ... the whole performance was exquisite and an honour to the English stage.[80]

Playwright Christopher Fry recalled a colleague's comment on Ashwell's realism: apparently she had 'unconsciously' traced the carpet pattern with her foot as she tried not to make eye contact with her interrogator.[81] The *Standard* thought the play enabled her 'to realise the high expectations formed by those who long ago predicted that only opportunity was wanted to place her on an equality with the best of our emotional actresses'.[82] Dramatic critic William Archer, while acknowledging that Ashwell's talent had been recognised before this production, considered the reason for the current acclaim was because this was the best play she had appeared in, and it was important that criticism acknowledge the creator as well as the interpreter.[83]

Irene Vanbrugh later wrote: 'Mrs Dane was played with remarkable understanding by Lena Ashwell – an actress who held a unique position at that time. She was very sensitive with a quiet method and an interesting voice and expressive face. She depended entirely on her own way to gain her effects and undoubtedly succeeded in giving to any part she played a depth of feeling which she controlled with a technique of underplaying which was very successful.'[84] Ashwell acknowledged Wyndham's help in this successful 'underplaying'. He insisted her costumes be simple and innocent, despite Mrs Dane's past, and encouraged her to use quietness rather than hysteria to increase tension when her past is discovered. She had recognised immediately the great opportunity Jones had given her and resolved to take advantage of it. This was her first association with Wyndham and he was the personification of kindness. She appreciated and acknowledged his advice and sympathy.

1.6 Ashwell (Mrs Dane) in *Mrs Dane's Defence*, Wyndham's, 1900
(Biograph Studio, author's collection)

King Edward and the Prince of Wales attended performances and the theatre was full most nights. There were many picture postcards of Ashwell as Mrs Dane in circulation: she found it nerve-wracking that she was so widely recognised and was astonished that suddenly she was 'asked out to all sorts of parties by people whom I knew, and those I had never met or heard of: praise from everyone'.[85] The *Weekly Register* summed up her rise in status:

Perhaps the pleasantest event of the theatrical year has been the discovery of the general public of Miss Ashwell … a young artist who has for years beautified, not with her talent only, but with her whole-hearted and intelligent devotion, every bit of work entrusted to her. So her head will not turn when she is told she has reached the summit of her art, she has climbed too steadily to be deceived.[86]

At the end of the year *Mrs Dane's Defence* was a continuing success. The *Era* considered it to be 'the modern play of the year'.[87] All this came to an abrupt end with the death of Queen Victoria on 22 January 1901. Theatres closed as a mark of respect, and the play's run ended. Despite her ensuing unemployment, she was not idle: her rise in status as an actress led to greater participation in professional organisations and charitable events, and pressure to give opinions on matters pertaining to the stage and on wider social and political issues.[88] Frequently she shared the bill with distinguished colleagues, reciting poetry or performing dramatic monologues at benefit matinees for the Royal General Theatrical Fund, the Actors' Orphanage and other theatrical charities, as well as for children's and medical causes. She was also familiar as a long-standing member of the Theatrical Ladies' Guild, attending annual summer theatrical sports days and garden parties which brought members of the profession together.

After overcoming initial nervousness, Ashwell was engaged regularly as an after-dinner speaker, following her success at the O.P. (Old Playgoers) Club Ladies' Inaugural Dinner on 16 December 1900:

We of the stage are traditionally nervous on first nights, and as I gather that this is your first night, and as I have never before spoken in public off the stage; it is emphatically mine … In my heart of hearts I am not quite sure it is a woman's business to lecture – in public; it may spoil her method on other occasions. And method is a thing on which I set great store, because on the stage method is our greatest gift.[89]

Throughout her career Ashwell gave considerable thought to the nature of acting. Her approach was through realism and she recognised there were limits to the range of roles she and others could play: 'I would beg you to remember this when judging the efforts of those whose business it is to please and amuse you. An actor or an actress may not really be acting badly – he may be utterly unsuited by temperament to the particular task of the moment.'[90]

At the end of 1900 the stage was increasingly reflecting a war-changed world. Such change, as Ashwell was reaching her peak as an actress, provided her with opportunities to be noticed and heard. Cecil Raleigh, the O.P. Club's guest lecturer before Ashwell, had stated that the balance in the West End was shifting from melodrama and 'cheap clap-trappy and commercial drama' to more serious drama, influenced by developments in education and the work of Irving, Tree, Alexander and the Kendals.[91] These were her mentors, with whose management she was familiar as she considered her longer-term career. The Boer War was affecting everyone's lives and Ashwell was becoming active in the stage's role of showing itself

once more to be in close touch with the national life … there has been a marked change in the character and quality of the plays produced … the art of dramatic writing cannot be sacrificed to conventional prudery. And in all of the plays – problem and otherwise … we noticed a great increase in …'humanity' … the mere fact of a subject being 'painful' will not prevent its being used as the theme of a very successful play. The idea people only go to theatre to be made to laugh has been completely exploded by the continued success of some of the saddest stories imaginable … acted with deep, convincing earnestness. For one of the most remarkable phenomena is the number of young artists of serious aims who have arisen, and … the facility with which those actors whose reputations were made in thinner and lighter work have adapted themselves to the modern demand of purposeful and problematic plays. Who, when Mr Wyndham was best known to fame as the much-engaged Bob Sackett,[92] could have prophesied he would develop into the most rational of *raisonneurs* and the stern unbending judge of *Mrs Dane's Defence*? And who could have foretold the sort of successes made … by actresses like Miss Vanbrugh and Miss Ashwell? … the year … has been commendably free from effeminate triflings and unedifying follies … to sum up…[a] year for the stage, as for the nation … of heart. It has been a time of energy and emotion.[93]

Ashwell's next West End appearance was a year and a day after the opening of *Mrs Dane's Defence*. This was a hard act to follow, but Isaac Henderson's *The Mummy and the Humming Bird*, which re-opened Wyndham's for the 1901 autumn season, did reasonably well.[94] Ashwell played the wife of a scientist (Wyndham), who falls under the spell of the Humming Bird (Taber). The *Era* found it

curious, touching two extremes – that of domestic melodrama and that of analytical and ironic comedy … the humiliation of the husband is his just punishment for not having looked after his wife better … no actor could have borne himself with more dignity [than Wyndham]. Miss Ashwell … evidently unnerved by the warmth and fervour of the reception … on her first entry, played Lady Lumley with that nervous intensity which she employs with so much effect; and, as an exhibition of feminine fire and 'temper', her speech and exit in the second act were irreproachable.[95]

Country Life considered she gave to her character 'that intense but wonderfully restrained emotionalism, that astonishing naturalness and reality, that suggestion of height and depth in modern passion, masked by modern impassivity, for which she is always remarkable'.[96] Before Christmas this production made brief forays to Brighton and Birmingham, and returned to London on 6 January 1902. The first act of the play was Wyndham's contribution to the annual General Theatrical Fund matinee at Drury Lane. After *The Mummy and the Humming Bird*, Ashwell stepped in at short notice (and the waiving of her fee) for ten days to help Mrs Tree, who was ill at the beginning of her management season at Wyndham's.[97] In *Caesar's Wife*, a translation of *L'Enigme* by Paul Hervieu, which was one of three short plays opening on 1 March, Ashwell played Leonore, 'a guilty wife' caught out after an affair with a young man staying at her husband's chateau. After defending her innocence, she confesses her guilt and is made to suffer remorse. 'Ashwell's depiction of bitter indignation was extremely keen and powerful.'[98]

Early in her career Ashwell recognised the need to diversify and to work on her vocal presentation, especially given criticism of her limitations as a young actress. This, coupled with her love of poetry and the English language, led her to develop and perform regular recital programmes. She considered poetry to be something which 'lifts ugly actions out of the sordid because it recognises the torture and anguish of the spirit'.[99] At the Royal Academy of Music she formed a long-standing partnership and friendship with pianist/composer Stanley Hawley.

> At the time, she had a light soprano speaking voice, but with help from Comyns Carr and Hawley, added an octave to the lower register, and this extra octave gave her the instrument required for emotional roles. As Miss Ashwell intoned a dramatic passage, Hawley played chords on the piano, until the actress began to respond to the harmonies and realise how thin her stage voice really was. The final discovery was that the voice which belonged to her emotional self was fully an octave lower.[100]

Ashwell was grateful for Hawley's contribution: later he set Elizabethan love lyrics and other poems to music which she described as

> lovely barred music through which the poem was increased in beauty; we used to imagine that somewhat in this way the old Troubadours spoke to their harps. It was hard work, but the result, entirely due to the help that Stanley gave me, has been that my 'squall'[101] was changed into a controlled instrument ... It is not only pronunciation and enunciation and the other technicalities so often mentioned; it is music that can make an instrument if we can feel it and work with it. All poetry is a song.[102]

Over the years they gave many recitals, some for charity events, others, such as the matinee recital on 1 May 1902 at the Bechstein (now Wigmore) Hall with vocalist

Thomas Meux, organised as commercial ventures. Not everyone appreciated their style. 'Miss Ashwell's beautiful voice and pathetic intensity were appreciated to the full by a large and fashionable audience,' wrote the *Era* on 3 May, 'but we must confess our dislike to a musical accompaniment played in a manner that drowns even one single word of the text. Mr Hawley's music is often charming and generally appropriate; but as it is illustrative, the composer, who is also the executant, should know it must be kept well under the voice.' The duo performed frequently with Royal Academy of Music colleagues, and their contacts and knowledge of the repertoire, to be put to good use later at the Kingsway and for the Concert Parties during the First World War, developed at this time. Recognised as a successful, committed graduate of the Academy, Ashwell was made a Fellow in 1901.

In early 1902 she was anticipating a new play written for her by Jones. She would not reveal too much about the play, although she was very eager to play the role. She was preparing for a revival of Jones' *Mrs Dane's Defence* with Wyndham, which opened on 5 June. Although this was only a short season, Ashwell remained in the public eye, reciting at a reception during Sarah Bernhardt's London season on 23 June. The *World of Dress* interviewed Ashwell, claiming 'important' insights into her stage dress. She sought realism rather than fashion. To avoid the obvious she had decided to wear blue rather than white for Mrs Dane's confession scene, as she did not want the audience to be given any early indication as to what would happen. She never wore green on stage and considered hats and gloves hampered her.[103] Dress was an important key to any character and she always thought out her own costumes. With *Mrs Dane's Defence* she had demonstrated an innate sense of exactly how far she could break theatrical conventions (including costume) without losing the respect of her audience and colleagues. She was growing in confidence on and off the stage.

Jones read *Chance, The Idol* to G.B. and Charlotte Shaw in the summer of 1902. The Shaws were unable, or perhaps unwilling, to attend the Wyndham's opening on 9 September. Shaw wrote: 'the theatre only exasperates me when I care about the play. I have almost come to the conclusion that actual performance is only advisable as the last resource of a thoroughly undramatic bungle ... However, you are not so badly off as you might easily be elsewhere. Lena is a squawker; but she is a squawker of genius.'[104] For some reviewers, the theme of the play – compulsive gambling as an illness – could only incite pity, not dramatic sympathy, and worked against its success, particularly as the inner processes of the gambler were not explored. Ellen Farndon (Ashwell) gambles to pay debts of her former lover Alan, with whom she has a child and who has abandoned her. Since the Examiner of Plays could only pass the play if the gambler loses, for the *Times* it appeared 'too predictable'.[105] The *Era* reported that 'Ashwell ... [who] has established a "speciality" in the depiction of neurotic, hyper-sensitive and morbid young females, was quite in her element ... kept the audience in constant anticipation of an emotional outpouring on the part of the erratic and excitable erring one ... [she] never faltered, flagged or failed'.[106] The *Daily Mail*, disappointed in the play, thought Ashwell's 'power of conveying conviction, of earnestness and genuine feeling, is not surpassed by any actress on the English stage'.[107] She was so convincing at one performance that someone called out to Alan (W. Graham Browne), 'You dirty cad! Marry her!'[108] *Chance, the Idol* ran until late October, during which month Ashwell, who was absent through illness for some performances, had begun rehearsals for Emilia, in *Othello*.

Forbes Robertson's *Othello*, with Gertrude Elliott as Desdemona and Taber as Iago, opened on 15 December 1902 at the Lyric. *Country Life* considered that the casting of Ashwell as Emilia struck one 'as having most interesting possibilities', and it was she who received the best reviews.[109] 'She is earnest and sincere; her denunciation of her husband; her wrath against Othello, and bitter contempt for his blindness were expressed with real vigour and truth … quite in the spirit of the tragedy.'[110] Summing up the 1902 theatrical year, the *Era* declared that

> a noticeable feature of the year has been the poor figure which has been cut by our old established playwrights. Mr H.A. Jones' only contributions have been *The Princess's Nose* and *Chance, the Idol*, which was only saved from immediate failure by the emotional acting of Miss Ashwell … Forbes Robertson's revival of *Othello* was, perhaps, an error of judgement as far as he himself was concerned [he lacked the physique, vigour and voice]: but as an experiment in temperament it was interesting and Miss Ashwell's Emilia was certainly superb.[111]

Ashwell was engaged to play in Tolstoy's *Resurrection* with Tree in the spring of 1903, to be followed by *Dante* with Irving at Drury Lane. It was the first time Tolstoy's work would be seen on the London stage and there was considerable interest in the Russianness of the story, the music and the visual effects. Despite the degradation portrayed, it was considered to be a very moral play. The *Anglo-Russian* featured it in great detail over three months, looking at the production's background, publishing cast pictures and reprinting highlights from press reviews.[112] *Resurrection* opened at His Majesty's on 17 February 1903, with Tree as Prince Dmitry and Ashwell as Katusha. '[She] showed herself to be our greatest emotional actress, for, taken as a whole, I do not see anyone else upon the stage at the present moment who could have rendered those varying moods of that wild soul with so faithful an intensity.'[113] Apparently the play did not bear much resemblance to the novel, but many aspects were effective and the acting and scenic effects were clever.[114] Again Ashwell was featured on postcards depicting scenes from the play. Katusha gave her the opportunity to demonstrate

> the extensive boundaries of her art. We know her as the falsehearted butterfly of society, with padded movements and purring, lying tongue, such … as she played in *Wheels within Wheels*. We have seen her display great power in 'strong' scenes … in *Othello*, but never before have we seen her as an abandoned, drunken *'fille de joie'*. Voice, gestures, and a swinging dissolute stride, all contributed to a clever piece of character-acting. Unfortunately, the attempt to adapt Tolstoi has resulted in a melodramatic compromise with an unsatisfactory ending, thus

1.7 Ashwell (Katusha) in her peasant's
costume for Act I, *Resurrection*,
His Majesty's, 1903
(Raphael Tuck, author's collection)

1.8 Ashwell (Katusha) in *Resurrection*,
His Majesty's, 1903
(Raphael Tuck, author's collection)

robbing the situation in which Maslova [Katusha] finds herself of much of its
original intensity.[115]

Ashwell relished her role, but did not find Tree inspiring to work with: 'He was
difficult to act with for his emotion never felt sincere, and he was always liable to
clown.' He may well have robbed her of some of that intensity: during the first-act
love scene he would amuse himself by unfastening the hooks at the back of her
peasant's dress and the only deterrent was for her to be sewn into the costume.
As she observed, his failure in memorising meant he seldom really knew his part.
Compared to her experiences with Irving and Wyndham, she felt Tree 'had never
been through the mill and remained in many ways an amateur'.[116]

In early March, the *World* published an interview with Ashwell at home at Port-man Mansions, Baker Street. She was 'about medium height, with a grave face and a quiet, serious, rather nervous manner', making it hard for the interviewer to imagine how she was capable of 'such versatility'. She was 'pre-eminently English-looking and English-mannered', prompting praise for her ability to give such a thrilling depiction of 'the agony, the terror, and the shame of a life such as that of Maslova, the poor outcast of Russian society'.[117] Now well into rehearsals for *Dante*, Ashwell presided at a Playgoers' Club meeting in early April. Journalist Foster Fraser lectured on 'The Stage Siberia and the Real'. Introducing him, Ashwell, perhaps nervous that he would be critical, reminded him that '*Resurrection* described life in Russia … thirty years ago, and that probably great changes had taken place since then'.[118] Fraser illustrated his talk with lantern slides of Russian scenes and Siberian prisons. Slavonic songs and the Russian national anthem were sung by the Russian Choir, which also sang before performances.

Ashwell and Tree were pleased that *Resurrection* was one of three plays in 1903 to prompt the claim that 'so far from being moribund, modern English drama has only just begun to live … No one can say Tolstoy's work is not "of the time". It is the twentieth century in excelsis – with its deep melancholy, its wide sensitive sympathies, and its relentless questioning.'[119]

At this time Ashwell's attention was drawn to increased activity in the women's movement. On the same page as its review of *Resurrection*, the *Anglo-Russian* published 'Woman Among the Nations', describing women's suffrage in Europe, the USA, Australia, Argentina, and India and Ashwell noted, as a new season of Parliament approached, the journal's urging:

At the commencement of this new session the women of Great Britain and Ireland should be on the alert and press forward their just claim for full political repre-sentation on an equality with men. If the majority of women studied economic questions beyond their own little domain of domestic expenditure, they would realise the growing necessity for the services of capable efficient women in every department of the State.[120]

Irving's *Dante* was eagerly anticipated. Elaborate preparations were underway at Drury Lane: the scenery was painted by three French artists who worked on it for months, and Xavier Leroux composed special incidental music. For the forty-nine speaking roles and many extras there were frequent rehearsals, despite uncertainty about the opening date, postponed from 23 April as Irving was unwell. Ashwell left *Resurrection* on 22 April and was replaced by Lily Brayton for its remaining month. With the first night announced for 30 April, she joined the *Dante* com-pany for two rehearsals a day. The playwrights, although 'Dante was a poet rather than a man of action …[had] made [him] an active reformer, a man ahead of his time, and distinctly modern in his views and sentiments.' They had decided to personify in him a lover of liberty, a fierce hater of persecution, of oppression and of clerical domination … not the historical Dante; but the moral Dante … Irving's Dante was a creation of surpassing power, impressive interest, and grand and noble elevation … the part is not a very strong one; it was the art of impersonation employed by the actor that made his performance such a success. Miss Ashwell depicted the anguish of Pia del Tolomei and the impulsive energy of Gemma with all the striking talent which has made her so popular; but neither role exacted to the very utmost her remarkable abilities.[121]

After 82 performances, *Dante* closed on 18 July. A few days before, Ashwell appeared in the Casket and Trial scenes of *The Merchant of Venice*, with Irving and Terry, for an Actors' Association benefit matinee at Drury Lane which raised over £1,000.[122] During a few months' break, at the actor John Billington's farewell testimonial at the Haymarket on 6 October, Ashwell played an old woman in the premiere of *The Monkey's Paw*.[123] This dark, dramatically intense little tale about the power of a monkey's paw to grant wishes, was adapted by Louis Parker from W.W. Jacobs' story. Ashwell, who performed it with Cyril Maude and Sydney Valentine, revived the play in later years as a curtain-raiser.[124]

On 10 October, after a regional tour, the 65-year-old Irving embarked on a gruelling twelve-month American tour, with Nora Lancaster replacing Ashwell. *Dante* was not successful, and Irving abandoned this vast production early on. In London the memory lingered, featuring prominently in the *Era*'s seasonal summing up: 'The fact that, despite the difficulty of making a dramatic play out of the life of the Italian poet, Sir Henry was able to draw thousands to this immense theatre proves the marvellous spell exercised by his genius and his personality.' Tree's *Resurrection* was also praised as a 'bold and fearless enterprise … the performances of himself and Miss Ashwell made an indelible impression on all who saw them. By the presentation of this great work – thrilling, impressive, and human – Mr Tree conferred a benefit upon London playgoers and proved that courage is the best policy in theatrical management.'[125]

At the same time as she was cast in her next West End production, Ashwell was the guest speaker, on 7 November, for the New Vagabonds' Club. Voicing her growing awareness of issues that were concerning her, but not on completely safe ground, she observed theatre to be in a period of transition and declared that 'only a few years ago theatres were much larger and much more dimly lighted'. The *Era* took issue with this, wanting 'to know the names of the "much larger" theatres to which Miss Ashwell alludes. We fancy their size is as imaginary as the "general feeling of dissatisfaction with plays and actors" which she has discovered.' She had observed, in relation to her own acting, that better theatre lighting brought the stage and audience into a much closer relationship, making it possible to present plays of a more delicate and real nature. She hoped for 'a municipal theatre, built by the County Council on the banks of the Serpentine' and spoke of the difficulties for young women seeking theatre work. Mr Tree's proposed school of acting, to improve standards and to provide early opportunity for talent to be developed or another career sought, was an important initiative.[126] 'It seems to me ... we would all prefer a little more technique and a little less of that vague thing called personality that irritates us as much oftener than it satisfies us. If an actor gets swamped by technique, it is simply a proof that his personality is ultimately not strong enough to rise above it.'[127]

Ashwell was soon preoccupied with issues such as the status and conditions of employment for theatrical workers: although she reached a high position in her profession relatively quickly, she knew the struggle for financial independence. In 1900 actresses' salaries were generally between £1 and £3 a week. With no union fighting for a basic minimum wage, managers could exploit an overpopulated profession. Already her vision for the future of theatre was much wider than just an ambition to develop as an actress. Hearing more about German municipal theatres, she was interested in their operation and funding from local and state government and endowments from the wealthy. It was a difficult concept for the English to grasp. Many could not envisage County Councils working with theatre managers and assumed ratepayers would be reluctant to contribute. Since 1900 the London County Council (LCC) had been proactive in the implementation of regulations for theatre licensing and safety and the *Era* considered the Theatres and Music Halls' Committee unsympathetic to managers in requiring expensive safety upgrades to venues.[128] In September 1902 the Lord Chamberlain, previously a buffer between theatre managers and the LCC, announced licences would not be granted for stage plays unless managers produced 'a representation in writing from the LCC that [their] theatre was "properly safe" from the danger of fire, or the decision of an arbitrator to that effect, appointed in the manner provided in the Act of 1878'.[129] Irving had spent many thousands getting the Lyceum to regulation standard, and new owner Comyns Carr now had to undertake £20,000 of further work. Other managers were similarly affected and the *Era* urged managers to unite against this, otherwise unsympathetic, inexperienced and changing councillors and officers would make their lives a misery.

At the same time, assumptions were being made that publicly funded theatre must, by definition, be dull and worthy. Linked with the municipal theatre idea was that of a national theatre, along the lines of the Comédie-Française in Paris. This was not embraced wholeheartedly:

Like the prevailing epidemic of smallpox, the 'movement' in favour of an English National Theatre must, we suppose, 'run its course'. There is no vaccinatory protection possible against the contagion of misguided enthusiasm; and the advocacy of a National Theatre must occupy its allotted period before it is replaced by some fresh proposal for the elevation and improvement of the British drama ... An establishment like the Comédie-Française cannot be inaugurated by the raising of a subscription or even the passing of a Parliamentary Bill. It must be the growth of years of national life and development ... subsidy should be the crown of the edifice, not its foundation stone ... the very essence of a National Theatre is that it shall be the expression of national aspiration.[130]

It appeared national theatre agitators were grumblers who sat at home and would not support it anyway. 'The result would be that the National Theatre would become the home of conscientious failure. Its name would be a synonym for respectable dullness; and it would share with the pulpit an unenviable reputation for the cure of insomnia.'[131]

The London casting of Tree's leading actress for *The Darling of the Gods*, which had premiered in New York in late 1902, created much discussion. Cora Urquhart Brown-Potter was a strong possibility, until 'it was finally decided the Tosca part should be offered to the heroine of *Resurrection* – to wit, the brilliant ... Lena Ashwell ... [and it is] likely to be another sensational success for [her]'.[132] The production opened at His Majesty's on 28 December 1903 and was still drawing crowded houses after its hundredth performance in late March 1904. Yo-San (Ashwell), Prince of Tosan's daughter, and Kara (Basil Gill), the outlaw band leader sought by Minister of State, Zakkuri (Tree), are in love. Yo-San conceals Kara, deceiving the Minister as to his whereabouts, but her action is eventually discovered by her father, who betrays Kara. He is tortured and Yo-San, to save his life, reveals the gang's hideout. They are destroyed, Kara commits suicide and Yo-San, condemned to purgatory for a thousand years, commits suicide. In the final scene she ascends to heaven to join her beloved Kara.

Critics were divided on Ashwell's contribution. *Black & White Magazine* felt 'cold print cannot convey an adequate idea of her admirable work in a distinctly difficult part. Whatever pathos the piece possesses is wholly in her hands, and [she] rises above the part to heights of womanhood where, perhaps, no other actress today could follow her',[133] whereas *Queen* was convinced her 'picture of this poor little product of the land of the chrysanthemum is thoroughly Western in treatment [and like] a Japanese vase made in Birmingham'.[134] Just as *Resurrection* had provoked interest in and discussion about the veracity of the portrayal of things Russian, *The Darling of the Gods* did the same for things Japanese. The *Daily Mirror* had been 'informed' by Ashwell's 'writer brother', Roger Pocock, that 'his sister's make-up and dress were accurate copies from those of the sister of Japanese artist and "Samuri", Mr Markimo, who had carefully superintended every detail of the production'.[135] Much of the debate was related to developing realism in the theatre as authenticity was sought in design as well as acting. *Yo-San's Song*, sung by Ashwell in Acts III and IV – 'There are fleet loves and sweet loves and loves of all season and loves without reason and great loves like mine when the heart aches, the heart breaks, that vows can be slighted, when love has been plighted, red roses can never make wine'[136] – is more authentically American musical than anything Japanese.

In March, during the run of *The Darling of the Gods*, Ashwell was devastated to learn of Robert Taber's death in America aged 38. She was planning to go into management with him: their first production was to have been *Leah Kleschna*. If successful, they intended to present productions in England and America. Taber had encouraged her to believe in her work, saying she 'might do much. He was a very brilliant actor and taught me many of my parts, showing me line by line the effects that could be made, so that the technical side of the art was revealed to me.'[137] In 1903 they had worked with playwright C.S. McLellan on *Leah Kleschna*, but 'our dreams were smashed like an egg-shell ... when it was found he had advanced tuberculosis of the throat and could never act again ... One of those very rare souls; one of the very brave, the very true.'[138] Besides grief, Taber's death left Ashwell with many problems. Had he lived, they might have created a stage partnership which would have given her wider recognition. As it was, she was never associated with any leading actor as his leading lady – an association of which there were many examples at the time – except on a play-by-play basis. She had reached a critical point in her career. While still a supporter of the system of the actor-manager, there were disadvantages:

When I had been ill and unable to play the public had asked for their money to be returned. There was nothing ungenerous or unreasonable in the fact that the actor-manager needed to keep the attention of the public on himself ... For that reason – or perhaps at the moment there were no criminals ready for me to act – I bought a French play, re-named *Marguerite*, and took the plunge into management alone ... I was afraid of London and went on tour, thinking I should gain the experience I needed cheaper, as all touring is on sharing terms. There I made a mistake as I was known and loved by many in London but was practically unknown in the provinces.[139]

Notes

1   E. Terry, *The Story of My Life* (London, 1908), 247–8.
2   The Pocock family memorial plaque, Holy Trinity Church, Cookham, England. Father: Charles Ashwell Boteler Pocock (1829–99). Mother: Sarah Margaret Stevens (Cole on *her* mother's side, 1839–87). Of her siblings, Lena was closest in age to Henry Roger (1865–1941), Ethel Georgiana (1867–1924) and Hilda Frances (1871–1964). Her eldest brother Francis Agnew (born 1858) lived in America. Her eldest sister Rosalie (1860–1941) married Canadian civil engineer Samuel Keefer.
3   For years Lena pretended that she was younger than Hilda, so most obituaries give her year of birth as 1872.
4   L. Ashwell, *Myself a Player* (London, 1936), 13.
5   *Ibid.*, 25.
6   *Ibid.*, 27.
7   *Ibid.*, 44.
8   Ethel studied at the Slade School of Art and Hilda trained at Alexandra Hospital for children. Before graduating from the Academy, Ashwell had recited *Bergliot*, a dramatic poem with orchestral accompaniment by Grieg, at a public concert. This successful rendition was repeated at a Sir Henry Wood Promenade Concert in 1891 when she was a member of the Greek Church Choir, Bayswater, earning a small salary and enjoying 'sitting up in the gallery singing the unaccompanied chants' (*ibid.*, 56).
9   *Ibid.*, 55.
10 *The Pharisee*, by Malcolm Watson and Mrs (Ellen) Lancaster-Wallis, ran for a two-week Easter holiday season.
11 Letter from Harrison to Ashwell, 17 June 1891 (Lena Ashwell Papers, Department of Rare Books, Special Collections and Preservation, University of Rochester, Rochester N.Y.). *That Dreadful Doctor* was a comedietta by Charles Young given in a special matinee at the Opera Comique in July 1891, on the same bill as Dan Leno, Vesta Tilley and Arthur Playfair. This play also toured to Cambridge and Oxford. It was through Malcolm Watson that Ashwell was engaged by Arthur Bourchier for this production. Her nervousness prompted his advice, 'You are a very NICE little girl, but take my advice and give it up' (Ashwell, *Myself a Player*, 58). This statement later became a long-running shared joke between Ashwell and Bourchier.
12 Ashwell, *Myself a Player*, 59.
13 Amy Roselle (1852–95) and husband Arthur Dacre (1851–95) were English comic actors. They died in Australia in a murder-suicide following an unsuccessful, financially disastrous nine-month tour.
14 *Referee*, 26 March 1893.
15 E. Moore, *Exits and Entrances* (London, 1923), 35.
16 Winifred Emery (1862–1924), born into a theatrical family, made her debut aged 8, and became one of the most versatile and popular actresses of her time. She premiered *Lady Windermere's Fan* (1892) and *The Little Minister* (1897). She married actor Cyril Maude. *Oxford Companion to the Theatre*, ed. P. Hartnoll (Oxford, 1983), 247.
17 Sydney Grundy (1848–1914), playwright, journalist and critic, initiated the private or club performance in 1882 to beat the censorship.
18 Mrs (Alice) Comyns Carr, *Mrs J. Comyns Carr's Reminiscences*, ed. Eve Adam (London, 1926), 229.
19 *Ibid.*
20 Ashwell, *Myself a Player*, 62.

21 Golding Bright became a theatrical agent and author representative; by the early 1920s he was well-known, shrewd, popular but lazy, apparently sleeping through many first nights. 'He was a small, quiet, very well dressed man, of considerable charm, public school and Oxford ... He always wore white kid gloves at first nights, which he never removed.' B. Mantle and G.P. Sherwood, *The Footlights Flickered*, (London, 1975), 30.

22 Letter, 20 March 1894 (Lena Ashwell Papers, Department of Rare Books, Special Collections and Preservation, University of Rochester, Rochester, N.Y.).

23 Letter, 3 April 1894 (Lena Ashwell Papers, Department of Rare Books, Special Collections and Preservation, University of Rochester, Rochester, N.Y.).

24 *Daily Telegraph*, 18 May 1894.

25 Ashwell, *Myself a Player*, 64.

26 *Irish Times*, 14 August 1894.

27 Letter from Glover to Ashwell, 14 August 1894 (Lena Ashwell Papers, Department of Rare Books, Special Collections and Preservation, University of Rochester, Rochester, N.Y.).

28 *Blackpool Gazette*, 28 September 1894.

29 *Topical Times*, 6 October 1894.

30 *Queen*, 19 January 1895.

31 *Daily Telegraph*, 13 January 1895.

32 L. Irving, *Henry Irving: The Actor and His World* (London, 1951), 595. Laurence was a friend of Ashwell's, and presumably this is an anecdote told directly to him.

33 *Ibid.*

34 Letter from Golding Bright to Ashwell, 16 January 1895 (Lena Ashwell Papers, Department of Rare Books, Special Collections and Preservation, University of Rochester, Rochester, N.Y.).

35 Ashwell, *Myself a Player*, 79.

36 *Ibid.*, 80.

37 *Ibid.*, 81.

38 *Ibid.*, 82.

39 *Era*, 29 May 1895.

40 Ashwell claimed 'a severe indisposition compelled me to leave the cast after the first month' (*Illustrated Sporting and Dramatic News*, 2 November 1895), but the extant playbills indicate she was still in the cast in mid-July and until September when replaced by Doris Templeton.

41 Letter from Golding Bright to Ashwell, 23 May 1895 (Lena Ashwell Papers, Department of Rare Books, Special Collections and Preservation, University of Rochester, Rochester, N.Y.).

42 *St James's Gazette*, 17 June 1895.

43 *Illustrated Sporting and Dramatic News*, 2 November 1895.

44 *Today*, 23 November 1895.

45 *Saturday Review*, 1 February 1896.

46 *Carmen* is Henry Hamilton's dramatic version of Prosper Mérimée's novel.

47 *Queen*, 13 June 1896.

48 *Daily Telegraph*, 21 December 1896.

49 *Saturday Review*, 26 December 1896.

50 *World*, 3 March 1903.

51 Irving, *Henry Irving*, 602. Ashwell also refers to this in *Reflections from Shakespeare*, ed. R. Pocock (London, 1926), 8–9.

52 *Daily Mail*, 17 August 1897.

53 Louis N. Parker (1852–1944) studied at the Royal Academy of Music and was Director of Music at Sherborne School for 19 years. A composer of cantatas and songs as well as a playwright, he was made a Fellow of the RAM in 1898. A great admirer of Ibsen, he translated foreign plays and collaborated with other writers (*Era*, 23 February 1907).

54 *Stage*, 21 October 1897.

55 *Saturday Review*, 12 March 1898.

56 C. Scott, *The Drama of Yesterday and Today* (London, 1899), 347.

57 *Daily Telegraph*, 7 November 1898.

58 *Morning Leader*, 7 November 1898. Actress Madge Kendal (1848–1935) and her partner and husband William Kendal, were highly respected members of their profession for more than forty years. Ashwell quoted Dame Madge as saying, '"the art of acting was concentrated imagination", and in fact when the image is felt the words do become alive' (Ashwell, *Myself A Player*, 51).

59 Ashwell, *Myself A Player*, 113.

60 *Ibid.*, 114.

61 J.H. Barnes, *Forty Years on the Stage* (London, 1914), 226–7.

62 M. Beerbohm, *Around Theatres* (London, 1953), 23.

63 Ashwell, *Myself a Player*, 105.

64 Letter from Parker to Ashwell, 25 February 1899 (Lena Ashwell Papers, Department of Rare Books, Special Collections and Preservation, University of Rochester, Rochester, N.Y.).

65 Ashwell, *Myself a Player*, 93.

66 *Liverpool Daily Post*, 25 April 1899.

67 *Manchester Evening News*, 22 April 1899.

68 R.C. Carton was a *nom de plume* for Richard Claude Critchett (1856–1928).

69 *Globe*, 24 May 1899.

70 *Weekly Dispatch*, 8 October 1899.

71 *Pilot*, 17 March 1900.

72 *Westminster Gazette*, 12 March 1900. Ashwell described meeting Malcolm Watson: 'I was so terrified that I tore the gimp off the arm of a chair and, realising what I had done, became absolutely speechless, praying that he had not noticed the destruction. I think that my agony softened his heart' (Ashwell, *Myself a Player*, 57).

73 *St James's Gazette*, 7 May 1900.

74 Beerbohm, *Around Theatres*, 76.

75 *Daily Mail*, 7 May 1900.

76 *News of the Week*, 8 September 1900.

77 *Saturday Review* on *Chance, The Idol*, 13 September 1902.

78 Ashwell, *Myself a Player*, 117–18.

79 *Ibid.*, 118.

80 *Morning Post*, 10 October 1900.

81 A description given by Christopher Fry to the author in 1994.

82 *Standard*, 27 December 1900.

83 *Morning Leader*, 20 October 1900.

84 I. Vanbrugh, *To Tell My Story* (London, 1948), 185.

85 Ashwell, *Myself a Player*, 118.

86 *Weekly Register*, 11 January 1901.

87 Other plays in this category included *Mr and Mrs Daventry*; Beerbohm Tree's production of Stephen Philips' poetical drama *Herod*; and J.M. Barrie's *The Wedding Guest* (*Era*, 29 December 1900).

88 Ashwell began appearing on guest lists for civic and social occasions, including the Lord Mayor's Ball at the Mansion House for Lord Mayors, Lord Provosts, Mayors and Provosts of the United Kingdom on 22 November 1901, and was accepted into fashionable society, making important contacts she was to exploit later.

89 *Daily News*, 17 December 1900.

90 *Topical Times*, 22 December 1900.

91 *Era*, 24 November 1900.

92 Wyndham played this character in *Brighton*, Frank Marshall's anglicised version of *Saratoga* by Bronson Howard. It was a great box office success, but considered by many, including William Archer, to be 'unbearably vulgar'. See W. Trewin, *All On Stage: Charles Wyndham and the Alberys* (London, 1980), 59–60.

93 *Era*, 22 December 1900.

94 Isaac Henderson was an American journalist (*New York Evening Post*), novelist and playwright. Another of his plays, *The Silent Battle*, produced by Wyndham at the Criterion Theatre in 1892, was an adaptation of his novel *Agatha Page*.

95 *Era*, 12 October 1901.

96 *Country Life*, 14 October 1901. At this time there were substantial reviews of London productions in regional newspapers, often in anticipation of tours.

97 Helen Maud Holt (1863–1937), Tree's wife, worked in close association with him.

98 *Era*, 8 March 1902.

99 Ashwell, *Myself a Player*, 72.

100 E. Short, *Introducing the Theatre* (London, 1949), 284.

101 G.B. Shaw's description of Ashwell's vocal technique (*Saturday Review*, 26 December 1896).

102 Ashwell, *Myself a Player*, 112–13.

103 *World of Dress*, August 1902.

104 Letter from Shaw to Jones, Norfolk, 31 August 1902, in D.A. Jones, *Life and Letters of Henry Arthur Jones* (London, 1930), 220.

105 *Times*, 10 September 1902.

106 *Era*, 13 September 1902.

107 *Daily Mail*, 10 September 1902.

108 *Era*, 4 October 1902.

109 *Country Life*, November 1902. Ashwell's scrapbook for this period contains sketches and paintings of her as Emilia by various artists (London: Victoria & Albert Museum – Theatre Museum: Lena Ashwell Scrapbooks 1891 to 1914: TM 6055).

110 *Standard*, 16 December 1902.

111 *Era*, 3 January 1903.

112 *Anglo-Russian*, February, March and April 1903.

113 *Truth*, 26 February 1903.

114 *Sketch*, 25 February 1903.

115 *Sun*, 19 February 1903. When a French company brought *Resurrection* to the Royalty Theatre, London, in 1906, critics found Berthe Bady as Katusha less impressive than Ashwell. Reviews are included in Lena Ashwell Scrapbooks 1891 to 1914: TM 6055.

116 Ashwell, *Myself a Player*, 123.

117 *World*, 3 March 1903.

118 *Daily Chronicle*, 6 April 1903.

119 The other plays were Pinero's *Letty* and Ernest Willett's *A White Passion Flower* (*Era*, 9 January 1904).

120 *Anglo-Russian*, March–April 1903.

121 *Era*, 2 May 1903.

122 *Era*, 18 July 1903.

123 In May 1908 Ashwell organised a similar benefit occasion at the Kingsway for Billington's actress wife.

124 Sydney Valentine (1865–1919), a popular actor, accompanied Wyndham and Irving on American tours and had an extensive career in London and New York. He was largely responsible for the Valentine Touring Contract drawn up by the Stage Guild in 1919.

125 *Era*, 15 August 1903.

126 Tree established the Academy of Dramatic Art in Gower St, Central London, in 1904. Now the Royal Academy of Dramatic Art.

127 *Era*, 14 November 1903.

128 *Era*, 20 August 1901.

129 *Era*, 6 September 1902.

130 *Era*, 1 February 1902.

131 *Ibid*.

132 *M.A.P.*, 28 November 1903.

133 *Black & White Magazine*, 2 January 1904.

134 *Queen*, 2 January 1904.

135 *Daily Mirror*, 25 January 1904.

136 In Ashwell's scrapbook there are copies of sheet music, some handwritten and dedicated to Ashwell. These include the *Yo San Waltz* by Antonia Doring with a picture of Ashwell as Yo-San, published by E. Donajowski, and William Furst's waltzes and Yo-San's theme and other tunes 'as played at His Majesty's Theatre', published by Charles Sheard & Co., Anglo-American Music Publishers (Lena Ashwell Scrapbooks 1891 to 1914: TM 6063).

137 Ashwell, *Myself a Player*, 115–16.

138 *Ibid*., 129.

139 *Ibid*., 131–2.

2

Actress-manager

By mid-1904 Ashwell was confidently assuming the role of actress-manager. She announced that 'under the prevailing system I cannot get the characters I am ambitious to appear in, and my ambition will not be satisfied until I have a theatre in London at which I can produce serious works, and prove there is as big a public for them, when they are of the right sort and properly presented'.[1] Convinced that 'long runs exercise a baneful influence upon dramatic art', she intended 'to strike out on fresh lines, giving the public plays in quick succession'.[2] There was great interest in her plans and the *Era* reported that she had secured the English rights to *Les Oiseaux de passage* after its successful run in Paris, but she did not take this further.[3] Meanwhile, *Marguerite*'s cast at the Coronet Theatre was announced on 30 July. Ashwell was rehearsing energetically,

> advising, superintending, giving a hint here and making a suggestion there, as though she had played the difficult part of actress-manager for years … 'Rehearsing is hard work, of course, but I feel ever so much better for my short trip to America[4] … I love rehearsals. For me they never lose their interest and fascination … I sometimes wish we could go on rehearsing and put off that dreadful first night indefinitely. I cannot tell you how terrified I am when I think of it … apart from that, I love my work intensely, and am never so unhappy as when I have nothing to do. It seems to me that to be one's own manager is the only way to be constantly employed.[5]

There was a discouraging note of caution from Frank Curzon: too many theatres with not enough good plays to fill them, with the thin line between success and failure dependent on many factors including theatre location, production costs and ticket prices.[6] Undaunted, Ashwell described the play as having a strong appeal. She encouraged young playwright Michael Morton to adapt *Marguerite*; the result, differing in many ways from Madame Réjane's version, convinced Ashwell the original title, *La Montansier*, would be misleading.[7] Morton described the play as anticipating 'the coming of the [French] Revolution … Marguerite … is a woman of the world, an actress of importance … at the head of her own theatre … the first deep note of drama is struck when the woman reveals stronger elements of her character, and

2.1 Ashwell in the title role of *Marguerite*, Coronet, 1904
(Rotophot, author's collection)

proves her loyalty to her friends'.[8] These qualities attracted Ashwell, but its histori-cal setting was expensive to stage. Marguerite's leading actor, Neuville, and an old comedian, Saint-Phar, are both in love with her. She shelters a Royalist, Phillippe, whom she loves, when Robespierre and Saint-Just are in power. Saint-Just discovers her secret and offers her the choice of becoming his mistress or being guillotined. To avoid this, she induces her company, and Phillippe, to join the army of the Republic. Phillippe deserts and Neuville demands he be shot. Marguerite threatens to run in front of the guns. Neuville threatens suicide, forcing her to order the attack in which Phillippe is wounded. Finally, Marguerite and Neuville are reconciled through re-hearsing a love scene. *Marguerite* opened on 5 September. The following day, while the *Daily Telegraph* declared Ashwell had made 'a brilliant debut in her new career as manageress' and 'if last night's audience, with their cordiality, their continuous applause, and their generous enthusiasm, afford any future omens, she is assured of popularity and success', there were reservations about the choice of play.

Ashwell had been acclaimed as a 'serious, modern woman' and critics were reluctant to allow her to diversify. William Archer thought the role unsuitable for her: 'It demands brightness, versatility, even volatility of expression, whereas Miss Ashwell's gift lies rather in the direction of suppressed intensity of feeling. No one can rival her in portraying the anguish of a tortured soul; but there is very little of that … in the part of Marguerite.'[9] The *Tatler* thought it 'a showy piece made for Madame Réjane who is essentially a comedienne. Now among many excellences Miss Ashwell's forte is not comedy. Temperamentally she is nothing if not a modern woman of almost neurotic earnestness … The play is a hotch-potch of caprice, tragedy, comedy, burlesque; in fact all the features in which a player can shine have been selected and planted as it were in a pot (boiler).'[10] Other reviewers agreed that Ashwell was 'incapable of playing comedy … Her voice, her appearance, her manner, her atmosphere – all strike the note of tragedy. She needs some strong emotional stimulus to bring out the best in her … If she be wise, she will choose parts which give scope for this wonderful talent of hers. Nature designed her for tragedy.'[11]

The one-week London season was followed by ten weeks of provincial touring.[12] This was a risky enterprise: Ashwell had not appeared very much outside London. For the first four venues, she played *Marguerite* for the full week, adding *Mrs Dane's Defence* in Nottingham as *Marguerite* was not attracting sufficient audiences. Even for the flying matinee of *Mrs Dane's Defence* in Belfast, the *Irish News* reported that 'The higher priced portions of the Palace Theatre were very well filled yesterday afternoon … but other parts of the house were sparsely occupied.'[13] Reviews for her performances and those of the company were good, expressing pleasure that Ashwell was 'not one of those short-sighted managers who hold that their own ability justifies them in engaging unknown or incompetent artists for lesser parts, so that her company will be found to include several tried and trusty favourites'.[14]

Initially Ashwell was optimistic about finding good plays: until she went into management she had not received or read so many manuscripts. While aware there were many playwrights, she was finding very few 'who can write the acceptable

Tragedy.

MISS LENA ASHWELL.
DRAWN BY G. C. WILMSHURST.

2.2 Tragedy: Miss Lena Ashwell, *The Sketch*, 18 October 1905

work' and was still 'waiting for the play which shall combine amusement for the masses and instruction for the serious'.[15] On 5 October the *Liverpool Echo* reported she had designs on Shakespeare and was eager to appear as Rosalind and Juliet. Apparently she said she 'should hate to play Lady Macbeth. No one appreciates its great possibilities more than I, but ... the role of Rosalind appeals more to me than any of Shakespeare's characters.'[16] She also stated that

> I have entered upon my present undertaking with serious intention ... I want to extend my outlook, to face a wider public ... I want to hazard my fortune to make or mar it ... I have discovered a good deal. The insularity of some big provincial centres amazes me. Their reserve, their haughtiness, their coldness towards strangers, their self-reliance. These are qualities supremely English I know ... but I felt, at first, like an adventurous traveller in a foreign land, unknown, unwelcomed, and viewed even with suspicion ... But the public is to be won.[17]

As she was planning provincial tours each autumn, and January London seasons, she hoped audiences, tiring of popular music hall, would return to theatre. Asked about the stage as a career for women, she was adamant that hardships should be appreciated from the beginning: 'the very obstacles in one's path are a sort of insurance against waste of time. The girl who has sufficient patience and enthusiasm and grit to surmount the difficulties of the first year has probably something of genius – assuming that genius really is an "infinite capacity for taking pains."'[18] Despite her own experience, she felt that in London one ran the risk of becoming an imitator and that the provinces were a better training ground.

Ashwell's first experience of management ended in failure in mid-November. She 'returned to London with experience and nothing else'. The next six months were very difficult. Before the production of *Leah Kleschna*, 'there were months of worry and anxiety ... There were three of us to keep, myself, my sister Ethel, and a small child [Honor Stevens[19]] I adopted.' Ashwell describes how this provoked much gossip: 'It is always more amusing to say shocking things about people than humdrum ordinary ones.' The child's parents, Ashwell's cousin Charlie Stevens and his wife, 'died within a month of each other ... no one wanted the child. We were neither of us really capable of bringing her up ... [but] without any legal formalities, we sent for the baby.'[20]

Ashwell was frustrated, principally, by the New York success of *Leah Kleschna*. 'I had tried to get Charles Frohman to produce *Leah Kleschna*, but he laughed at the idea that a thief could, as a heroine, prove of interest ... [The] play was sold to that magnificent actress, Mrs Fiske. Mr Frohman had to buy the English rights for a very large sum.'[21] In February 1905 it was confirmed that Frohman hoped to produce it with Wyndham. Although McLellan had written the role for Ashwell, there were rumours Minnie Maddern Fiske would play it again. Relieved when casting was agreed, Ashwell announced deferment of 'her own managerial scheme' in partnership with business manager William Greet.[22]

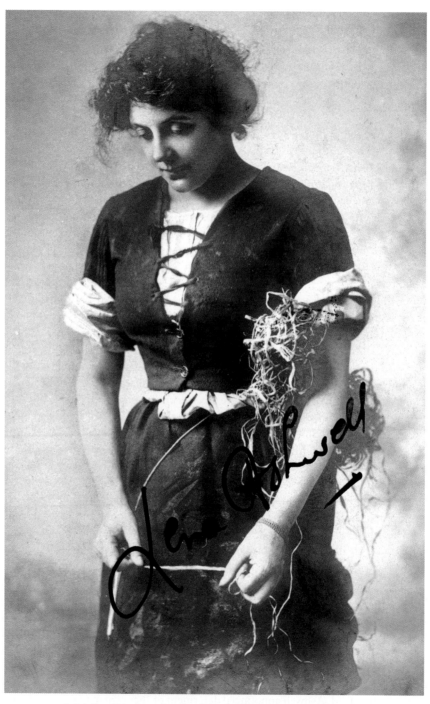

2.3 Ashwell in the title role of *Leah Kleschna*, New Theatre, 1905
(Ellis & Walery, author's collection)

Rehearsals for *Leah Kleschna* were underway when Wyndham was injured in New York. Leonard Boyne was announced as his replacement, with Dion Boucicault directing. The opening night at the New was delayed from Easter Monday (24 April) until 2 May, creating an unusually long rehearsal period. Familiarity with the role paid off. Ashwell 'acted with all the quiet naturalness and wonderful reality which are her own particular gifts. She suggested throughout the unknown longings of the girl; there was a spirituality about her, shining through her every look and action.'[23] Leah has been trained, by her professional burglar father, to break into Parisian houses; in this instance to take jewels from Paul Sylvaine, a kind French deputy, admired by Leah since he rescued the Kleschnas from a shipwreck. Leah does not know it is Paul's house until he apprehends her and then releases her. Meanwhile Raoul, worthless brother of Paul's fiancée, steals the jewels. Paul suspects him and tells Raoul's father. The marriage does not take place. Reformed by Paul's actions, Leah threatens suicide rather than continuing a life of crime. She escapes to work on the land, where Paul seeks her, presumably with a view to marriage.

The success of this production was a vindication of Ashwell's strong commitment to the play. She had 'long been recognised as a fine emotional actress, but never has she had a better chance to make good her claims to the foremost place among actresses of this type'.[24] She was no longer Lena Ashwell but 'a fierce, abandoned, daring woman, finally softened by love into humanity but prepared even then to end her life if that great deed be requisite to her new purpose. The sensation of terror and pity which this very marvellous young girl is able to produce in this part is an imperishable memory.'[25]

Leah Kleschna is a 'safe success'. It combines all the strong, close construction, and tense sensationalism of a melodrama, with the deep human interest of a modern 'social regeneration' play. The union is irresistible ... Miss Ashwell, so to speak, has been in training for this role for some time. She was, it seems, born to play the part. The passion, the sadness, and the fury of the mixed and warped nature of the girl are all shown by the actress, now in the prime of her artistic development, with marvellous force, freedom and sweetness ... its subtleties are in danger of being overlooked in the very intensity of its sensation.[26]

Alan Dale, writing in the *New York American*, compared, disparagingly, this production with the New York version. He thought Mrs Fiske 'would smile in a luxury of humor if she could see the almost burlesque imitation of her own work offered by Ashwell ... [who was] quite unintelligible ... She talked in a sort of graphophonic snappiness with a blur to it ... Miss Ashwell's performance ... was a whole bunch of feathers in Mrs Fiske's cap.'[27] Dale conceded the production had been well received in London, but denied the enthusiastic English response. This had no impact on London audiences and by early August 100 performances had been given. The *Era* reviewed the production again on 5 August. 'It says much for the staying powers of Mr McLellan's clever play that it has survived the "nipping

2.4: Ashwell in the title role of *Leah Kleschna*, New Theatre, 1905
(*Play Pictorial*, May 1905)

air" of an exceptionally depressed and depressing theatrical season … An intensely interesting story is cleverly developed, and the audience are brought face to face with a social problem of the highest importance.' On 23 September the *Era* noted the hundred and fiftieth performance and some alteration to the final act, previously considered the weakest. Leah was now discovered, at curtain rise, working in the field, rather than entering to meet Paul. Most newspapers printed brief reviews, which further boosted publicity. In early October Ashwell was unwell and Lillian Waldegrave played a number of performances. This may have affected attendance, for the production did not continue for much longer.

On 13 October Henry Irving died in Bradford. The next day, theatres across the country acknowledged his great contribution to the stage. The *Era*'s elaborate farewell quotes Ashwell: 'What tribute can be worthy when the greatest artist of our time, the truest gentleman, the kindest, best, and most wonderful friend has gone, except to pray we may not forget the great artistic lesson of his life? Personally, I feel the only fitting tribute is at least an effort towards a municipal theatre.'[28] While touring in *Marguerite*, Ashwell saw Irving for the last time in Sunderland. She told Laurence Irving that Henry was

> frail and very tired. Yet he talked to her earnestly and prophetically. The decay of theatres in the provinces was inevitable. Already commercialism was threatening to debase a great art into a catch-penny industry … He urged her to believe in the spiritual power of theatre in a changing world to educate the hearts of men … he so imbued her with a sense of mission thereafter she devoted the greater part of her theatrical life to bringing the higher drama to the poor and hitherto neglected districts of London and to provincial towns where normally theatre no longer thrived.[29]

Ashwell always carried Sir Henry's portrait with her: 'I can never forget the noble, big-souled artist who gave me such generous inspiration.'[30] The passing of Irving was the end of an era: the actor-manager was no longer a dominant force and the drama was in a state of transition. Playwrights, the *Era* proclaimed, would also have to respond to change:

> Under the old dispensation … a leading manager could nearly always rely upon … Pinero or H.A. Jones to supply him with a suitable piece … each actor had his line of business … But the modern actor of eminence is forced … to be an experimentalist. He is absolutely driven out of his groove by change … The modern play-going public is unspeakably difficult to cater for. They are just advanced enough to feel the old fashioned method of playwriting is insipid, and not yet educated up to the point of appreciating reality for its own sake … In the old days it was sufficient to play a certain line of parts perfectly to satisfy the most cultured section of the public … In the last generation people were satisfied with the outsides of individuals … or, at any rate, with the revelation

of the top stratum of their souls. Now they want to go right down to what the Americans call 'bed-rock'... The coming dramatist will be all-wise, but at the same time all-merciful; so intelligent as not to want to show it, and so strong and sapient as not to be cruel or cynical ... The development of the English stage in the next ten or twelve years will be extremely interesting; full of variety, impulse, adventure – and uncertainty.[31]

Irving had helped change public perception of the theatrical profession. With his passing came respect and increased status for members of the profession at a time when Ashwell was ready to take on a wider public role. In early March she secured a lease on London's Savoy Theatre, undaunted by the *Era*'s view of 'the arduous existence and never-ceasing, Sisyphus-toil of the actor-manager'. She was joining those who had 'to be play-selector, rehearser, producer, and leading actor, besides giving "an eye to the box-office", and an occasional hour to society and speech-making. How dull a place London would be without him and his enterprises. Surely it is enough that, with all the fluctuations of theatrical business, these bold adventurers are not driven from the field.'[32] Despite her first, unsuccessful management attempt, her aspirations in this direction were seen as almost inevitable: 'the brilliant work she has accomplished in the past few years, the popularity she has won by virtue of a very rare and exquisite talent, the appeal she never fails to make to those who delight in powerfully emotional acting, all these things rendered her appearance in a theatre controlled by herself only a question of time'.[33]

On 19 April her new season began with Clothilde Graves' comedy *The Bond of Ninon*. Ashwell's heroine was Ninon de L'Enclos with Henry Ainley as the young soldier of fortune who comes to Paris in 1662 to establish his claim to title and property, unjustly taken from him. Once again Ashwell enjoyed the rehearsal process: her company worked 'so loyally together that they have made my position as manageress very easy and pleasant ... After having endured on stage so many tragedies I simply revel in a comedy part ... you will be relieved to hear I do not commit murder. Nor do I burgle, nor become intoxicated ... nor seriously misbehave myself as it has been my fate in many plays of late.'[34] Graves had found a small volume of stained pages, entitled 'Lettres de Ninon ... once the property of the Earl of Eglinton', which inspired her character. Research was undertaken to ensure costumes were historically correct; Percy Fletcher composed the music and Stanley Hawley wrote a song.

The reception was not what they had hoped for. The *Pall Mall Gazette* reported booing which it attributed to the play being too short (performance began at 8.15pm, concluding at 10.30pm) and to 'some periods of boredom and of several ineptitudes that had provoked titters'.

Probably the qualified success was due to the fact that both author and manager were ladies. We can hardly imagine any male author writing *The Bond of Ninon* ... [or] producing it ... The result is a show characteristically feminine. Ladies

2.5 Ashwell (Ninon de L'Enclos) and Henry Ainley (Chevalier de Bellormé) in *The Bond of Ninon*, Savoy, 1906 (Rotary Photo, courtesy of Stuart Gough)

are fond of dress ... a most picturesque period, that of Louis XIV ... Chevalier de Bellormé ... before going (to the wars) asks [Ninon] to execute a matrimonial 'bond' in his favour. He gets her to write 'a chit' declaring she will love nobody but 'the bearer' which he wears as a decoration ... The audience expresses its incredulity, and when the eccentricity of the 'bond' was commented on by various characters afterwards, the audience expressed no dissent. We are at a loss to know why Miss Graves invented this remarkable document.[35]

This view was taken up by B.W. Findon, who declared that 'had Miss Ashwell had a man of keen intelligence to direct her – one who knew her limitations, and how far it was safe to trade on her powers – he would never have allowed her to choose a style of play for which she had no predilections'.[36] Some critics felt Ashwell did well in a light comic role, but for others it was not her forte. There were conflicting responses but the best gauge was box office income. This was not enough to keep the play running for more than three-and-a-half weeks and it closed on 10 May.

For Ashwell's next production, Edward Knoblock dramatised *The Shulamite*, by serial romance authors Claude and Alice Askew. According to Knoblock, 'It was a simple production with only six characters ... The cheapness of producing my play luckily attracted her syndicate [and it] was put on ... at the Savoy on May 12th, 1906.'[37] While the play differed somewhat from the Transvaal-set novel, the story remained 'morbid, feverish, overstrung'.[38] The tyrannical Simeon Krillet beats his wife Deborah, who falls in love with a young Englishman (Waring) learning farming from Krillet. Waring attempts to conquer his passion by leaving, but a lightning strike kills his horse, forcing his return. Krillet has found Waring's diary declaring his love for Deborah. Waring, saving her, in self-defence kills Krillet. They take his body to the horse and he is assumed killed by lightning. Waring plans to return to his dying alcoholic wife in England, but a jealous Deborah reveals to Simeon's sister the real cause of her husband's death. Silence is bought with the promise they not meet again, condemning both to lives of misery. Waring departs while Deborah prays for strength to keep her oath. The *Era* was enthusiastic:

> One of those plays that hold the audience in a pincer-like grip, that wring the heart and strain the nerves ... few, if any, actresses on the English stage could have so well rendered the indignant revolt, the mad passion, and the intense agony ... Norman McKinnel[39] gave a grandly simple and nobly rugged impersonation of the stern, cruel, deeply serious Boer ... impressive, acted with tremendous fervour and intensity.[40]

The *Evening Standard* welcomed Ashwell's performance with high praise:

> Lena Ashwell is a great actress. She fills the stage. You can look at nothing else but her pale face. And you must not let your attention wander from that for a moment, or you will lose the play. It is all told in her face. The story comes out in the little smile of pleasure, the quiet, unhurried voice, the face of pain, the paralysis of torture that is choked in silence. There is no noise, no rant. The tangled hands tell the tale – the sharp, violent bit of lightning gesture, the spasm of clenched teeth, then silence! No one gets so much out of silence as Lena Ashwell ... Young actresses should go and sit at Miss Ashwell's feet.[41]

There was another opinion from J. T. Grein: 'Whether it is wise to give a certificate of greatness to an actress whose elocution and deportment are not beyond reproach may be fitly left to the conscience of those who indulge in this extravagance.'[42] Grein was never in agreement with other critics as to Ashwell's abilities, and he found the piece melodramatic and in poor taste.

The third act, considered to be the play's weakness, was rewritten with a happy ending and replaced the original act on 12 June. Ashwell was given the opportunity to comment in the *Sketch*, particularly with regard to the revised ending. She provided a very articulate statement about the essential criterion by which to judge a play:

> It interests the public because of the truth it contains. It interests the actors for the same reason, not for the opportunities ... it offers them in exhibiting a certain strenuousness of which they may be capable ... The old plays held the stage because of the prestige of the actor in the part ... A modern play holds the stage in such measure as it reflects life, but it must reflect life dramatically. That is quite different from reflecting it theatrically.[43]

This was Ashwell's response, perhaps, to the *Era*'s lament, in May 1906, for the lost period of Victorian 'innocence' embodied by Terry in the 1870s. Plays, actresses

2.6 Ashwell (Deborah Krillet) in *The Shulamite*, Savoy, 1906
(Rotary Photo, author's collection)

2.7 Ashwell (Deborah Krillet) in *The Shulamite*, Savoy, 1906
(Rotary Photo, author's collection)

and audience expectations had shifted considerably towards greater sophistication. Ashwell was a representative of this change, despite Terry's great influence on her:

> At present the stage is 'struggling between two worlds'… We make an experimental dash into the analytic, then we have a revulsion of feeling for the merely interesting and picturesque … Miss Terry's truly feminine charm, her wayward, winning ways, her nervous but not neurotic temperament, her bright, eupeptic, amiable individuality, her fine physical organisation, and her technical excellence are qualities which were commoner in the 'seventies' than they are at present, and are growing rarer.[44]

That summer the theatrical profession celebrated Terry's fiftieth year on the stage with a Jubilee matinee and other tributes. Ashwell was on the Jubilee Fund committee and performed in one of the twelve all-women *Tableaux Vivants* at Drury Lane on 12 June. On 2 June the *Era* announced the Shubert brothers would tour *The Shulamite* with Ashwell throughout America. While preparing for the production's short English tour, managed by William Greet and starting in Plymouth on 20 August, she helped out at various summer charitable events, including a Botanical Gardens recital for her brother's Legion of Frontiersmen.

Ashwell was fulfilling a keen ambition to perform in America and conforming to fairly standard practice at the time. Many managements subsidised London seasons with provincial and American tours where success was more predictable. Ashwell was not well known there and being promoted by a local management was the only viable option. It was also an opportunity to lift her spirits. At this time 'a great sorrow befell me. Ethel [her sister] became ill … she had to spend the next few years in hospitals and nursing homes. I went to America to get away from myself, and gave up my flat so that I might get away from memories which accentuated my loneliness.'[45]

In early October her arrival was announced in the American press. She had been 'looking forward for years to coming here … [with the] first play I have had I can do in both England and the United States'.[46] Rehearsals began at the Majestic, where Ashwell was interviewed by the *New York Times*:

> Though she speaks of her art with the utmost earnestness, she is notably a woman with an active interest in current affairs. She possesses a spontaneity, and her range of thought is not confined to matters of the stage … [She was] not in a position to make any valuable comparison between English and American offerings … '[I] have only seen two plays during the few days I have been in the city … *The Girl of the Golden West* [Belasco] and *The Hypocrites* [English] … I liked the Belasco piece very much.'[47]

For the two-week season at the Garrick, Chicago, Ashwell was billed as 'The Great English Emotional Actress in the Latest Success of the English Stage in American debut'.[48] The city gave her the best reception of the tour, despite an inauspicious start. The production opened on Sunday 14 October 1906. Sunday night traditionally attracted a rowdy and uncouth, pleasure-seeking audience, for whom *The Shulamite* was unsuitable fare. It was a stressful start and an indication of her ignorance about the American stage.

> Miss Ashwell paid a bitter penalty in yielding to the greed and bad taste of her managers and submitting the beautiful message of her art to an assemblage dominated by ribald fools who have made the phrase 'A Chicago Sunday night audience', a by-word and a scandal throughout the land. For these dunces ... the loveliest, subtlest moments of this fiery poetess had no meaning. The passion and beauty of her acting were as the pearls of proverb ... [She] faced ... the hopeless silliness and stupidity of an American assemblage of playgoers who missed every delicate point ... who heeded not the hisses of the furious minority and who inflicted upon that minority a sense of shame and pain ... Nobly the actress from England ... finally beat down the cackle and the guffaw. At last she silenced the oafs, never seeming to lose a grip on herself – though she must have been suffering – and she sent the people away impressed. It was an unmistakable and a beautiful triumph.[49]

The *Chicago Daily News* was fascinated by her voice:

> She speaks with a slur of tone most musical and touches her trainante voice with a sharp, high nasal minor full of choked-back tears and tragedy. It is a peculiar voice, but eloquent in sadness and starry in prettier moments of tenderness and content ... makes all her points through clearly intelligent gracious mental suasion. She neither hammers ideas at her audience nor obviously acts, but in delicate elegance of technique thrills and touches, influences and stirs her audience.[50]

Ultimately, Ashwell was unsuccessful in America, perhaps because she was 'unlike any other who has come to us from abroad. We have none at home with whom she may be compared, although she does not excel the greatest of our own actresses.'[51] She was too much an individual and a threat to more conventional actresses. Some critics likened aspects of her work to Mrs Fiske, Mrs Patrick Campbell and Margaret Anglin.[52] The London *Daily Express* reported that 'Chicago has showered all its endearing adjectives upon Miss Ashwell ... she and *The Shulamite* have taken the fancy of the Chicagoese ... the theatre has been crowded nightly with men and women who cheer her and weep with her. One Windy City critic declares ... [she] brought the thrill of poetry and passion.'[53]

While Ashwell 'longed for [London actors] McKinnel and Harry Ainley',[54] the company played a month at the Lyric, Manhattan, transferring to the Shubert, Brooklyn, for a week in early December. The Chicago press included 'triumph' in most reviews, but New York stressed 'gloomy'. The *New York Evening Journal*

began with 'For those who care to take their theatrical pleasures sadly and seriously *The Shulamite* will suit.'[55] Ashwell was generally praised, but the play was
apparently too depressing:

> For no better reason that I can discover than the fact that Chicago liked the play,
> New York has refused to accept Lena Ashwell in *The Shulamite*. The reviewers
> urge the piece is gloomy – a fault that, with equal justice, might be found in
> *Hamlet*. I can't help wondering if they expected Knoblauch's powerful story of
> illicit passion to be eked out by an Irish comedian and a pony ballet.[56]

The Shulamite did not draw hoped-for audiences and on 31 October, after hasty
negotiations, two 'impromptu' matinees of *Mrs Dane's Defence* were announced
with Ashwell and Margaret Anglin.[57] Guy Standing, English, and well-known in
America, played Wyndham's role in *Mrs Dane*, and Waring in *The Shulamite*.[58]
Anglin held the New York rights to *Mrs Dane's Defence*; contractually she had
to appear whenever it was presented. She offered to play Lady Eastney, so that
Ashwell could play Mrs Dane. Ashwell was obliged to return the compliment,
although neither actress had played Lady Eastney before. Ashwell described these
as 'competition matinees … a stunt, like a boxing match, a fight as to who was the
better in the part'.[59] The press generally preferred Anglin, considering her Lady
Eastney to be more appropriate. New York critics were polite, recognising Ashwell
had created the role of Mrs Dane, but on tour she was highly praised. H.A. Jones,
coincidentally lecturing in America, was present: 'Miss Anglin gave a much better
performance as Lady Eastney than Miss Ashwell did, but … God made Lena Ashwell for Mrs Dane, just as he made Mrs Pat Campbell for Mrs Tanqueray.'[60] The
New York Dramatic Mirror identified their differences: 'In both characters Miss
Anglin appeals most strongly to the sentimental human side of her audience … Miss
Ashwell on the contrary, makes her appeal to the intellect of her hearer.'[61] A full
production of *Mrs Dane's Defence* was speedily prepared for Ashwell to perform
in repertoire with *The Shulamite* at the Shubert in December and then in Boston.

Ashwell was much sought after for interviews and guest appearances and the
pressure was on. There were extra rehearsals for *Mrs Dane* and she had been 'so
wined and dined and feted … she has not quite been able to make up her mind
whether she is a theatrical star or a pink tea prize'.[62] She declined many invitations
as she attempted to maintain energy for rehearsals and performances amidst the
pace of life in America. 'Everything must be done in a hurry. In England we take
time sufficiently to digest our plans … One doesn't seem to have time to think, and
yet nothing could be better. Perhaps we think too much in London.'[63] During this
tour she was very dependent on her sister Hilda, and on Beryl Mercer, who played
the kaffir slave girl in *The Shulamite*:[64]

> On many occasions when my heart failed me for fear I was pulled through by
> … Beryl Mercer … [She] was a kind of Ariel to me in times of confusion and

uncertainty, for she would suddenly tell me quite definitely and circumstantially the events which were about to happen ... [There were] many occasions her visions prevented me from taking hurried actions which would have landed me in difficulties.[65]

After New York, the Majestic, Boston, was home to the company for two weeks until Christmas. Here, the audience and critical response were much warmer:

Ashwell is the greatest English-speaking actress, the only one on the stage who can be compared with Duse without suffering ... so quiet are her methods she never seems to be acting at all ... this is the reason why Miss Ashwell made no stir in New York ... A taste that has been debauched by ladies who act all over the stage, act by main strength from the rise of the curtain ... It is interesting and significant to record that outside the metropolis Miss Ashwell was far better understood and appreciated.[66]

Between Christmas and the opening of *Mrs Dane's Defence* at the Pittsburgh Belasco on 31 December, Ashwell performed in Worcester and Springfield. 'Miss Ashwell's Mrs Dane was a revelation ... with Miss Anglin, we have seen the part acted in a theatrical manner ... the actress dominated ... while Miss Ashwell got beneath the mere speeches and gave us the real, hunted creature over whose head was always suspended by a hair the double-edged sword of her past ... It was real emotional acting.'[67]

Ashwell returned to the Studebaker, Chicago, on 7 January 1907. On 13 January the *Chicago Tribune* announced that she would premiere Hartley Manners' comedy *The Wooing of Eve*. Three days later the management had decided to continue with *The Shulamite*. On the same day, the *Chicago Post* announced that Victor Mapes'[68] new play *The Undercurrent*, produced by Ashwell, would open on 22 January. Confusion and uncertainty compounded a busy and stressful time. There were rushed rehearsals and Ashwell's lack of experience was creating problems. '*The Undercurrent* proved to be ... a mediocre and illogical story excellently told by Miss Ashwell and Mr Guy Standing.'[69] The tour was becoming ever more disheartening. On 28 January Ashwell collapsed, ill with exhaustion. The tour was abandoned and the press had a field day: 'While the excuse has been given out that Lena Ashwell is in ill health, the fact is she has been grievously disappointed over her American tour.'[70] For the *Chicago Daily Journal* she had set herself an insurmountable handicap – that of bringing only one play, 'which, only half succeeding, left her in a dilemma'.[71] It appeared she should have come better equipped with roles in which she had proved incomparable. Ashwell wrote later: 'It was when again in Chicago my health collapsed and with it the tour. Narrowly escaping brain-fever, I was taken into the home of Henry Holt, the well-known publisher, where Florence, his wife, sister to Robert Taber, nursed me back to health. So I returned to England [on 27 February] and the most interesting period of my life.'[72]

After recovering some strength, in late April she underwent surgery. During her lengthy convalescence, two significant events occurred. She met her future husband, Dr Henry Simson, an eminent Scottish obstetrician to whom she had been sent for medical treatment: she knew almost immediately he was her soulmate.[73] Then, while staying at a friend's house, her future plans took shape. In the light of the outcome, she refers to the two main protagonists at this time by names other than their real ones. Although there has been speculation as to their identity, there were no press statements about her benefactors, nor any reference to their support in her theatre programmes. The only account of these events is in her autobiography, *Myself a Player*:

> Jane [Emerson] I had known the longest. She was an American and a million-airess, a sensitive idealist, delicate, intelligent, anxious to use her power wisely … Before she met Lady Caroline one would never have thought she was even a rich woman … I used to go to lunch and babble about all the wonderful things which could be done: co-operative companies working together for years … producing plays by unknown authors to break down the commercial ring. Full of the ideals of democracy as promulgated by … George Bernard Shaw, I would sweep the profession clean of all artificial standards of value, all inhibiting control by the aristocracy of the profession.[74]

Ashwell discovered much later that Jane had anonymously sent her £500 during the difficult *Marguerite* tour.

> Lady Caroline belonged to a different world. At our first meeting I disliked her … [but she] was so kind to my much-loved sister, Ethel, that … my uneasy feeling left me … She was definite, shrewd, and obsessed with the desire for power … over people, to direct and arrange their lives, most kindly and generously, but, they must follow the course which seemed best to her … Jane Emerson and Lady Caroline first met at my flat. They disliked each other, but soon we were meeting frequently, all very happy and jolly.[75]

When Ashwell returned from America she found a dominant Lady Caroline installed with Jane (whose companion of many years had left), who arranged the lease on a house in Cowley Street, W1, for Ashwell after her convalescence.

> The prospect Jane laid out for me was like a fairy-tale. I was to take a long lease of a theatre, engage a company which would be the nucleus from which to cast any play, engage these actors by the year to do away with the casual labour method and give the sense of security so necessary to sound work. I was to produce plays by unknown authors, finding young writers, poets, thinkers … I was to be allowed to create with her money behind me … I was to have the opportunity of freeing theatre from the domination of the mass-mind, 'what the public wants', and of

giving some vision of what the artist wanted, which seemed saner and wiser, for art should lead, not be led. What a dream to try to fulfil! The first instalment, £3000, was to purchase a lease and redecorate a theatre and work out all the details to perfection. A fund in the hands of trustees was created to provide for my sister. A definite income was to be paid to me so that, whatever my earnings in the theatre might amount to, I would not have to use my brains for the sordid details of existence.[76]

As she began to pursue her dream, there were many opportunities for Ashwell to appreciate the implications of her undertaking. She wanted work from new, young playwrights, while recognising that her role as an established actress-manager was an essential ingredient for success: it was a fine line to walk if she was to survive financially and she would have to choose her plays carefully. She was not alone: Annie Horniman's Manchester repertory had similar vision and determination, and others were attempting to establish non-commercial people's theatres. Ashwell would learn quickly that managers were trying to find ways, such as musical 'overtures', curtain-raisers and publicising an earlier start time than actually happened, to create an appropriate environment for a thinking-man's theatre inspired by Shaw and Ibsen. Meanwhile, the *Era* was seeking reasons for 'the theatrical "bad business", of which most managers had been complaining of late', attributing it 'to the general want of money'.[77] A more hopeful George Alexander considered that 'the vast well-to-do middle-class are the real supporters of the theatre … They have neither the audacity nor the motive to be mean (they don't beg for free tickets or pay only for the Pit) … As a domestic emollient, a visit to the theatre has no rival; and, as it is usually undertaken for the sake of the "female element", the influence of that element on the fortunes of a playhouse is very great indeed.'[78]

On 6 July 1907, the *Era* announced that Ashwell was negotiating 'a lease of the Great Queen Street Theatre, the little house owned by Mr W.S. Penley, which during late years has been devoted to intermittent periods of German seasons and special performances'.[79] The 1882 theatre had a somewhat chequered history as the Novelty, the Joddrell and the Eden Palace of Varieties before it became known as the Great Queen Street Theatre. Actor-manager William Penley renovated it in 1900, 'with the money [he] made out of *The Private Secretary* and *Charley's Aunt*, and up to now [it] has proved a white elephant'.[80] It was also 'the theatre which will be remembered chiefly as the place where with *A Doll's House* [in 1889] Ibsen worship began'.[81] Ashwell, ever the pragmatist, renamed it the Kingsway, clearly identifying it with the recently constructed main thoroughfare near which the theatre was situated, slightly off the beaten West End track.[82] While embracing the opportunity, Ashwell feared obligation, especially when she signed the ninety-nine-year lease. At the age of 38, when colleagues were consolidating their careers as actresses, she took on the major task of renovating and managing a theatre. Plans to provide a new stalls' buffet, enlarge the orchestra and change the entrance vestibule were drawn up by Frederick Foster and submitted to the LCC Theatres and Music Halls Committee on

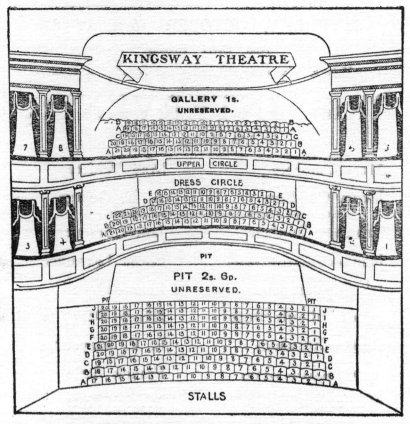

2.8 The Kingsway seating plan, *Iris Intervenes* programme, 1915 (author's collection)

30 July.[83] There was no objection to these plans provided they complied with certain conditions. Work began almost immediately. On 10 August the *Era* reported that

the Kingsway is in the hands of workmen, who have already done wonders … [and is] fast assuming a very pretty appearance. White, with gold scroll work, is to be the prevailing colour, a contrast being effected by the carpets, hangings, and seats, which are all to be in red. The large foyer is being converted into a pleasant lounge … the spacious entrance hall (on dress circle level and including the box office) has been greatly improved, and there is every indication the theatre will be among the cosiest and best appointed in the metropolis.

A major transformation was taking place: 'The rearrangement of the seating in all parts of the house is a feature of the reconstruction ... the gallery seats are also designed for comfort, while the boxes are nooks of sheer snugness.'[84]

While redecoration was in progress, Ashwell 'was sent to Madeira to get strong'. Returning, she discovered the Cowley Street house was actually owned by Lady Caroline and all the money for the theatre was Lady Caroline's, not Jane's. 'All the arrangements came through her, and the accounts rendered began to arrive. Although I had much work to do at the theatre, I must go when called to the country, to recite, to lunch or dine ... I was in her debt and expected to pay in full.' She also felt the schemes put to her by Lady Caroline were intended to part her from Dr Simson. 'All communications ... were to be made direct to Lady Caroline, the excuse being Jane's indifferent health ... She made her terms very definite, and they amounted to my being a slave, a puppet, a kept creature. The alternative was equally definite, for if I dared to refuse she would ruin me socially, financially, and artistically.' Ashwell refused to bow to her terms and 'to the outer world I was made to appear all that she said I was; ungrateful, dishonest. But it is useless, to my mind, to be influenced by "what people will say".'[85] She tried to leave the house but only managed to pay outstanding bills and have her name restored as the owner. She did not see Jane again and even Ashwell's solicitor was prevented from speaking with Jane.

No matter how personally apprehensive she may have been, the mood was positive:

The Great Queen Street Theatre never did 'find its *voie*,' in an artistic sense. The Kingsway ... has its *voie* definitely marked out by Miss Ashwell in advance; and ... it will be a road and a way that will be easily found by the public. The tiers of seats from the front row of the dress circle to the uppermost row of the gallery rise one behind the other in degrees sufficiently abrupt to baffle the most fatuous of females capable of imagining her misnamed 'picture' hat is an object of interest. Elegance and simplicity characterise the scheme of decoration ... a clear view of the stage is to be obtained from even the seats at the extreme side.[86]

Patron comfort was a priority: as well as free cloakroom facilities, Ashwell intended to oversee the refreshments, including matinee afternoon teas. The stage was flat with a raked auditorium. There was a new electric light installation and 'stage equipments [which] are as complete as any in Europe'.[87] The theatre was not a large one, with a capacity for 'nearly 550 exclusive of the boxes [an additional 50 seats]. There were 84 gallery seats, 144 [tip-up seats] for the pit, 64 upper circle, 96 dress circle and 154 stalls.'[88] All seats were numbered and bookable in advance. Ashwell set about promoting the Kingsway's accessibility to public transport. Close to the theatre 'L.C.C. trams and a fine service of horse and motor 'buses [run]. Another line of 'buses running from Victoria to Kings Cross passes the very door.' The

2.9 Kingsway programme cover, *The Truants*, 1908 (author's collection)

theatre was a short walk from the British Museum and Holborn stations. 'The cab fare from nearly all the principal hotels and railway stations is 1s.'[89]

As the building took shape, artistic plans were gradually released to the press. The first play, *Irene Wycherley*, 'presents a powerful study of a woman forced by the brutality of her husband to leave him, a tragic denouement being reached when the two are by accident brought together again'.[90] A young Irishman, Anthony Wharton,[91] after seeing *Leah Kleschna*, sent a one-act play to Ashwell. Although she thought it unsuitable, she advised him to write 'something more ambitious. *Irene Wycherley* is the result. Miss Ashwell describes it as a strong serious modern comedy of *The Walls of Jericho* type.'[92] As the opening night approached, press releases were published throughout the country. Much was made of her stated intention

> 'to alternate plays of serious interest with comedies, and to produce at matinees, pieces which, while ... of artistic merit, would not perhaps interest a sufficient number of the public to warrant their being placed in the regular evening bill ... I hope to form a repertoire of plays likely to appeal to the varied tastes of my patrons.' This, it will be noticed, is an endorsement of the Vedrenne-Barker[93] policy, which will be good news, both to the public ... and to authors who yearn for the production of interesting plays which do not necessarily appeal to the box office. Miss Ashwell's consideration for the comfort of audiences extends to the orchestra. There is to be no resounding brass; it will be composed solely of stringed instruments, and the music is to include 'selections from the works of younger composers, who are struggling for a hearing'.[94]

Ashwell intended to maintain the nucleus of a permanent company of actors, directors and musicians. With Edward Knoblock, Stanley Hawley and Norman McKinnel (head of production) as her creative team, they worked hard. McKinnel was a respected actor and producer, with a considerable following and strong credibility. His contribution on stage and behind the scenes was significant and fully acknowledged by Ashwell. 'We were all young still but had had experience in our profession, and we were whole-hearted in what we wanted to achieve.'[95] Again the press responded positively:

> In truth, with ... Miss Muriel Wylford, Miss Frances Ivor, Mr Henry Vibart, Mr C.M. Holland and Mr Dennis Eadie, she has already around her as intelligent and capable and clever a band of players as could be chosen from the London stage ... Every care will be taken to make the productions scenically choice, though, of course, the smallness of the stage will give but little opportunity for anything very ambitious in a spectacular way.[96]

Six days before the opening, Ashwell held an afternoon 'At Home' private view. Accompanied by the Band of the Coldstream Guards, she 'welcomed the endless stream of visitors ... Social, theatrical and musical London gathered in hundreds to give the popular lady lessee and manager a hearty "Send off".'[97] Also present – it would have been perilous to ignore them – were members of three playgoers' clubs: 'the O.P., the Playgoers' and the Gallery First Nighters – and others without whom no first-night audience in the capital would appear complete'.[98] The theatre's transformation and welcoming, positive atmosphere were made much of, as were the support and encouragement of Ashwell's colleagues. Everyone was willing her to succeed and prosper. There was no mention of her benefactress, nor of Lady Caroline's response to Ashwell's refusal to play the game any longer. Ashwell writes, 'London was plastered with new and original advertisements, a striped pink and white background with a miniature frame inserted to hold my portrait[99] … All the time we were planning and rehearsing I did my best to keep Jane and Lady Caroline in touch, but without response. The Kingsway opened on Friday the thirteenth, with thirteen in the cast.'[100] (Ashwell's sense of drama got away from her here – the theatre actually opened on Wednesday 9 October 1907 – the 13th was a Sunday, but there were 13 in the cast.)

With no further money from Lady Caroline, all other expenses had to be met from the box office. It was not going to be easy. With eight performances a week, the maximum weekly income at full capacity would be approximately £1,600, not a great deal to break even, let alone operate a profit, on short runs of plays. In 1906, the annual rates charge for the Great Queen Street Theatre had been £500 (Wyndham's was £2,500, the Savoy £2,914 and the Coronet £875[101]), and this no doubt increased with the improvements Ashwell made.

On 9 October the curtain-raiser was a revival of Alfred Sutro's *Maker of Men*. The audience and critics were there for *Irene Wycherley*. Irene has left her brutal, degenerate husband Philip and lives in London. When he is blinded in a shooting incident, Irene returns to her former country home. Feeling nothing but revulsion, she unwittingly sets in train his retribution by inviting, at his request, his former mistress and her new husband to visit. It transpires the suspicious husband was responsible for Wycherley's injury. Realising this, Irene orders the woman from the house. The husband's suspicions confirmed, he shoots Philip and then himself. At the end, Irene is defending herself against the entreaties of Harry Chesterton who wants her to leave the wretched Wycherley family to its fate. Ashwell had secured

> a strong play for the opening … Mr Wharton has given us a ghastly but deeply impressive tragedy of domestic life, which, though it shocks and horrifies, still tends towards righteousness … written and played throughout with relentless, but irresistible, realism … Every trait of emotion, every passing cloud of sorrow, were shown by Miss Ashwell with an elevated art … an impersonation on the highest plane of histrionic art.[102]

There was high praise for the rest of the cast, particularly for Norman McKinnel as Philip, but the *Yorkshire Post* heard

> 'disagreeable', 'ghastly', 'awful' … [from] many in the audience … when the curtain fell on the second act … Yet no one could gainsay the truth underlying the actions of the principal characters of this modern society drama … [It] started well … but developed into mere drawing-room melodrama of the most virulent type, and ended in the commonplace manner of the shilling shocker … The applause diminished … and the audience was evidently disappointed with the development of the play.[103]

The *Manchester Dispatch* admitted 'It was not a play for all markets, but its power, its truth, and its sincerity were manifest despite its obvious weaknesses, and the

2.10 *l–r* C.M. Hallard (Harry Chesterton), Ashwell (Irene), Henry Vibart (Charles
Summers), Norman McKinnel (Philip Wycherley) and Dennis Eadie (Sir Peter Wycherley)
in Act III, *Irene Wycherley*, Kingsway, 1907
(Dover Street Studios, Production Souvenir Folder, author's collection)

fact that, from lack of experience, the author has not yet acquired full mastery
over his resources. Still … his capacity to depict character, and to tell a moving
modern story in vivid and natural dialogue give high hopes of his future.'[104] For
many, it was Ashwell's and McKinnel's acting 'which thrilled last night's audience
to its centre'.[105]

Irene Wycherley was an ideal vehicle for Ashwell – she had chosen well. She was
indisputably an emotional actress, capable of expressing the existence of an intense
inner life, and was at the peak of her career, under pressure and given extra impetus
by off stage difficulties and the very real need to succeed. It is not possible to assess
the extent of Ashwell's and Knoblock's contribution to the play's final script, but
given her experience and the opportunity and incentive to influence the outcome,
it can be assumed she played an active role. Some reviewers implied this was likely
and speculated on the true identity of the author. 'The wicked husband is painted
as black as possible – so black one is inclined to believe a woman responsible for
his creation … In a play so admirably written and beautifully acted it is difficult to
say exactly how much the actress owes to the author, the author to the actress.'[106]
Ashwell wrote that Wharton sent her parts of the play over time and she made

'suggestions as to the advisability of some scenes and alterations of others. I had great faith in it for it was so full of vitality and sparkling dialogue, and contained much humour … [I] offered it to the Shubert Brothers; but they had no time to read it. After production the American rights were valuable … the theatre benefited.'[107] Later Wharton, to his regret and still retaining his admiration for her, fell out with Ashwell over the artistic and financial success of the play. He wrote on 6 April 1908 protesting she snubbed him in a restaurant where he heard her saying 'It's mine', presumably in relation to his play. He thought she was 'behaving generally in a most uncalled for and high handed manner'.[108] He was seeking continued success as a playwright, but admitted having difficulty with ideas for his next work.[109]

Irene Wycherley certainly created interest, although J.T. Grein was not overly impressed: 'As a rule she rises to a great scene and slurs the smaller ones', but he admitted that 'despite its flaws, [it] is a play worth seeing, because it indicates the drift of the young generation: because it shows an ambition to cut the cables to insular convention'.[110] This verdict was endorsed by H.G. Hibbert, who argued that puritanical critics, in this case those who dismissed *Irene Wycherley* 'with the remark that it contained passages of such impropriety as to impose silence', were misconstruing the responsibilities of journalism. This play must be seen, not censored. Mostly the Censor got it right, rejecting plays

> by their dirt; but usually, also, by their dullness. It would have been a calamity had not *Irene Wycherley* appealed to him … it would be a disgrace to the playgoer were he … diverted from a proper admiration of the play … by the yappings of puritanical critics … There is no situation on stage at the moment comparable in strength and sadness with that expounded in *Irene Wycherley* … I have no belief in criticism as a dominant force in the shaping of a theatrical fortune. The playgoer usually makes up his own mind quickly … ninety-nine visits to the play are a weariness of the flesh – there is the hundredth night, potentially bearing that triumph of the playwright or the player which pays for all; which gives … a sense of delight to which all other pleasures of the imagination are incomparable.[111]

Despite the bleak realism of the play, Ashwell and the Kingsway were newsworthy and fashionable, with three royal visits early in the season. King Edward attended a performance in late November. All this was important for Ashwell's initial success. In fact, demand was so great for higher-priced seats she 'found it necessary to add an extra row of stalls and there is every indication of the run being a long one'.[112]

Ashwell was congratulated on her start in management: 'She has done it in a businesslike and ambitious style, providing comfort and luxury in her theatre, and promising us enterprises on truly artistic lines. Even her little programme is a novelty; of a small handy size, prettily got up, full of information and free from advertisements, it is worth the sixpence charged for it.'[113] Her opinion on English drama was quoted at length:

I believe a big revival has set in. People are thinking more. There are more theatres devoted to the legitimate drama of thought than … five years ago … I believe in British brains. I believe there are still many undiscovered geniuses who can write a strong, intense, human play. It is a fallacy to suppose … that the humble author of a curtain-raiser cannot expand his talents to a three or four act play.[114]

However, this belief faltered the more she sought appropriate new plays, particularly curtain-raisers, to precede *Irene Wycherley*. Audiences demanded a lot for their money and were not content to be sent home too early. After five weeks of *Maker of Men*, she presented a new work, *A Stroke of Business*, by Arthur Morrison and Horace Newte, adapted from Morrison's short story, *Divers Tales*. A story of mean-mindedness and greed, reviewers generally considered it unworthy of the main production, so it was replaced on 20 December with a revival of McKinnel's one act play, *The Bishop's Candlesticks*, a version of the well-known incident in Hugo's *Les Misérables*, which had premiered in August 1901.

Although not long enough to fill a whole evening, 'Irene Wycherley' seems to be doing almost as well as it deserves. It is a wonderfully able play, and one of the things which may be seen and studied several times with advantage.'[115] As well as noting her success, the *Morning Advertiser* provided an insight into audiences of the day. 'Miss Ashwell has shown courage and sound discrimination in choosing a work by an unknown man, and it goes to prove how little the public is concerned with the writer of the play. It is always pleasing to see a new management – more especially when the head of it is a young and popular actress – make a lucky hit.'[116]

Not content to conquer the West End, Ashwell undertook a series of 'flying matinees' outside London. The first was relatively close by in Eastbourne. In November there were matinees in Birmingham and Richmond, followed by Cardiff on 12 December.[117] 'The last mentioned is a bold adventure, but by dint of utilising two dressing saloons attached to the 5.0 pm express and a service of motor cars at Paddington, Miss Ashwell is confident of reaching the Kingsway without delaying the rising of the curtain at the advertised time.'[118] Commentator B.W. Findon did not consider the Cardiff 'flying matinee' a bold adventure. He believed combined travel and performing, no matter how good or 'painstaking' the actors may have been, adversely affected the London evening performance, and considered Ashwell's motives were due to a record-breaking spirit and an attempt to emulate rival managements. While he considered Brighton within reasonable distance to undertake a 'flying matinee', Cardiff was too far and it would be more appropriate for the company to tour there.[119] Ashwell, anticipating further Kingsway tours, was intent on creating awareness and generating demand. The *Daily Graphic* called it 'A Record in Stage Annals':

A director of the Great Western Railway will accompany the artists, special printed notices will be circulated … to the officials all along the line, instructing them to keep the line clear, and four racing motor cars will convey the company from Paddington to the Kingsway along a route which will be specially watched by the police. Every second is precious to make this record breaking performance a complete success. The fourteen artists and five assistants will change dresses and makeup in a specially fitted saloon while travelling at sixty miles an hour. It will be one long, nerve straining, strenuous struggle which only the highest physiques could endure. But it will be done – unless fog makes quick travelling impossible.[120]

The *Daily Express* announced breathlessly that Ashwell intended 'to break all previous records for "flying matinees" today … the following is the timetable: Leave Paddington 8.45 am, Arrive Cardiff 11.35 am, Matinee begins 2.0 pm, curtain falls 4.20, Leave Cardiff 5.5 pm, arrive Paddington 8.30 pm, Arrive Kingsway Theatre 8.45pm'.[121] After playing to a full house, the company found 'a large crowd at Cardiff Station … the London express, due at 4.57, was in three minutes before time, and the special saloons and dining car … were speedily run on behind the train. All the company had entrained by 5 o'clock, and hearty cheers were raised when the train started. Miss Ashwell smilingly bowed her acknowledgements.'[122] In January there was a further 'flying matinee' to Coventry, when once again the itinerary and details of elaborate planning were newsworthy.

The success of *Irene Wycherley* gave Ashwell time to consolidate her position at the Kingsway. The box office was doing well, so there was no rush to find her next play. As she did not intend to settle into long runs, by early December there was speculation as to what she would produce next. Not be drawn on future plans, she made no announcements until January 1908. Meanwhile, she had sufficient income for building improvements, submitting a plan to retain a projecting shelter in front of the theatre and another 'to reduce the height of a barrier behind the gallery seating, and to fix two seats in recesses at the back of the pit and gallery', both of which were agreed to by the LCC.[123]

Nightly performances and theatre management did not preclude her involvement in wider concerns. Asked for her thoughts on censorship as discouragement for young playwrights, she declared 'no particular quarrel with the Censor … I would prefer him to a committee of experts or any substitute which the dramatists themselves might suggest.'[124] Plays were considered by the Lord Chamberlain before performance was permitted, on the basis of the 1843 Theatres Act. There was a growing debate on the role of the Censor, many feeling that the system needed reassessment and change. A letter Ashwell had written to the *Morning Leader* was quoted by the *Era* when debating whether the licence clause forbidding smoking in theatres but not music halls would stand up in law, especially as some managers, facing competition for audiences, wanted to be able to introduce smoking as an additional 'comfort' in their theatre:

The question … is rather one of feeling; and Miss Ashwell may be believed to express the general sentiment of her class when she writes: '… if it is safe to allow smoking in music halls I cannot see it is any more dangerous to grant the same privilege in a theatre ... Personally, I should very much object to smoking in the auditorium during the performance. In the plays with which I hope to be associated, complete absorption in the performance ... not only of the actors, but also of the audience, is almost an absolute necessity. Theatre-goers will easily recall when ... the sudden striking of a match in the auditorium would completely destroy the illusion of the scene, and the enjoyment of the entire audience, besides being distracting to the artists. I do not believe playgoers want to smoke during the performance.'[125]

She pointed out that at the Kingsway she had endeavoured to provide suitable facilities for smokers as she rather liked a cigarette herself. In December, the LCC removed the no smoking clause from theatre licences under its control, thereafter leaving smoking in theatres to the discretion of individual managers at such sub-urban theatres as the Coronet and the Kings, Hammersmith.[126]

As 1907 drew to a close, Ashwell agreed with Granville-Barker, when he addressed the Oxford Fabian Society: 'If anything was to be done for theatre it must be organised as a State affair ... a municipal theatre should be similar to a hospital. It must be in the charge of an expert, but should be free from rent, rates, and light charges.'[127] Given the daunting financial situation she faced after the withdrawal of her backers, she hoped this might eventuate quickly. Happily, she was in the ascendant artistically. The *Daily Express* included *Irene Wycherley* in its best six plays of the year, in the company of Hubert Henry Davies' *The Mollusc*, Maugham's *Lady Frederick*, Granville-Barker's *Waste*, Sutro's *John Glayde's Honour* and Shaw's *Caesar and Cleopatra*.[128]

Notes

1   *Illustrated Sporting and Dramatic News*, 3 September 1904.

2   *Manchester Courier*, 6 September 1904.

3   *Era*, 10 September 1904.

4   This visit is likely to have taken place in July, the first opportunity Ashwell had to visit Robert Taber's family.

5   *Pall Mall Gazette*, 3 September 1904.

6   *Era*, 3 September 1904.

7   *La Montansier* by M.G.A. de Caillavet, Robert de Flers and M. Jeoffrin.

8   *Pall Mall Gazette*, 3 September 1904.

9   *World*, 13 September 1904.

10   *Tatler*, 16 September 1904.

11   *Land and Water*, 10 September 1904.

12   The itinerary was Manchester Theatre Royal, Queens Theatre in Leeds, Glasgow Royal, Liverpool Royal Court, Nottingham Royal, Newcastle Royal, Sunderland Avenue Theatre, Middlesbrough Royal, Dublin Royal, and Princes Theatre, Bristol. Flying matinees were presented in Manchester and Belfast.

13   *Irish News*, 3 November 1904.

14   *Sunderland Weekly Echo*, 22 October 1904. Her company included Frank Mills, Charles Groves, Thomas Holding, Charles Doran and Miss Sydney Fairbrother.

15   *Sunday Chronicle*, 18 September 1904.

16   Lady Macbeth was one of the few Shakespearean roles Ashwell did play, during the First World War.

17   *Nottingham Express*, 12 October 1904.

18   *Bristol Western Press*, 16 November 1904.

19   Honor Stevens married the actor and production manager Harley Merica, who was a member of the Lena Ashwell Players; not much else is known about this couple. An Honor Cole was a member of the Players in 1922–3, at the same time as Harley Merica. She played fairly minor roles. It is likely she was Honor Stevens, taking the stage name Cole, from her ancestors on Ashwell's mother's side of the family (Ashwell, *Myself a Player*, 18).

20   *Ibid.*, 132–3.

21   *Ibid.*, 131–2.

22   *Sketch*, 15 February 1905. William Greet (1851–1914), was theatre manager at the Avenue, Lyric and Savoy Theatres (including D'Oyly Carte Opera Company) as well as a producer of musical comedies and operettas at the Adelphi, Lyric and Vaudeville Theatres.

23   *Standard*, 3 May 1905.

24   *Daily Mirror*, 14 May 1905.

25   *M.A.P.*, June 1905.

26   *Era*, 6 May 1905.

27   *New York American*, 27 July 1905.

28   *Era*, 21 October 1905.

29   Irving, *Henry Irving*, 656.

30   *New York Telegraph*, 4 November 1906.

31   *Era*, 18 November 1905.

32   *Era*, 17 February 1906.

33   *Daily Telegraph*, 20 April 1906.

34 *Era*, 14 April 1906. Ashwell's company at this time included H.V. Esmond, Edward Sass (also the production's director), Helen Ferrars, Beatrice Terry and Vincent Sternroyd.

35 *Pall Mall Gazette*, 20 April 1906.

36 *Morning Advertiser*, 5 May 1906.

37 E. Knoblock, *Round the Room: An Autobiography* (London, 1939), 80–1.

38 *Era*, 19 May 1906.

39 Norman McKinnel was described as 'the typical great actor of the naturalistic school … a Galsworthy actor … a symbol of the time's acting. It was virile and natural acting. It aimed at truth as opposed to effect'. F. Vernon, *The Twentieth Century Theatre* (London, 1924), 101–7.

40 *Era*, 19 May 1906.

41 *Evening Standard*, 14 May 1906.

42 *Ladies' Field*, 26 May 1906.

43 *Sketch*, 13 June 1906.

44 *Era*, 5 May 1906.

45 Ashwell, *Myself a Player*, 142. She makes no mention of who cared for the young Honor Stevens at this time.

46 An unidentified article (Lena Ashwell Scrapbooks: TM 6056, 1891–1914).

47 *New York Times*, 7 October 1906.

48 Quoted from the programme and playbill (Lena Ashwell Scrapbooks: TM 6056, 1891–1914).

49 James O'Donnell Bennett, *Record Herald*, 15 October 1906.

50 *Chicago Daily News*, 15 October 1906.

51 *Chicago Daily Journal*, 15 October 1906.

52 *Chicago Daily News* and *Inter Ocean*, 15 October 1906.

53 *Daily Express*, 7 November 1906.

54 Ashwell, *Myself a Player*, 138.

55 *New York Evening Journal*, 30 October 1906.

56 Quoted from an unidentified newspaper from Houston, Texas (Lena Ashwell Scrapbooks: TM 6056 1891–1914).

57 Margaret Anglin had played Mrs Dane in the American production five years previously.

58 Guy Standing (1873–1937), London-born, spent his early career in America. He played leading roles in London from 1909 to 1913 before returning to New York. He had a short film career in America from 1933. Awarded the KBE for services as a member of the British War Mission to the USA, 1914–18.

59 Ashwell, *Myself a Player*, 120.

60 Jones, *Henry Arthur Jones*, 21.

61 *New York Dramatic Mirror*, 24 November 1906.

62 Undated *Chicago Daily News* article from 1906 (Lena Ashwell Scrapbooks: TM 6056 1891–1914).

63 *Washington Herald*, 2 December 1906.

64 Beryl Mercer, born in Spain on 13 August 1882, was an actress from the age of four. She understudied Ashwell in 1904, and lived and worked in America from 1916 until her death in July 1939.

65 Ashwell, *Myself a Player*, 135.

66 Undated *New York Everybody's Magazine* article of 1906 (Lena Ashwell Scrapbooks: TM 6056, 1891–1914).

67 *Pittsburgh Post*, 6 January 1907.

68 Victor Mapes, a lecturer on theatre and supporter of American plays, had written some plays in French for the Comédie-Française. He was director of the New Theatre, Chicago (1906–7).

69 *Chicago Post*, 23 January 1907.

70 *New York Dramatic News*, 9 February 1907.

71 *Chicago Daily Journal*, 2 February 1907.

72 Ashwell, *Myself a Player*, 140.

73 *Ibid.*, 143–5. Sir Henry John Forbes Simson (1872–1932) studied at Edinburgh University and was Hon. Consulting Surgeon to the Hospital for Women, Soho Square, London.

74 *Ibid.*, 141.

75 *Ibid.*, 141–2.

76 *Ibid.*, 145–6.

77 *Era*, 6 April 1907.

78 *Era*, 8 June 1907.

79 'Mr W.S. Penley's cosy little theatre in Great Queen Street was opened under the management of Hans Andresen and Max Behrend. This is the fourth season of the German theatre in London, and, it is hoped, will prove successful' (*Public Opinion*, 28 November 1902, 691).

80 *Gazette Times* (Pittsburgh, USA), 1 September 1907.

81 *Referee*, 6 October 1907.

82 It remained the Kingsway until it was damaged by bombing during the Second World War (having closed in May 1941) and was finally demolished in the late 1950s.

83 These alterations were not as extensive or radical, certainly on the exterior, as Ashwell claimed, although the interior was made more comfortable. According to R. Mander and J. Mitchenson, *The Lost Theatres of London* (London, 1968, 232–3), the proscenium was set back a few feet, improving the proportions of the house.

84 *Standard*, 4 October 1907. See also *Era*, 5 October 1907: 'The style of the decorations is Louis XVI, and the impression created is that of artistic simplicity, the prevailing tones being cream and terracotta. The handsome central hall is approached by a flight of white marble steps, and everything has been done in detail that can add to the comfort and convenience of Miss Ashwell's audience.'

85 Ashwell, *Myself a Player*, 145–9.

86 *Morning Advertiser*, 4 October 1907.

87 *Sportsman*, 4 October 1907.

88 *Cork Times & Echo*, 6 October 1907.

89 Quoted from a manifesto issued by Ashwell on 23 September 1907, in Mander and Mitchenson, *Lost Theatres of London*, 232–3.

90 *Era*, 10 August 1907.

91 Anthony P. Wharton (*nom de plume* for Alister/Alexander P. McAllister), a 27-year-old Dubliner working in a business capacity at the Royal University, was without previous theatre experience. He had written other plays, but this, supposedly written in three weeks, was the first to see the light of day in London.

92 *Daily Chronicle*, 4 October 1907.

93 John Eugene Vedrenne (1867–1930) and Harley Granville-Barker (1877–1946) formed a joint management team which had success at the Savoy Theatre, presenting new plays in repertory, including works by Shaw.

94 *Globe*, 3 October 1907.

95 Ashwell, *Myself a Player*, 149.

96 *Daily Chronicle*, 4 October 1907.

97   *Standard*, 4 October 1907.

98   *Birmingham Post*, 4 October 1907.

99   The same colours and design were used on her programmes. These were picked up by the *Illustrated Sporting and Dramatic News* in its review on 23 November 1907, which included sketches of the actors in character in 'miniature' frames on striped backgrounds.

100 Ashwell, *Myself a Player*, 149–50.

101 *Era*, 6 October 1906.

102 *Era*, 12 October 1907.

103 *Yorkshire Post*, 10 October 1907.

104 *Manchester Dispatch*, 10 October 1907.

105 On 23 October 1907 the *Sketch* featured the play with 'The Most Criticised Moment in a Much Criticised Play', including a picture of Ashwell as Irene sitting stiffly on McKinnel's knee. 'Wycherley seeks to renew relations with his wife. Philip: "Let's have a second honeymoon". The incident here depicted, when the brutal Wycherley, blinded by a gun-shot wound and beast rather than man, seeks to resume his former relations with his wife, has aroused a great deal of comment and a good deal of discussion.' Ashwell's reaction of revulsion was realistic and dramatic – and was something not previously depicted with such force on the stage.

106 *Brighton Standard*, 22 October 1907.

107 Ashwell, *Myself a Player*, 150–1. No evidence has been found of an American production but it may not have been mainstream or in New York.

108 Letter from Wharton to Ashwell (Lena Ashwell Papers, Department of Rare Books, Special Collections and Preservation, University of Rochester, Rochester, N.Y.).

109 Wharton's next success appears to be *At The Barn*, premiered at the Prince of Wales, 11 April 1912, and performed by Ashwell's company in 1928. In contrast to *Irene Wycherley* it is a light and conventional love story.

110 *Sunday Times*, 13 October 1907.

111 *Mammon*, 16 October 1907. There was further observation of the play's heightened realism and break with conventional behaviour when Lady Kate, writing in *Brighton Society*, 30 November 1907, commented that in real life 'it is an uncommon thing for a woman to state her age after she has reached twenty-five, but on the stage there is not the same reluctance shown. In *Irene Wycherley* you hear Miss Ashwell mention the fact that she is 29, though the character is made up to look much older; and I hear that Mr Maugham, in his new play, *Lady Frederick*, makes his heroine confess to 35. This is a nasty jar to one's feelings, considering that such a thing could not possibly happen in real life.'

112 *Dublin Evening Telegraph*, 22 October 1907.

113 *Hour Glass*, 23 October 1907.

114 *Daily News & Leader*, 30 October 1907.

115 *Westminster Gazette*, 21 December 1907.

116 *Morning Advertiser*, 28 December 1907.

117 M.A.P., 16 November 1907, reported apropos the Birmingham matinee, under the heading 'An Actor's Spoiled Face': 'Miss Lena Ashwell just had an amusing experience with her printers but she does not, in this particular respect, lay claim to originality. Proofs of the illustrated bills she had ordered for Birmingham … a fortnight or so before the day of the *Irene Wycherley* visit, had not arrived at the Kingsway … and she telephoned to know the cause of the delay. The printers phoned back to say that the delay was not their fault at all, but was caused through the difficulty they had had with the photograph of Mr McKinnel, whose forehead was all over scratches, and they had been obliged to "paint them in", "in order to get a clear reproduction"! And after the

whole world – the whole play-going world at any rate, had been discussing the wounds on Philip Wycherley's brow!'

118 *Era*, 9 November 1907.
119 *Morning Advertiser*, 9 November 1907.
120 *Daily Graphic*, 20 November 1907.
121 *Daily Express*, 12 December 1907.
122 *South Wales Daily News*, 13 December 1907.
123 *Era*, 7 December 1907.
124 *Daily News*, 30 October 1907.
125 *Era*, 12 October 1907.
126 A year later, in December 1908, the Lord Chamberlain withdrew his prohibition of smoking in theatres under his control.
127 *Era*, 9 November 1907.
128 *Daily Express*, 30 December 1907.

3

Pioneer, 1908 to 1914

The years 1908 to the outbreak of war in 1914 were some of Ashwell's busiest and most productive, described in her autobiography under the heading 'Wider Vistas'. She celebrated her hundredth performance in *Irene Wycherley* on 7 January 1908 and soon after this a second company, performing the same repertoire, began a long spring tour in Folkestone. Throughout her Kingsway management there were usually two or three companies on the road, taking successful productions as far afield as Dublin. For this she was reliant on the skill and commitment of Norman McKinnel and tour managers Lawson Lambert and H.B. Fitzgibbon, who collaborated with the Kingsway business manager, Walter Maxwell.

As a new theatre manager developing a repertory company and actively encouraging new writers, Ashwell was of great interest to the press. Her feminine touch, attention to detail and consideration of theatre patrons were noted. The Kingsway was pleasantly comfortable, with a clear approach to ticket pricing and free lists, although attempts, which she supported, at a united approach to abolishing free lists and 'papering' the house to deal with 'deadheads'[1] – people who attended only when given free seats – were unsuccessful. At a time when both the Theatrical Managers' Association and the 1908 breakaway group, Society of West End Theatre Managers,[2] led by Charles Wyndham, virtually excluded women, Ashwell, as a female manager, relished her reputation as an individual. She was not a member of these organisations despite active participation in other professional associations.

A consistently independent personality, working tirelessly for a variety of causes aimed at improving the lives of many, she nevertheless recognised the importance of working with colleagues on the professional issues of the day. As ever, drama was perceived to be in a state of decline. Questions of public taste were raised, alongside the revival of the idea of a national theatre and a non-commercial, 'serious' theatre to improve quality and respectability. Theatre licensing and censorship were hotly debated and the professional actor's employment conditions were an important consideration. In January 1908 the *Era* noted an apparent dearth of serious dramatists and the rise of music hall popularity,[3] while praising Ashwell for her 'energy and ability' in reviving the Kingsway's fortunes. Although originally published in Italian, Mario Borsa's view of the British drama's decay, in *The English Stage of To-day*, lost nothing in translation: 'The system of long runs,

MARIE TEMPEST STILL LEADS
BUT MARY MOORE HAS TAKEN SECOND PLACE

WHO IS LONDON'S BEST DRESSED ACTRESS?

A Handsome Prize will be presented to the Actress who, from this date until March 15, 1908, receives from her admirers the greatest number of votes in this competition. Announcement of exact nature of prize will be made later.

All you have to do in order to express your preference is to cut out the accompanying blank, fill in properly the name of your favourite and send to the publication office. Any number of votes can be sent, the number to depend only on the coupons clipped from this page. Name and address of sender are not essential.

Voting at the time of going to Press:—

Name	No. of Votes
MARIE TEMPEST	409
MARY MOORE	368
KITTY GORDON	336
LENA ASHWELL	305
ELLIS JEFFREYS	275
MARIE LOHR	241
MARIE ILLINGTON	231
GABRIELLE RAY	221
VIOLET VANBRUGH	186
GABY DESLYS	184
LILLAH McCARTHY	162
LILY BRAYTON	154
MAUDI DARRELL	125
CONSTANCE COLLIER	122
ALEXANDRA CARLISLE	103
ELLALINE TERRISS	98
LILY ELSIE	91
MARGUERITE LESLIE	89
JULIA NEILSON	84
HILDA ANTHONY	67
ISABEL JAY	33
CORALIE BLYTHE	31
MIRIAM CLEMENTS	31
ZENA DARE	29
PAULINE CHASE	20
MISS HOEY	14
MARIE LINTON	12
EVELYN MILLARD	11

Names will be added to this List only when TEN or more Votes are placed to their credit.

"LONDON SKETCHES,"
92 Fleet Street, London, E.C.

I vote for ....
as London's Best Dressed Actress

Sender's Name..

Address ....

(NOTE.—IT IS OPTIONAL WITH SENDER WHETHER NAME AND ADDRESS SHALL BE GIVEN.)

3.1 Who is London's Best Dressed Actress?
London Sketches, 7 March 1908

of actor-managers, and restaurateurs-proprietors, the competition of music hall, Puritanism, censorship, the middle-class and conventional customs of playgoers, the want of interest displayed by the state, explain up to a certain point – if they explain anything at all – the lack of serious, refined, and artistic drama.' For a full explanation, it was necessary to look at the public itself which is 'the creature of the modern industrial civilisation, with ideas, sentiments and tastes moulded by its environment'.[4] Borsa argued that as general conditions of living had risen, diffused wealth brought comfort within the reach of the masses while at the same time creating a uniformity of behaviour and ideas. It seemed to him that 'none of the great questions which have agitated the Continent during the past fifty years has made an impression, even skin deep upon the "great British public" ... [demonstrating an] incapacity for feeling or appreciating serious and thoughtful art, uniformity and banality of its tastes'.[5] Unlike German and French theatre, which received government subsidy, London theatre was commercially motivated, dependent on long runs. It was predicted that even Ashwell, 'attempting to found a repertoire theatre ... will probably fall a victim to the long run'.[6] Dramatist Alfred Sutro corroborated Borsa's pessimism:

The dramatist who would have influence on his generation may lift one eye to Heaven, the other must squint at the box-office. From that callous and entirely unemotional machine he learns the expense of running a theatre amounts to £800 or £900 a week; and that taking into account the sum spent on production, receipts must average £1100 or £1200 a week as a minimum for his play to enjoy a run. This means roughly six thousand people must elect every week to go to his play.[7]

The difficulties in achieving success were further highlighted by actors' pay conditions. When the Actors' Association resolved to set a minimum weekly wage of £2 for an actor with a speaking role,[8] current rates for leading players were up to £12 in some companies, although less was more usual, with most actors earning between £2 and £5. Unless a play was a period or costumed piece, players provided and maintained their own clothes for a role. This was expensive and often stressful for actresses; many journals filled whole columns with dress details, preferring to comment on these rather than the quality of the acting.[9]

However, in *Irene Wycherley* Ashwell had a thought-provoking drama and some box office security while adding to her successful identification with strong or troubled women, many of whom she described as 'criminals', who broke convention emotionally or socially:

Whatever the degradation of the life, the emphasis was placed on the imperishable beauty and indestructibility of the human soul. It was always with this in my mind I played the range of criminals that came my way. For years I played criminals and broke all the commandments ... having so many illegitimate babies that at last I felt I would have to murder one or two to get even.[10]

3.2 *l–r* Nannie Bennett (Miss Smithers), Ashwell (Diana), Christine Silver (Miss Brant),
Doris Lytton (Miss Morton) and Muriel Vox (Miss Joy)
in Act I, *Diana of Dobson's*, Kingsway, 1908
(Dover Street Studios, courtesy of Stuart Gough)

Regardless of her personal reputation, she sought new plays and those expressing
the concerns, interests and spirit of the time. Given these criteria and her personal
beliefs, it is inevitable that she was attracted to plays dealing with women's issues,
such as suffrage, financial independence and equality.

Cicely Hamilton, an ardent suffrage supporter, journalist and young actress with
the Play Actors,[11] sent Ashwell a one-act play, *The Sixth Commandment*, in 1907.
Impressed, she suggested Hamilton write something else for consideration. Originally licensed as *The Adventuress*, *Diana of Dobson's*, Hamilton's first full-length
play to be produced, opened at the Kingsway on 12 February 1908. Ashwell played
an exhausted but rebellious shop girl, Diana, who, on receiving a legacy of £300,
decides to leave her job at the drapery – for which she receives 'five bob a week for
fourteen hours' work a day – five bob a week for the use of my health and strength
– five bob a week for my life. And I haven't a doubt that a good many others here
are in the same box'[12] – and to live life to the full for a month, knowing she will
have to return to a life of drudgery once the money runs out. Ashwell was 'thankful
to be allowed to play a comedy! [and] revelled in every second, enjoyed every line
[she] had to speak', partly in recognition of her personal need for laughter and
happiness.[13] She thought the story was 'a slight one, with ... a beautiful love interest
... [however] the authoress can hit hard when she likes, and some of the scenes are
written in a spirit that can only be described as exceedingly sarcastic and satirical'.

The play created much discussion about work conditions for women, forced to
live-in at their place of work, enduring unpleasant conditions and low wages with
little hope of change in their circumstances, except through marriage.[14] Reviews
anticipated, and fuelled, its great success. There was much enthusiasm for the scene

3.3 Ashwell in the title role of *Diana of Dobson's*, Kingsway, 1908
(Dover Street Studios, author's collection)

in which Diana, after a month of playing a wealthy widow visiting Switzerland, issues a challenge to her would-be suitor, an unemployed ex-Guardsman unable to live on £600 a year and seeking his livelihood through marriage to a wealthy woman: to see if he can live as she will have to on her return to England:

> I cannot understand how you and your like have the impertinence to look down on me and mine? When you thought I had married an old man for his money, you considered I had acted in a seemly and womanly manner – when you heard that, instead of selling myself in the marriage market – I have earned my living honestly, you consider me impossible. And yet, I have done for half a dozen years what you couldn't do for half a dozen months.[15]

J. T. Grein was effusive: 'If there had been nothing more in this remarkable play than this one speech, which is one of the finest and sincerest to be found in … modern English drama, I should hail the advent of Miss Hamilton with unbounded joy.'[16] The lovers' affection is genuine, and when they meet again later on London's Embankment, both out of work and hungry, he is a changed man. Taking up her challenge, he realises he can live on his allowance, and proposes to share it in marriage with Diana. Grein continued:

> *Diana of Dobson's* is exactly the type of play which we have been yearning for, it depicts life of today, it cuts into the lower stratum, it is hallowed by a touch of romance … the greatest merit of all … is the veracity, the simplicity, and directness of the play … [It] will rank in the life-work of Miss Ashwell; she rises to every situation; she is touching in her scenes of emotion; she is the woman who battles, and in her hour of glory never forgets the inherent sadness of her life.[17]

The beginning of Ashwell's association with the suffrage movement coincided with *Diana of Dobson's*. At this initial stage she was quoted as judging suffragettes by results – 'If the tactics adopted are successful, they may be justifiable, if not, they must be ridiculous'[18] – and her own tactics involved the choice of plays she presented, rather than overt campaigning.

During the run of *Diana*, the Kingsway presented six special matinees of new one-act plays – another move to encourage playwrights and diversify activities. A comedy by Judge Edward Parry, a 'fantastic play' by Anthony Wharton, a 'serious comedy' by Eva Anstruther and a tragedy by Mrs W.K. Clifford were launched. Ashwell was looking for curtain-raisers, such as Wilfred T. Coleby's new work, introduced into the repertoire in early May, which prompted *Public Opinion* to ask:

> How does Miss Ashwell do it? Here is another new play, *The Likes O' Me*, by a new author, which is 'fresh, unconventional, amusing, pathetic and technically right' … If this most wonderful actress-manager is not very careful, she will cut the ground from under the feet of the agitators for an 'intellectual theatre', added

3.4 C.M. Hallard (Captain Bretherton) and Ashwell (Diana) in *Diana of Dobson's*,
Kingsway, 1908 (Dover Street Studios, courtesy of Stuart Gough)

to which she is making her intellectual theatre pay, which they don't profess to
hope to be able to do.[19]

'What a nursery of new ideas the Kingsway has become',[20] *London Opinion* ex-
claimed. Reviewers generally took an interest in Ashwell's policy of encouraging
writers while attempting a mixed bill. However, regular programmes of short plays
could not draw audiences or sustain a West End theatre.

By the turn of the century many charitable organisations were using theatrical personalities to attract donors to fund-raising events. Ashwell, very active on
the charity circuit, lent her name and presence to health causes, particularly Dr
Simson's Women's Hospital in Soho, as well as to the Church and, increasingly, to
those concerned with women's needs and special interests. She frequently made
the Kingsway available for special matinees, charging only costs, not a hire fee. In
May 1908 she masterminded a benefit matinee for an elderly actress, Mrs John
Billington. The all-female entertainment included Jonson's masque *The Vision of
Delight*, Act I of *Diana of Dobson's*, Tennyson's *The Falcon*, a new short play by
Cosmo Hamilton and songs, recitations and dances. As a member of the executive
of the Actors' Orphanage Fund, she took part in the annual summer Regent's Park
Theatrical Garden Party, an important social event.[21] Most prominent members of
the profession were present, serving tea, judging funny hats, performing sketches
and running raffles.

During the 1908 spring season, 24 new productions in London achieved less
than 95 performances but *Irene Wycherley* (140) and *Diana of Dobson's* (141)
were in the top ten longest-running productions.[22] Encouraged by success, Ashwell
obtained LCC approval to enlarge the Kingsway box office to accommodate three

booking clerks to handle increased ticket sales. She introduced numbered, book-able 5/- seats, positioned between the pit and the stalls and priced accordingly, intended for playgoers 'who, while finding it inconvenient to go home and dress (for example, men who work in the City), are unwilling to appear unconventionally attired'.[23] The number of these seats was flexible, according to demand. This was a risky practice, open to abuse by those wanting to sit near the stalls while paying less, but Ashwell made it a successful initiative. The Kingsway was constantly in the news through her regular national distribution of press statements. During the summer closure period, an auditorium ceiling ventilation fan was installed.[24] At the re-opening in September it was revealed the gallery had become a commodious upper circle, entailing a slight increase in admission prices. Ashwell was now sole lessee, following the transfer of Penley's share to her. Increased box office income was essential to make the theatre pay.

> In place of the shilling seat on a 'knife board', there will be two-shilling tip up seats ... she [Ashwell] always takes her patrons into her confidence about her plans. She does so on this particular occasion with her accustomed grace – 'I am sorry I have had to abolish the gallery. During my whole career I have received nothing but kindness from "the gods". The theatre is small and the old gallery was not comfortable. I hope "the gods" will recognise that, although I have raised my prices, I have provided ... increased comfort, and they will continue to look down benignly upon me in the future from the upper circle.'[25]

The Gallery First Nighters' Club, however, did not look benignly on the changes and, recording a strong vote of disapproval of the alterations and price increase, suggested a boycott of the Kingsway. Despite this, Ashwell addressed her audience confidently:

> During the past year I have experienced nothing but encouragement at your hands; so great indeed has been your kindly interest in our venture that I feel justified in believing the little Kingsway Theatre has gained a warm place in your affections, and I can assure you that I shall leave no stone unturned to make that feeling permanent.[26]

Some of Ashwell's best work as an actress was during the years when she was also a manager. Working with playwrights, she encouraged them to exploit her particular qualities. She found and built characters which influenced public perception of her on stage as well as subsequent casting by other managers. Undoubtedly these char-acters gave her off stage confidence in her management and community activities. She acquired a reputation for being

> a marvellous feeler of the public pulse, and people have striven to account for the secret of her successful judgement in various ways ... she allows the [initial] reading to be done for her, and then makes a choice that will suit herself, while

other managers and players attempt to choose entirely 'off their own bat'. Selecting merely a piece that will afford good display for a 'star' is found in nine cases out of ten to be a failure, while an all-round, well-knit work comes not only to stay, but runs along into the provinces, and somehow or other plays itself and lives on for many seasons.[27]

Happiness in her personal life was a contributing factor to her energy and courage as an actress, manager and active member of society. Immediately after her divorce from Playfair, on 31 October 1908, she married Dr Simson in a quiet ceremony between a matinee and evening performance. She described their years together as 'complete happiness … however battered and weary I felt, I came home to absolute harmony, safety and love'.[28]

Much of the debate about an 'intellectual'/non-commercial theatre focused on what the *Era* called 'The National Theatre Question' in its many reports on meetings which Ashwell attended over the decade. The idea of an English National Theatre had its origins in Garrick's Stratford-upon-Avon Jubilee celebration in 1769 and was later supported by Irving. In yet another attempt to take the idea further, in May 1908, the Lyceum hosted a meeting of 3,000 members of the profession. They agreed to combine the resources and intentions of the Shakespeare Memorial Committee, set up to celebrate anniversaries of Shakespeare's life and work, with a National Theatre Committee, seeking a permanent home for the British theatre. Ashwell was a member of the very large, unwieldy committee, chaired by the Earl of Lytton, appointed to draft the Shakespeare Memorial National Theatre scheme.[29]

Besides new writing talent, Ashwell sought actors committed to working together and developing a stock company style. At the 1908 Academy of Dramatic Art Prize Giving, a young actress, Athene Seyler, won the Gold Medal. Ashwell and Sutro were the judges. Seyler impressed: Ashwell invited her to join the company in 1909 and they remained strong lifelong supporters of each other's work. (Another prize-winner, Wilfred Fletcher, later worked with the Lena Ashwell Players.) At Ashwell's memorial service on 20 March 1957, Seyler paid tribute:

I speak of Lena as my greatest theatrical friend, as one who as an actress, I realise now, formed in me any taste I had, any feeling of responsibility about the theatre, any feeling that my job was in any sense a calling. People do not speak much about her acting now because they say she was before their time. I feel like a contemporary. She gave me my first job on the stage.[30]

Seyler's career was a distinguished one and included many highly praised comic stage and film roles. In 1908, perhaps with youthful success fresh in her mind, a 'hopeful' Ashwell was quoted in an article on 'The Stage for Girls':

I think the stage is a very good profession – for some girls. For the kind of girl … who is possessed of considerable personal attractions, charm or manner, a good voice, an iron constitution, a determination to 'get there' in spite of all difficulties and above all, a sense of humour. Of course she must have some histrionic talent … granted the above qualifications, a girl may make quite a good living on the stage, so why shouldn't she adopt it as a profession?[31]

Responding to the frequently asked question, 'Is an Actress Influenced by Her Part?', she wrote a brief, sensitive analysis of her craft. She believed an actress must be able to

separate her private self from the character she is impersonating … but not her personality. For her purpose is to represent through her own personality a particular kind of woman under certain definite dramatic circumstances … it was absurd to suggest an actress became the person she was playing. I act what I feel. The characters I represent are very real … to me while I am playing them. If they were not, they would cease to convince.[32]

The following year, a Body of Associates, including Ashwell, was appointed to the council of the Academy of Dramatic Art. They undertook honorary part-time teaching and rehearsal supervision as well as making other contributions to the Academy's work.

Following the run of *Diana*, as the company prepared for nine weeks of touring and the closure of the Kingsway spring season on 20 June 1908, the National Union of Women's Suffrage Societies organised a mass procession of women through London. Ashwell did not take part in this event on 13 June but was included in the *Era*'s list of 'other actresses who advocate and work for Women's Suffrage'.[33] Involving many of the same actresses, but in stark contrast to the marches – indicative of the contradictions of the age – the king's annual Windsor Castle Garden Party, which Ashwell attended, took place on 20 June. Her position as an advocate for the women's cause was no doubt difficult. A few months later she married the royal family's gynaecologist and faced social dilemmas familiar to colleagues in similar circumstances. Their willingness and determination to use their positions for the cause, while risking loss in social status, was significant.

Diana of Dobson's was the Kingsway's most successful production, revived by Ashwell in 1909, and Diana is the role she is most identified with in accounts of her career. Kingsway companies performed it throughout the United Kingdom and by October 1908 arrangements were underway for productions in America, Australia, India, South Africa and European countries. Hamilton had sold Ashwell the rights and did not share the stage royalties. She blamed lack of confidence in her work for this unfortunate financial decision (later, Ashwell shared film royalties with Hamilton):

The Kingsway management read its plays with a commendable swiftness, and I think it was only a week or two after I had sent off my manuscript I received a letter asking me to call at the theatre … my first reaction to that letter was in-

3.5 Ashwell (Lady Kilross) and Master Philip Tonge (Freddie Cartwright) in *The Sway Boat*, Kingsway, 1908 (Dover Street Studios, courtesy of Stuart Gough)

credulity … It was impossible any one should think that play, that bungled play, was good enough to put on – and in London! … so I fell to the temptation of £100 down – which was more, far more than I had ever earned in a lump. With more sense I should have made some thousands out of Diana.[34]

As Ashwell prepared to take *Diana* to major regional theatres,[35] alongside a smaller cities and seaside resorts tour of the London repertoire, opening on August Bank Holiday, she received excellent reviews for her two companies already on the road. The autumn season, including Coleby's new full-length play *The Sway Boat*, was rehearsed on tour and opened in London on 9 October, exactly a year after the Kingsway's opening. Ashwell described Coleby as 'a most brilliant and delightful schoolmaster who wrote his plays in French. It was, I feel, a remarkable play, most tragic too, unhappy perhaps, but undoubtedly true.'[36]

The Sway Boat depicted the tragic story of Lady Kilross (Ashwell), previously married to a man who drank himself to death and whose young daughter had also died. Formerly drug dependent and desperate for children, she had married the fussy Lord Kilross. He is swayed by an imperious mother, who is in turn swayed by her doctor. When Lady Kilross's liaison with her young nephew's tutor is discovered, she returns to her drug habit and commits suicide by drowning. Only her devoted nephew realises she has found peace in death. The *Penny Illustrated Paper* considered the play would 'attract crowds of ladies who are interested in that type of play, where all sorts and conditions of affairs are discussed – affairs concerning marriage very largely – with unusual frankness'.[37] Ashwell's performance was 'highly interesting, intelligent and sympathetic, and as a piece of acting should be seen',[38] but within a few days it was announced that mid-week matinees would be abandoned due to the strain of Ashwell's role.[39] *The Sway Boat* closed on 21 November after a six-week season, falling far short of the success of previous plays.

The *Onlooker* was convinced 'it failed because its chief interest was abnormal and pathological … public taste is still wholesome enough to eschew the pathological drama'.[40] Ashwell may have misjudged the readiness of her audience to deal with such stories after the light-hearted experience of *Diana* had brought a new audience into her theatre – an audience not ready to deal with such challenging subject matter.

Three days later, *Grit* opened. Ashwell confessed she thought

a longer period would have elapsed before it became necessary to launch another production on the uncertain sea of public favour; but *The Sway Boat*, though it attracted favourable attention and achieved an undoubted success artistically, was perhaps scarcely of the texture to appeal to those who sustain a rooted objection to being forced to dive deeply into psychological problems. I now present *Grit*, a play in four acts by Mr H. Herman Chilton, for your approval. It is no longer a novelty at this theatre for you to be called upon to judge the first work of a new author, and my past experience tells me Mr Chilton could not possibly be called upon to face a more impartial and kindly tribunal.[41]

The comic plot of *Grit* involves an honest, kind carpenter (McKinnel) who saved an old gentleman from drowning. When the man dies, he leaves a large fortune to be divided equally between his rescuer and a friend's daughter (Ashwell), on condition these two, who have never met, marry. The ceremony takes place and the carpenter is prepared to let his wife continue her friendship with a young man. Finding an earlier will of the old man which leaves all his wealth to the young woman, the carpenter offers to set her free. Touched by his gesture, she dismisses the hapless young man and accepts the true value of her marriage. Some critics implied that a 'happy ending' scenario was now rather beneath Ashwell and out of keeping with her previous productions. Although described as 'an honest, well-intentioned piece', reviews did not anticipate a great success for the production, which ran through December.[42]

In its review of the Dramatic Year 1908, the *Era* considered it was becoming more difficult to concoct a good play for the London market, although *Diana of Dobson's*, along with Pinero's *The Thunderbolt* and Shaw's *Getting Married*, were significant additions to the repertoire, with Hamilton's play described as 'a clever comedy and a scathing indictment of our social system'.[43] This praise was timely: the Kingsway revival of *Diana*, with most of the original cast, was announced for 11 January 1909. Once again the reviews were enthusiastic. On 17 January Ashwell wrote to the *Referee* on 'The Dearth of Good Plays', which drew a number of responses on 24 January. Over 2,000 new plays had been submitted to the Kingsway since autumn 1907:

These plays deal with modern life only as I have made it a rule to consider no plays in verse or on historical subjects, costume or musical plays. Out of these … experience has proved scarcely more than one percent have been worth the trouble of reading or even the clerical labour entailed in registration, acknowledgement, postage etc. Now, of this one percent, quite half have been one-act plays, so that only half percent represent three act plays. Or in other words, a good actable play which is worth producing is as one in two hundred.

She suggested unknown authors, or submissions without a recommendation from a recognised literary or dramatic person, should pay a reading fee. Thorpe Mayne was moved to establish an Unacted Authors' Association aiming to have managers decide productions by ballot and play-reading committees, with public readings to bring attention to members' work. The Playwrights' Association, formed as 'a direct result of Miss Ashwell's unfortunate suggestion that a reading fee of a guinea should be charged',[44] enlisted an expert reader to select and promote plays but after some 100 plays had been received, 'no nuggets' had yet been found. Later, Knoblock described his role at the Kingsway:

I read 7,000 plays in two years, about ten a day, working from 9 a.m. to 1 a.m. and Sundays from 9 a.m. to 4 p.m. I also re-wrote about twelve plays and saw to the scenery and costumes for the actors. I received what was then considered a very high salary in England for play-reading – £4 a week, finally raised to £6![45]

Ashwell continued to promote new plays, premiering Coleby's *The Truants* on 11 February, followed four days later with spring tours of *Grit* and *Diana Of Dobson's* opening in Folkestone, Grange and Croydon. *The Truants* was in a much lighter vein than *The Sway Boat*:

It is brightly written, it makes mild fun of the 'Salome' dance craze, and it has one splash into melodrama … Miss Ashwell handles a revolver prettily … *The Truants* … are a couple of young lovers who plan to run off for no very good reason, but who are persuaded by Freda Savile [Ashwell] to respect the conventionalities … Freda chances to have a secret – not at all dishonourable – which the youth … has discovered, and it is when he threatens to make ill use of it that the revolver is brought in to clinch the argument.[46]

All ends happily: Freda is able to marry her betrothed, who now knows about her child from a previous marriage, which she did not know at the time was a bogus union, while the young girl (Seyler), previously influenced by Freda's apparently independent attitude, marries her lover, rather than being a 'truant'. Reviews were mixed, with some critics finding a melodramatic farce sat uneasily in the theatre's repertoire. All praised unanimously Seyler's debut, predicting a great future for her. Ashwell was criticised for not giving the inexperienced Coleby more dramaturgical help, which she appeared to have given to earlier productions. 'That it is no longer provided augurs ill for the stability of the Kingsway management', claimed H. Hamilton Fyfe. 'Brains are as much needed in theatrical enterprises as others.' When theatre managers perceive this, 'they will pay their actors less, and with the money they save keep a staff of skilled dramatic editors, who will help beginners with ideas to get their efforts right'.[47] Ashwell, in an attempt reduce her workload, published some pointed advice to playwrights. 'Get a good, simple story and do not let too many things of import happen before the rise of the curtain. Centre your interest on one or two people. Learn to criticise your own work. Do not change your scene in the middle of an act. Write on modern life if possible.'[48]

Ashwell could not deny her musical background and, despite theatre music conventions, she attracted attention by experimenting with the presentation of interludes normally performed by a resident orchestra. Young composers were encouraged to submit work, and from early November 1908 musical selections, directed by Hawley, replaced the curtain-raiser. Ashwell was 'pleased to announce an increasing number of M.S works by British Composers, some now to be performed for the first time, and others which, though of great merit, are too rarely heard'.[49] Hawley composed inter-act interludes to suggest the atmosphere of the following scene and an ensemble of chamber musicians performed before the play. Many theatregoers wanted to talk between acts and they could do this 'without offence when light orchestral music of the ordinary kind is being given; with a high class string quartet playing Beethoven or Schumann, it was quite different. People thought they ought to stop talking and listen, and to the unmusical at any rate, this was rather tiresome.'[50] Ever responsive to her audience, in February 1909, when *The Truants* was preceded by a revival of Coleby's *The Likes O' Me*, she abandoned this experiment. The London String Quartet left the Kingsway for the concert platform while the theatre's orchestra continued to provide the usual background pre-performance and interval music.

By now, however, the 'honeymoon' period was over. Although Ashwell had kept hoping 'the undertakings with regard to finance would be met when necessary, and that some time Jane would see that the work was worthwhile', there was no further word from her or Lady Caroline.[51] She realised that, while she had focused on the artistic work, her position had become desperate and 'financial ruin had begun. The next weeks were hideous torture. I could not digest my food or sleep at night.'[52] On 13 March 1909, with no reserves or sufficient income gained through longer runs, she was obliged to abandon solo management at the Kingsway when *The Truants* closed. As the *Standard* remarked:

The year 1909 has not been kind … The theatre which has suffered the most undeservedly from the slump … is the Kingsway. *Grit, Diana of Dobson's* (revival) and *The Truants* all deserved better of the too-exacting playgoer. *Grit* it is true ran for over two months, but *Diana of Dobson's* was worthy of more than thirty-two performances, and *The Truants* of more than thirty-six … McKinnel's carpenter hero in *Grit* ought to have drawn the town (in the Drama's presumptuosity days it would have done so) … Seyler's delightful ingenue and … Eadie's remarkable Bill Chetwood, in *The Truants*, might have made the fortune of a much less worthy play.[53]

But she did have one more significant play to premiere: J.B. Fagan's *The Earth*, written when he was 'burning with indignation over the unfair treatment of *Irene Wycherley* by a certain section of the Press, centred on the proprietor of a newspaper, indicating the enormous, and sometimes ruthless, power of the Press.'[54] Fortunately, Otho Stuart offered a generous co-production arrangement, making it possible for her to continue the season until the summer break.

The Earth's powerful proprietor, Sir Felix Janion, opposes MP Denzil Trevena's submission of a Fair Wages Bill to the government. He prepares to use information on the close friendship between Trevena and the unhappily married Lady Killone (Ashwell) to force withdrawal of the bill. When Lady Killone learns that Trevena will succumb in order to protect her reputation, she threatens to take the blackmail story to the Press Association. Janion is forced to return evidence of the relationship and the bill proceeds. The published play is dedicated to Stuart but clearly Lady Killone was written as another strong woman role for Ashwell. The character is 'a woman of remarkable beauty. Her manner outwardly is one of great reserve tinged with irony, but she is capable of intense enthusiasm and extreme vivacity.'[55] Two short speeches allow us to understand Lady Killone and the play's appeal to Ashwell. When Janion's sister says, 'You appear to feel very strongly about Mr Trevena's Bill,' her reply is, 'I should have thought all women would feel strongly about it. Part of it is designed to put an end to the sweating of women and children.'[56] Later, when Janion learns of her involvement with the Women's Political Union he sneers: 'Didn't know you were a suffragette, Lady Killone.' Her response is, 'Yes, with limitations. You needn't picture me as Andromeda chained to Downing Street railings, and waiting for Perseus, in the shape of a policeman, to wrench me free – I'm not that sort of suffragette.'[57] She proves equal to Janion in her understanding of the ways of the world and he admits he is beaten by her pluck. A hard-hitting play, it portrayed on stage for the first time the duel between the press and politics.

It was well received at the Torquay premiere, before a glittering opening night in London on 14 April. The 'remarkable impression' made by this play was 'confirmed at succeeding performances … the acting is unanimously voted as worthy of the high tradition … established under Miss Ashwell's management … one of the liveliest comedies of the day and one of the most striking recent contributions to the Theatre of Ideas'.[58]

The Earth created more news than just reviews. Shaw accused Fagan of plagiarism, claiming *The Earth* was stolen from Granville-Barker's prohibited play *Waste*. He knew Ashwell, protecting her licence, had declined *Waste* for the Kingsway. Declaring that both plays contained a cabinet minister who, 'on the eve of crowning his Parliamentary career by the introduction of a great Bill, is discovered to have been

3.6 Ashwell (Countess of Killone) and Allan Aynesworth (Denzil Trevena) in *The Earth*, Kingsway, 1909 (Dover Street Studios, courtesy of Stuart Gough)

engaged in an intrigue with a married woman,' he conveniently underplayed the very different issues dealt with in the two plays.[59] His quarrel was with the censorship, not Fagan, whose response indicated the weakness of Shaw's case, pointing out such similarity was equal to the observation that characters in both plays might have worn brown boots. The exchange attracted audiences to the Kingsway: in fact Fagan thanked Shaw for 'giving me an advertisement' by selecting 'The Earth as a convenient missile to hurl at the Censor'.[60]

At this time managers were confronting proposed changes to theatre licensing laws. Robert Harcourt's New Theatres Bill proposed the assignment to the LCC of the Lord Chamberlain's responsibility for licensing London theatres and also the abandonment of his censorship role for new plays. This met with almost unanimous disapproval from managers and dramatists, including Ashwell, who considered 'present conditions [in England] preferable' to countries without censorship.[61] There was little doubt the law needed to take into account changes in entertainment provision. The 1843 Theatres Act, still active, imposed restrictions on licence holders with regard to music and dancing. New, flexible legislation was needed to ensure more consistent employment for artists and uniformity for managers. Parliament set up a Licensing and Censorship enquiry and its deliberations were reported in the summer of 1909. Shaw, keen to abolish the Lord Chamberlain's power, was furious when the enquiry did not take his fifty-five-page tirade against the censorship as evidence.[62] The friendship between the Shaws and Ashwell must have been strained, especially as she was the first woman to give evidence, on 20 August, necessitating a break in rehearsals for her next play, Madame X. While personally somewhat ambivalent about censorship – on the one hand she felt 'the actor did need some protection, on the other hand, the interference of the Censor was often ridiculous'[63] – publicly Ashwell asserted censorship was desirable: 'It is wiser to have control before and not after the production of a play', as production involved many people who could be out of work as a result of police proceedings. She thought 'it would be fatal' for performers if control over plays was placed in the hands of local authorities, because they knew nothing about it. Ashwell was concerned provincial tours would no longer be viable if local authorities had censorship responsibility as some towns might not permit a play allowed elsewhere. Her suggestion was a committee of 'men of the world', to whom the Censor could refer if undecided and to whom an author could appeal. When asked whether there would be women on that committee, she replied with a simple, 'No, sir.' A few years later she was quoted on the Censor being a woman, but here she consciously avoided raising the women's issue when there were important professional issues at stake. The enquiry also sought views on the removal of distinctions between licences for theatres and for music halls. Her reply was: 'I object to their being on the same footing. They [music halls] should not be allowed to produce long dramatic plays … it would be very bad for the legitimate theatre.'[64] This view altered somewhat following her debut in vaudeville in 1911. The report on retaining censorship was issued in November 1909 and the Lord Chamberlain continued to administer the existing Theatres Act.

Ashwell had attended the newly formed Actresses' Franchise League (AFL) December 1908 meeting at the Criterion Restaurant, where Forbes Robertson, a long-time supporter of female suffrage, proposed 'this meeting of actresses calls upon the Government immediately to extend the franchise to women'.[65] By 16 April 1909, when she opened the Women's Freedom League fund-raising bazaar at Caxton Hall, she was committed to the cause, despite many pressures on her time. The Kingsway programme for *The Earth* carried a *Votes for Women* advertisement promoting the Royal Albert Hall public meeting on 29 April, organised by the Women's Social and Political Union. During the next two months, while playing nightly in *The Earth* and attracting full houses, Ashwell participated in suffrage, social and charity events as she dismantled her Kingsway management. Maxwell accepted an engagement at the Criterion and McKinnel was appointed producer-in-chief to Herbert Trench's Haymarket repertory. Jay & Mann secured rights for *The Truants* and negotiated a tour with most of the original cast.

In early June Ashwell and Dr Simson were guests of the New Vagabonds' Club, where she proved an entertaining after-dinner speaker; the press as far afield as Manchester quoted her anecdotes. While her role as a prominent actress-manager was coming to an end, she became a confident spokesperson and advocate for new ideas and causes.[66] Press notices from 17 June announced that Ashwell was ceasing management and letting the Kingsway, while retaining the ninety-nine-year lease. 'Management is terribly hard work. You have friends you cannot see and a home you cannot live in. But I have discovered new talents … That is enough for honour.'[67] The press saw it as 'a matter of regret that Ashwell could not see her way clear to continue'.[68]

> She and her advisers have made mistakes this season … but during her first season she brought an unpopular theatre into great popularity and very high esteem. She gave us good plays, good acting and good music and she seemed to have established a relationship between herself and her audience probably warmer and more intimate than that enjoyed by any of the other theatrical managers in London.[69]

By now it was known she would be leading actress in Charles Frohman's new company, at the Globe (previously the Hicks), presenting 'strong human plays', including Alexander Bisson's *La Femme X*.[70] Frohman could not resist joking: 'During the past season Miss Lena Ashwell has played in *The Earth*. From September onwards she will play in The Globe.'[71] Meanwhile, Fagan's play achieved its hundredth performance and there were plans for a New York production. It closed in early August, but with *Diana of Dobson's* still on tour, Ashwell's responsibilities continued. At this time she was discovering 'the world of the theatre was not the only world, and there were movements going on; for the seeds of revolution were germinating. There was much in the world that needed to be put right',[72] and she became immersed in the women's suffrage movement, offering her advocacy services and participating regularly in AFL monthly 'At Homes' which began in October 1909.

3.7 Ashwell (Jacqueline Fleuriot) and Arthur Wontner (Raymond Fleuriot) in *Madame X*, Globe, 1909 (Rotary Photo, courtesy of Stuart Gough)

3.8 C.M. Hallard (Laroque) and Ashwell (Jacqueline Fleuriot) in *Madame X*, Globe, 1909 (Rotary Photo, courtesy of Stuart Gough)

'Miss Ashwell's Triumph' proclaimed the *Daily Chronicle* on 2 September, following the opening night of *Madame X*. Jacqueline Fleuriot (Ashwell), twenty years after having been thrown out of her home for a failed romantic escapade by an unforgiving husband, Louis (Sydney Valentine), has sunk to the depths of despair. She is mistress to Laroque, friend of a blackmailer who attempts to obtain her dowry from Louis. Jacqueline refuses to take part and shoots Laroque. As the central melodramatic device, her young barrister son, Raymond, who does not know his mother (nor does she recognise him), defends her in court. Watched by Louis, Raymond eloquently succeeds in having her acquitted, unwittingly accusing his father of cruelty and merciless pride, changing their relationship forever. Following recognition between members of the family, Jacqueline dies a protracted death. Ashwell made an easy transition in performance style from the relative intimacy of the 560-seat Kingsway to the larger Globe auditorium, which accommodated over 1,000 patrons, and 'held the breathless attention of the house till the fall of the curtain, many of the audience being visibly affected, and one gentleman in the dress circle going into a fit'.[73] For Ashwell, the most significant acclaim came from Ellen Terry, who praised her 'high, high death' in this role.[74] She was heartened to receive such a response, given the past difficult months.

Madame X played for five weeks while Ashwell was rehearsing *The Great Mrs Alloway*, directed by Dion (Dot) Boucicault, which premiered on 8 November. Mrs Alloway, previously a notorious courtesan, has cut a revengeful swathe of broken hearts and ruined fortunes in India following her abandonment by the man she loved before the birth of their son George. Assuming the name of Mrs Hartland, she returns to England where George falls in love with Ethel and has the opportunity, through Sir Charles Hewitt-Gore, to learn more of the father he never knew. Sir Charles discovers Mrs Hartland is Mrs Alloway and demands the marriage be stopped. Defending her career, she puts the situation to Ethel, who decides to marry George and, in a bid for his happiness, leave him in ignorance. In so doing, she recognises his prejudices would never allow him to forgive his mother and condemns herself to a lifetime of concealing the truth. *The Great Mrs Alloway* was 'of mixed quality', appearing initially to be a domestic melodrama, but emerging as 'a play dealing very seriously with sex relations and women's wrongs'. Ashwell's central performance was

full of nervous animation and tense mental activity … [which] proved her to be one of the finest actresses on the English stage, and unapproachable in her especial sphere. The rising spirit of revolt in womanhood has no more picturesque exponent than Miss Ashwell, who is at her best when protesting with indignant scorn against cruelty and injustice.[75]

While now better able to concentrate on her acting, Ashwell was still responsible for promoting the Kingsway as a venue for hire. Her first booking for 1910 was a transfer of Besier's *Don* from the Haymarket and Criterion Theatres. She retained the principal lease on the Kingsway until after the First World War; between 1910 and 1920 she sub-leased it to Lillah McCarthy and Granville-Barker (early 1912 to April 1915) and then to the Vedrenne/Eadie management.[76]

Ashwell continued to work with Frohman in his repertory company at the Duke of York's. McCarthy and Irene Vanbrugh[77] were also members and she was not engaged full-time. Repertoire pieces were alternated during each week, so she was not performing every night. The season introduced subscription booking into ticket purchasing, and included plays by Shaw and J.M. Barrie, with Dot Boucicault and Granville-Barker directing. Shaw's production of *Misalliance*, with Ashwell playing juggler and trapeze artist Lina, opened on 23 February 1910. For the *Era* it was an 'undeniable success', with Ashwell delivering 'indignant tirades and ingenious explanations with all the requisite art and energy'.[78] J.T. Grein was less enthusiastic. A week later she opened in a triple bill, appearing in premieres of Barrie's short plays *Old Friends*, 'a gruesome and impressive dramatic homily on heredity, and the descent of sins [alcoholism] of the fathers upon the children', and *The Twelve Pound Look*, a comedietta which 'was both humorous and sarcastic, and was heartily enjoyed'.[79] In the latter she was Kate, an independent woman who had left her husband fourteen years earlier in order to retain her sense of self-worth. The play begins with the husband, now remarried, about to be knighted and employing a typist, Kate (with the typewriter that for £12 bought her freedom and the energy her ex-husband's new wife admires), to write thank you letters. Kate is still unimpressed by his success and tells him she did not leave him for another man, as he had assumed. Ashwell revived the play on a number of occasions and felt quite proprietorial about this role. She was distressed when *Misalliance* was taken out of the repertoire after only eleven performances. Her contract ended and the role of Kate passed to Vanbrugh, a permanent company member. Given his financial resources, Frohman might have succeeded had circumstances been more auspicious, but his repertory experiment concluded on 17 June when theatres were closed following the death of King Edward VII.

After an apparent period of dormancy, the National Theatre question re-emerged in 1910. An Executive Committee had been appointed and received an anonymous donation of £70,000, but further support proved elusive. King Edward VII, as a patron of the arts, was to be approached. As the *Era* urged support from the profession, Edward's death brought another hiatus. 'In view of the number of people who would be thrown out of employment by prolonged closing of theatres', King George V wanted theatres to be open, 'except on the day of his late Majesty's funeral'.[80] Managers nevertheless decided, as a mark of respect, that theatres would remain closed until after the funeral, re-opening on 18 May. A fund-raising Shakespeare Ball, planned for 27 June, was one of many events postponed. There was considerable demand on the Actors' Benevolent Fund. By the end of May theatres were suffering as audiences were kept away by the social pressure of the Court mourning which continued into June.

As life began to return to normal, on Saturday 18 June at the large Suffragist Procession through London, Ashwell was noticed. She recalled later:

long before the last women had left Cleopatra's Needle, the head of the orderly and well drilled army, carrying banners and flags of different societies, arrived at the Albert Hall. In the windows of clubs and along crowded streets were curious and contemptuous people. Well-dressed men, with ridicule in their eyes and the smile of superiority on their sneering lips, stared as we passed along. It really was infuriating and now it seems quite unbelievable. Lots of funny things happened to cheer us on that exhausting walk … Everyone was in mourning for King Edward, but for this procession we were asked to wear white dresses. Owing to a rush of work, I had no time to change, so there I was, conspicuous in black … and I heard a man say … 'You see 'er, there in the black? That there is the bad girl of the family.'[81]

Three days later she hosted an AFL fund-raising matinee at the Kingsway for the NUWSS. Hamilton's *How The Vote Was Won* and Shaw's *Press Cuttings* were performed. Participating in the Great Demonstration of Suffragettes in Hyde Park on 23 July, she was distressed by press comments reducing these events to entertainment: 'the crowd noted with cheers a little band of beautifully dressed women, among whom were Miss Ashwell … and several other suffragist sympathizers on the stage'.[82] Some twenty-five years later she wrote:

It is impossible to realise now the scorn which women who thought they should be recognised as citizens drew upon themselves from otherwise polite and sensible people. Managers, authors, pressmen became quite passionate in their resentment and, wise in their generation, did not associate themselves with this unpopular movement.[83]

Even Beerbohm Tree, a friend in many other ways, contemptuously rejected female suffrage as Ashwell's commitment to this and related women's causes grew.

In September 1910, Liebler and Company announced that Ashwell would appear in America in McLellan's drama *The Strong People*, retitled *Judith Zaraine*.[84] While preparing for her tour, she chaired an AFL meeting on 7 October and, as a belated contribution to Suffrage Week, the AFL presented a matinee on 18 November. Hamilton's *Pageant of Great Women*, directed by Edith Craig, with Ashwell as Florence Nightingale and many of her colleagues portraying the great women of history, was the finale. The packed, enthusiastic house, comprised mostly of women, was entertained also by 'Miss Ashwell's beautiful recital of some Elizabethan love lyrics [which] compelled an insistent encore'.[85] In December she sailed for America, leaving Dr Simson alone for Christmas.

Rehearsals, with an American cast in New York, began immediately. In London, the *Era* lamented the state of serious drama, explaining in part Ashwell's difficulty in sustaining longer runs at the Kingsway. 'The majority of playgoers go … to be amused, not to be enlightened or instructed. With our system of prices, theatre … has to be supported by the great prosperous middle class … the class which takes

3.9 Ashwell at the time of her second American tour, 1911
(Matzene, courtesy of Stuart Gough)

its wives and daughters … If a play pleases this class, it prospers; if it repels them, it fails.' The writer hoped critics would begin to provide more 'common sense criticism' and less intellectual analysis.[86] It was even harder in America. *Judith Zaraine* opened at the Astor on 16 January and closed two weeks later. Ashwell was praised for her portrayal combining 'intelligence and strength of purpose', but the play was not understood by critics or audiences, and Ashwell suffered another severe disappointment in America.[87] Originally intending not to return until May, she arrived back in time to recite at the AFL's 'At Home' on 3 March when Lord Robert Cecil urged suffragists to take on 'the rather dull, tedious work known as canvassing and persuading electors to put this question [the vote for women] before all others'.[88] He had the support of many, including Ashwell, when he stated that this method was more useful than militancy would ever be.

Almost immediately, she was cast in *The Master of Mrs Chilvers*, presented by the Vedrenne/Eadie management. She was delighted to be playing opposite good friend Dennis Eadie. J.K. Jerome's topical, political comedy, which treated the 'Women's Franchise question from a more serious standpoint than has been the case in most recent plays',[89] premiered at the Kings, Glasgow, on 10 April and at the Royalty, London, two weeks later. Chilvers, MP, supports his wife's involvement with the suffrage movement, but their lives are thrown into disarray by his needing to fight a by-election and his wife standing on behalf of the Women's Parliamentary Franchise League and pitting herself against him. She wins, but steps down when she learns she is pregnant. Unlike *Diana of Dobson's*, the work has not survived as a significant suffrage theatrical statement. It might have done, had Jerome pursued the issue of motherhood versus public life. During this season, on 3 May, at the annual Stratford-on-Avon Shakespeare Festival Ashwell made her long-wished-for debut as Rosalind in *As You Like It*. She had little time to prepare and it was not a critically acclaimed performance.

The New York visit was not an entirely negative experience. She had visited the Professional Woman's League residential club and returned determined to establish such a facility in London. With Eva Moore, Mrs Kendal and Princess Marie Louise (president), Ashwell, as chairman, began working towards a club to provide affordable, comfortable accommodation for young female artists needing residence in London during engagements. She found a centrally based venue in the former Marylebone Home for Cripples and raising financial support to adapt and furnish the building became her priority. Ashwell was a member of the Rehearsal Club – a retreat, founded in 1892, for actresses between rehearsals, matinees and evening performances. Her Three Arts Club intended 'to help those who are not yet firmly established on the ladder of success … it will also safeguard girls in the theatrical profession unused to London life'.[90] The Club's advisory board included the Lord Bishop of London, John Sargent, Elgar and Pinero and had many associate members who donated cash towards setting-up costs of £3,500. It was not a charity: charges would be reasonable, but once established, it would have to run on its income. The Club received a great deal of publicity, particularly for a special matinee on 19 May at St James's Theatre. The highlight was the revival of Jonson's *The Hue and Cry After Cupid*, with Ashwell playing Juno. Four hours in length, with scenes from well-known plays, one-act plays, a ballet and musical interludes, the event raised £500.

Ashwell, who often needed to be protective of her health and energy, did not march in the annual Great Procession of Women on Saturday 17 June 1911, but was supporting events representing the diversity of her interests and commitments, and appeared at the Kingsway with Terry and other distinguished actresses in Christopher St John's *The First Actress*,[91] which, with new plays by Hamilton and Margaret Wynne Nevinson, launched Edith Craig's Pioneer Players.[92]

The coronation of George V was celebrated by the theatrical profession at a Gala Performance on 27 June, attended by the king and queen, at His Majesty's Theatre. The evening ended with Jonson's masque *The Vision of Delight*, with Ashwell playing a 'romantic Phantasy' in 'a witty and brilliant epilogue to the Coronation festivities'.[93] The masque was a last-minute addition to the programme, included only after Ashwell's intervention. She took issue with the Managers' Association, which had ensured most of the leading actors would take part, with only a few women in supporting roles. She threatened to write to the queen, expressing regret the actresses had been excluded. The managers gave her twenty-four hours to organise a play for women. Having presented *The Vision of Delight* at the Kingsway in 1908, she quickly rallied support to re-stage it.

At this time, Ashwell was elected an AFL vice-president and the following months were particularly busy. The League had about 600 members and remained neutral on issues such as militancy. It used performances of plays to recruit members and enhance the franchise debate. This influenced Ashwell's choice of plays when manager John Halpin invited her to present a season at the Coronet from 18 September 1911. She began with a week of *Diana of Dobson's*, preceded by *The Likes O' Me* and followed by a week of *Madame X*, with some original cast members taking part. Both plays were well received: 'Miss Lena Ashwell has improved on her cleverly conceived and vividly executed study … she no longer lets her temperament run away with her tongue. In other words, she has checked that propensity to gabble that threatened to become a marked mannerism of one of our most accomplished actresses.'[94]

Immediately after this, on 2 October, Ashwell made her vaudeville/music hall debut at the Palace in Sutro's one-act play *The Man in the Stalls*. Given her attitude to plays in music halls during the censorship debate in 1909, she found her response to this new experience surprising. Observing other performers, such as a female Japanese tightrope walker, she was amazed at their training and 'efficiency'. She recognised quite suddenly the 'exquisitely definite and pointed' nature of a music hall performance, compared to the theatre, where 'we create our own atmosphere … but in the music-hall we have to come straight on and do our work pat, straight off'. Sharing the bill for over a month with the Kellino acrobats, Rinaldo the wandering violinist, and the Boganny Troupe, who presented an amusing scene in an opium den, she realised the hard work behind such entertainment and expressed appreciation for its variety, modernity and ability to bring 'all classes of the community together'.[95] Perceiving her changed attitude, the *Era* was quick to comment: 'The playing at a hall of Miss Ashwell … is one of those happenings that does more to hasten a solution of the question of plays in music halls than any number of diatribes or speeches from aggrieved authors.'[96] She wrote light-heartedly to Shaw: 'Please write me a music hall play! Something daring! and funny & please come and see *The Man in the Stalls* … Yours Lena Ashwell. P.S. I am the only Candida!'[97]

In October Ashwell, with Actors' Benevolent Fund and Royal General Theatrical Fund colleagues, examined the long-term financial security of members of her profession. She proposed a scheme of insurance against illness, unemployment and ill luck. Existing schemes were inappropriate and it was necessary to develop 'some freely organised pool into which those of us whose employment is as fitful as the breeze can put what we think or feel we can afford when we are in work, and out of which we can take as little as need be when the tiding over period arrives – the period between the expired engagement and the promised new one'.[98] Some touring companies already pooled a portion of wages from which could be drawn 'loans', repaid with a penny added for each shilling lent. At the end of the tour, the pennies 'interest' was divided equally. Clarence Derwent observed: 'Miss Ashwell's sympathies have always been with those who have got left in the struggle for fame.'[99] Ten months later the National Insurance Act was introduced, establishing a compulsory system for employees and workers generally. All theatrical workers were included, entailing a small contribution from earned wages with a similar contribution from management and the government. The Actors' Association took an active role in encouraging all members of the profession to be fully aware of this.

On 27 October 1911, the AFL presented a matinee of political parody at the Lyceum. The centre-piece was Laurence Housman's version of Lewis Carroll's story *Alice In Ganderland*. Ashwell recited Sidney Low's response to Kipling's poem 'The Female of the Species'. Soon after, she was one of four AFL representatives in a large Downing Street deputation to meet Prime Minister Asquith and Lloyd George. They sought to ascertain the government's intention on female suffrage given the planned Manhood Suffrage Bill.[100] Asquith declared he could not bring forward something he did not believe was in the country's best interests,[101] prompting Ashwell to write later that his expression made her 'think of that iron curtain which descends in the theatre to ensure the stage is completely shut off from the auditorium'.[102] Four days later there was a women's protest at the House of Commons and the divide between suffragist negotiators and militants widened. The AFL continued to use peaceful activities, such as its twelve performances of short plays, including *The Twelve Pound Look* with Ashwell reviving the role of Kate, at the early December WSPU Christmas Fair and Fête. On 8 December 1911, the Three Arts Club finally opened its doors. There was an initial membership of 500 and most of the 90 rooms were already booked. *Woman At Home* described the Club's initiators, facilities, governing body and advisory committees, rules and regulations: 'This new venture marks another step in the sensible social emancipation of women workers and their revolt against conditions of existence which would never be contemplated or endured by a man.'[103] To raise further funds, there was a magnificent Royal Albert Hall ball on 20 December. Arthur Bourchier played Santa Claus, with some 4,000 revellers in fancy dress dancing to music played by 120 musicians.

It was not all pleasure. In late November, former actor Charles Brookfield was appointed Joint Examiner of Plays with G.A. Redford. Within a month Redford resigned and the profession was responding. Ashwell's views were sought on whether the Censor should be a woman. 'I don't think it would hurt to have a woman who might represent the public more. I understand the Censor is there to protect the tastes of the public. There is only one reason for a Censor ... to protect people playing in a play suddenly being charged at Bow Street for some curious scruple of the Calvinistic conscience.'[104] Lillah McCarthy opposed any censorship other than public opinion and Cicely Hamilton feared a woman censor would be appointed on account of her looks, while Ashwell seemed to be 'almost alone in favouring the notion', doing so 'on broad feminist and not on narrow dramatic grounds'.[105] Her view was clear, however, in the *Pall Mall Gazette*: 'As to whether a woman censor is advisable and likely to license more freely than a man, everything would depend on the individual and that individual's limitations. The arbitrary division of sex in this matter will, I am sure, soon be another prehistoric joke.'[106] Confronting censorship issues close to home, Ashwell was compelled to apply for an injunction to restrain a performance of *The Secret Woman*, fearing it would endanger her Kingsway licence.[107] Granville-Barker was permitted to go ahead with a private performance only. Opposed to the views of colleagues such as authors Hamilton and Anthony Wharton, Ashwell was one of seventy-five managers and actors who were signatories to a letter to the king, dated 29 February 1912:

> We cannot help feeling that were such a censorship abolished, not only might undesirable plays be presented to the public, but the interference of the police, of municipal bodies, and various vigilance societies would render the conduct of theatres most irksome, and would be detrimental to the best interests of the drama. In this spirit we desire to express our confidence in the censorship as exercised under the Lord Chamberlain's supervision.[108]

The pro-censorship lobby believed theatre without censorship in France, and to some extent Germany, lacked decency and propriety. Such qualities were linked to serious purpose in the drama and to the idea of a municipal, non-commercial theatre. Many believed such a theatre would not draw its audience from the 'present play-going population' and municipal theatre would have a civic responsibility to provide a safe and respectable educative environment for young people and could cater for 'the class which takes life and literature seriously' by letting 'them have a theatre which is in accordance with their views and prejudices'.[109] The more recent

arguments for non-commercial, local theatre – access, affordability and other pleas-
urable associations such as 'entertainment' – did not enter into the debate. It was
hoped municipal theatre would create a new audience and provide the profession
with increased employment opportunities. Ashwell's view of theatre was a much
more inclusive one: she wanted to provide access to the best at affordable prices.

Once she embraced variety theatre, there was no stopping her. At the Palladium,
in February and March 1912, she directed Hamilton's one-act play *The Constant
Husband*, in which she played a smart businesswoman whose husband is a serial
eloper. Fed up with his returning to her, she visits the current object of his affec-
tions. Hoping this liaison will be permanent, she hands over her cookery books (his
return is frequently prompted by his need for her culinary expertise), and expresses
desire to get on with her own life. This was followed with a season of Act I of *Diana of Dobson's*, with Ashwell reviving Diana. On 15 March there was a protest
demonstration at the Opera House calling for the enfranchisement of women to
put an end to disorder. Regretting militancy, and seeking to distance organisations
such as the AFL from it, Ashwell was a signatory to a letter of sympathy to West
End tradesmen who suffered from 'the recent suffragette smashings'.[110] She also attended a WSPU Albert Hall demonstration on 29 March, strongly condemning 'the
attempt now being made by the Government to destroy by methods of repression
the agitation for the enfranchisement of women', and calling 'history to witness this
attempt to break the spirit of the freedom loving British people is doomed to fail'.[111]

Her main focus at this time was the Three Arts Club. On 11 May a matinee at
His Majesty's raised £375 towards furnishings. There was 'a bewildering array of
stars of the stage' and the programme included Jonson's *The Vision of Delight*, with
Ashwell as Phantasy. The Club had 700 members, was self-supporting and planned
regional bases once capital costs were covered. She identified the kind of 'charity'
they sought as the dictionary definition of 'universal love' rather than 'alms-giving
out of pity to the poor'.[112] Meanwhile, she was preparing for Wyndham's revival of
Mrs Dane's Defence, which opened in mid-May and ran until mid-July. Wyndham,
who was 75, suffered increasing memory loss and his distortion of lines made acting
with him difficult. 'Ashwell, so concentrated as Mrs Dane, could not handle the
situation'; for her, Wyndham's gap-filling could be 'excruciatingly funny as well as
miserably tragic'.[113] The nervous strain was intolerable, and she succumbed to an
attack of shingles. Ashwell had great admiration and affection for Wyndham but
the revival was 'a most ghastly experience'.[114] Throughout her career she suffered
a number of stress-related illnesses: Golding Bright's prediction that she was in
danger of overworking herself was not too wide of the mark. Except for public
speaking, she did not appear again on stage until November 1913. Often bedridden,
she wrote letters seeking financial support and guest speakers for the Club. Arranging a date for Shaw to lecture took a number of letters, and when he did speak, in
December 1912, she had been ill for nine weeks. Determined to promote the Club,
Ashwell invited distinguished guests, such as prima donna Nellie Melba, to speak
to residents while in London and the press was duly informed.[115]

On 5 July 1912 Vice-President Ashwell chaired an AFL meeting which considered the connection between the White Slave Traffic Bill and enfranchisement of women. The bill was before Parliament to consider amendments the AFL feared would weaken the existing act. Ashwell introduced the subject as one 'which women should know [about] and should face with courage and determination. So long as one woman remained a victim of the white slave traffic, women of the country must feel responsible.' A resolution was proposed and accepted: 'That this meeting, while welcoming any effort on the part of Parliament to minimize the terrible evil of the white slave traffic, calls upon the Government to deal a more fatal blow by granting the vote to women.'[116] While this meeting was not necessarily a turning point for Ashwell, it was a clear indication of her social commitment, although the rest of 1912 was a period of enforced inactivity for her. She gave a recital at the Kursaal, Harrogate, and, after giving notice she was applying for a music and dancing licence for the Kingsway, had an operation on 15 October to remove her appendix. She had intended to participate in a performance of St John's *The First Actress* on 29 November, but was 'for some time after her recent operation ... in a critical condition, [but] is now out of danger and on the road to recovery ... unable to resume her professional work before the New Year'.[117]

When Ashwell rejoined the fray, plans were underway for a suffrage 'Day of Meditation' on St Bride's Day, 1 February 1913. Organised by Reverend Clifford, Church leaders, Muriel de la Warr, Mrs Bramwell Booth (Salvation Army), the Forbes Robertsons, and Ashwell, it was a day of special meditation and intercession in Westminster Abbey, St Paul's Cathedral and numerous cathedrals and churches:

Men and women ... are asked to join in this common approach ... earnestly desiring the consciousness of the world may be so heightened that clear light may be gained on the difficult path, and increase of wisdom and power to achieve. Men and women especially interested in the matter are asked to keep five minutes at noon for silent remembrance and prayer, wherever they may be, during the days [20–7 January] upon which the suffrage question will be before the Commons.[118]

A few days later, at Queen's Hall, there was a meeting of the Federated Council of Suffrage Societies. Mrs Pethick Lawrence expressed the positive mood of the movement, declaring that recently there had been 'a tremendous access of public opinion to their side'.[119]

Although the fight for Women's Suffrage has been well documented, Ashwell's role in the theatrical profession's involvement has not. She focused on positive action and collaboration. While reacting strongly against the policy of forcible feeding of imprisoned suffragettes on hunger strike, like many colleagues she was somewhat ambivalent about the activities of the militants. She alienated Vanbrugh at the AFL Drury Lane meeting on 2 May when none of the speakers, with the bravely conspicuous exception of Miss Vanbrugh, thought it proper publicly to dissociate herself from the militant movement, whose reckless violence has shocked the conscience of every decent man and woman … The ladies who form this particular League stand in a peculiar position … their influence is great, and if they disapprove of methods which have so gravely compromised the fortunes of the legitimate movement for women suffrage, they should have the courage to say so.[120]

It was a difficult meeting, leading to Vanbrugh's resignation from the AFL. The resolution called on Asquith to bring in the vote by government measure to prevent disorder. Greeted by both cheers and hisses, Vanbrugh declared she had no sympathy with militancy. No other speaker supported her. She later wrote that Ashwell was the next speaker, saying 'while she appreciated my wishing to clarify my own attitude, it was not possible for the AFL to dissociate themselves from both sides in their campaign'.[121] Ashwell, who in June 1914 would acknowledge militant methods played a role in speeding up the campaign, then pleaded the cause of women workers, giving statistics on long hours and small wages. She urged those present 'not to be put off by any criticism, but to ask the anti-suffragist to meditate on the question, and get her to realise the one thing necessary to the women of this country was the vote'.[122]

Concurrently with her public statements for the AFL, Ashwell was a constant advocate for an accessible theatre. Addressing Bristol Playgoers' Club, she argued theatre had two great purposes to serve: widening the consciousness and awareness of its audience to gain them insight into the lives of others; and the awakening of feeling. On the subject of popular entertainment such as cinema, she felt 'the mass could never be the real judge of values, and the danger in modern civilisation was to confuse monetary success with real intrinsic value'. She wanted mechanical inventions (cinema) to stimulate people 'to demand from theatre something far greater, nobler and more important than it had yet been able to produce'. She concluded:

> when all artistes could express their individualism [instead of audiences seeking 'personalities'] … and without the only inspiration being that of one for gain, when they could construct a new standard which was not of monetary success … they would have in England a great theatre representing the hopes, desires and feelings of a really great nation.[123]

When the National Theatre question was debated in the House of Commons in April 1913, the Actors' Association urged the National Theatre Committee, of which Ashwell was a member, to organise a public appeal and begin planning the Shakespeare Tercentenary Year in 1916. A meeting on 15 May considered a progress report and balance sheet, but there was anger at the behaviour of those at the meeting, particularly Shaw's flippant response to the loss of £3,000 on the Earl's Court Shakespeare Exhibition in 1912.[124]

Ashwell no doubt left this meeting with good intentions but she was busy in many directions. Her part in the Women's Tax Resistance League[125] deputation to Treasury, on the subject of taxation of married women, was widely reported. In early June, seven women met with Chancellor Lloyd George to point out injustices in income tax law in relation to the recent Married Women's Property Act. The deputation considered it an indignity that a married woman was not properly responsible for her own affairs and urged that husbands and wives should be treated as separate taxable units. In a 'clever and amusing' speech, Ashwell explained after fifteen years of paying tax on her own earnings, this year tax papers were addressed to her husband at her place of business, the Kingsway. She was referred to in brackets as '(for wife)'. She explained:

> Her husband had never been an actor ... nor her manager, and had no desire to study the workings of a profession in which she had already made sums on which she had paid a considerable amount in income-tax before she was aware of his existence, although he assured her he was aware of hers. *[Laughter.]*... she could assure the Chancellor he would be quite incapable of giving a just return to the Government of her work, or the money she had made by it. If she was not a person, but an appendage, it should be impossible for her to be on the list of taxpayers. Surely anything which was simply a parenthesis should not be on the list of those who supported the expenses of this great nation.[126]

Other delegation members gave examples of indignities and injustice and Lloyd George promised, without conviction, to consider the issues. In *Votes for Women*, Ashwell argued it was 'through work people find themselves' and you cannot 'have a fine race of men when these very men are occupied in making slaves of women'. She felt that 'today the growth of imagination is going on in all classes; people are learning to visualise things, and so all sorts of old bad systems have got to go'. She declared she was not an advocate of militancy – 'I haven't the temperament for it' – but recognised the power of such tactics and could 'see it is horribly difficult to view things fairly when we are right in the middle of them ... and it is impossible for all women to work in the same way for their freedom'.[127]

In May, *Votes for Women* announced plans for a Co-operative Theatrical Scheme for Women, organised by the AFL's Inez Bensusan. The aim was to have the whole operation, including a theatrical agency, run by women, 'based on the co-operative principle'.[128] Once expenses were covered, all profits would be divided between the AFL and other guarantor suffrage societies. As its first big project, the Woman's Theatre booked the Court Theatre for a week with Ashwell cast in Charlotte Shaw's translation of Eugène Brieux's *La femme seule* (*Woman on Her Own*). So, apart from giving promotional press interviews, lecturing on Women and Work at the Women's Institute, chairing an AFL meeting at the Shaftesbury, and playing hostess at the Theatrical Ladies Guild Albert Hall Tea party, in November Ashwell was preparing the role of Thérèse, a woman on her own.

Now recognised as a significant public figure, she was receiving 'reviews' as a personality, and one article created a picture of a gracious and genteel Ashwell, living in a charming old-fashioned Grosvenor Street house. There was, however, 'something of the *révolté*, something of the *indignatio*, not *sorra*, but full of sentiment, which makes the reformer, the righter of wrongs and benefactress. Charity in Miss Ashwell's case begins at home, and with one's own sex.' She seized this opportunity to speak out on working conditions for actresses and declared the Three Arts Club to be 'an experiment no longer, but an established success', with over 1,000 members. To become a member 'you must be a bona-fide worker at one of the three arts ... it is of no use for *dilettante* or dabblers to try ... you must give evidence that you are a genuine labourer in the vineyards, not an amateur'.[129] Speaking at the Women's Institute, she felt it essential that everyone have opportunity to experience the 'intense joy of struggle and achievement' through work. But women

> must determine that conditions should be fair, and they must not do the community the great wrong of working without wages. One reason the work of the home-makers was so despised by men – although the home-makers were the most important people in the country – was that no money value had been placed on their work. Women were apt to distrust their own powers, to dwell too much on what they regarded as their limitations. There were no necessary limitations. Sex need be no bar in any direction. The main essential to success was a courageous belief in one's own powers and a determination to go forward.[130]

In *Flair* she was quoted as blaming producers for perpetrating the situation where beauty frequently prevailed over brains in the casting of women. Producers seem to forget all about

> an artist's power to become someone else ... a lot of the trouble arises from the dreadful habit of looking for 'types' ... I should never have won a prize at a beauty show ... By raising the intellectual standard of the actress we of the Woman's Theatre hope to do something to remedy the treatment of minor actresses who, in an overcrowded profession, were exploited for their looks and given little opportunity for continuity of work.[131]

Ashwell developed her observations on the acting profession further, contributing a chapter to *Women Workers in Seven Professions: A Survey of their Economic Conditions and Prospects*, published by the Fabian Women's Group.[132] She made it very clear there was little glamour for most actresses, pointing to the overcrowded nature of the profession and the need to develop 'a supplementary trade' to survive long periods out of work. She quoted an average annual income of £70 for a working actor, but declared that 'under present conditions, the average day for an average actress is one in which she looks for work'.[133] She gave examples of living and working conditions and a clear idea of frustrations and difficulties. She hoped this was a period of transition from which women would emerge stronger. As she said, on introducing a 'remarkable' AFL meeting at the Shaftesbury on 18 November, when all the speakers were men, she hoped male support would enable women to be given recognition of their citizenship: 'they had arrived, and they only asked for the recognition of their arrival'.[134]

Brieux's *Woman on Her Own* was not critically acclaimed at its Coronet opening on 8 December.[135] The *Times* thought the play could be called 'Round the Woman Question in two and a half Hours': 'The author seems to have looked up all the disabilities, real or imaginary, under which women labour in modern society, and to have determined his heroine shall endure them all.'[136] Thérèse, made penniless by an unscrupulous male lawyer and no longer a suitable wife for her weak fiancé, is forced onto her own resources. She works for a women's magazine, but when the editor makes advances towards her and pay and conditions worsen, she has to leave. In a bookbinding factory, she organises women into a union to obtain better conditions. The men threaten violence and damage; her boss requests her departure. At the end she returns to Paris, to live as mistress to her fiancé because they cannot marry without his parents' consent, or to turn to prostitution or another form of slavery to man. Some could not understand why Ashwell consented 'to enunciate this doctrine of inferiority ... she is herself a direct contradiction of the author's argument. Success by her own effort has been hers; she has shown herself enterprising and capable until she stands today as the woman's representative of her profession.'[137] There was praise for the production but not the play. It was a propaganda piece and 'like so many recent dramas, the whole thing is rather a statement of the difficulty than a solution, and though M. Brieux has attempted to state it honestly, there is over all a sense of hindrance and defeat'.[138]

After a week of performances, mainly to female audiences, *Woman on Her Own* was succeeded by *A Gauntlet* by Bjornstjerne Bjornson, originally produced by the Play Actors in 1913. The initial achievements of the Woman's Theatre, including its financial success, and the contributions of many actresses and writers, were praised. However, Ashwell was considered

> the most interesting personality of all ... she is a happy wife, the best friend in the world, a willing adviser and practical helper to any who seek her aid, an ardent fighter for the woman's cause, which she says is the only cause worth fighting for, and a charming hostess. She is the busiest woman imaginable, for she is a 'leading lady', has a theatre of her own, an interest in a hat shop, as well as a manicurist's, and a fine furniture shop[139] besides being a regular and welcome visitor to women's hospitals and a labourer for improved conditions for sweated women workers.[140]

Not surprisingly, on 30 December Ashwell was among thirteen distinguished women from all walks of life pictured on the *Daily Sketch*'s front page, considered suitable for inclusion on the king's Honours List – at the time open only to men.[141] Early in the New Year, the Three Arts Club Fancy Dress Ball at Covent Garden was one of very few light-hearted experiences for Ashwell and her colleagues in 1914. A fund-raising event, it focused on the work of women artists, with competitions for the best one-act play and for posters to be included in the Club's March Exhibition in London. The Club was producing *The Three Arts Journal*, a monthly periodical containing reviews, literary commentary, humour and illustrations, favourably reviewed in *Votes for Women*.[142]

In the first half of 1914 there was a considerable increase in suffragist activity. With the establishment of the United Suffragists in February, there were fifty-three organisations, involving both men and women. Ashwell headed the United Suffragists' committee of ten, who worked quickly and effectively in the Poplar by-election, helping, through meetings, canvassing and a demonstration, to reduce the majority of the Liberal candidate by some 1,600 votes.[143] Ashwell did not explain this apparent shift of allegiance from the AFL, but the United Suffragists was formed in the belief that men and women could usefully co-operate on equal terms for the enfranchisement of women, and regarded woman suffrage as the foremost bipartisan political issue of the day, so her purpose was clear. The intention was to lobby local constituencies to bring pressure to bear on government; to correct 'journalistic inexactitudes'; and to work in harmony with other leagues, while keeping in view 'the important truth that a merry heart goes all the way, and that a spirit of comradeship, good temper and sense of humour has always characterised the Woman's fight for freedom'.[144] Ashwell was also supporting an independent proposal for a deputation to Asquith and the Home Secretary to seek constitutional cessation of forcible feeding and withdrawal of the 'Cat and Mouse' Act.[145] Asquith refused to receive such a deputation and petitioning continued.

On 11 April, while Shaw was despairing of Tree's treatment of *Pygmalion*,[146] his wife Charlotte and Ashwell were en route to America for five weeks. They travelled with Chicago doctor and philosopher James Porter Mills, and his wife, who called herself 'Healer' and dabbled in Christian Science. Ashwell had been inspired by Adela Curtis's 'New Mysticism' and her methods of meditation adapted to Western religion. Through Curtis, Ashwell met Mills and quickly embraced his 'New Order of Meditation', based on what he called 'education of the intuition'. Mills lectured in England before the war and both Charlotte Shaw and Ashwell became his 'disciples,' even though he

> was not at all brilliant, not even clever. At times Charlotte thought him a rather snuffy, bad-tempered old man; but he had undeniable 'power', and he was 'different'. He could not write well, yet in the books he published, lacking clarity and without any vestige of style, he was able to convey something that caught and held the attention.[147]

Shaw published her understanding of his ideas in *Knowledge is the Door: A Forerunner*, which sold 1,000 copies.[148] For Ashwell, meeting Mills resulted in an amazing change which brought her life 'into a totally different focus and made it possible to carry on work which was far beyond my natural strength'. She found that 'Meditation was a faculty through which a new power within the mind could be given birth.' She had many lessons with him, and having learned to concentrate her attention in theatre, through meditation she gained insight and strength, accepting that 'all achievement meant real hard work, and there were mountains of difficulty in my nature and the smallness of my personal outlook. But I was shoved along that path by something stronger than myself.'[149]

As well as pursuing philosophical interests, they marched in a Boston suffrage procession; Ashwell described it as a 'tiny, well-ordered body passing through a polite and sympathetic crowd to be received at the Town Hall by the Mayor and Corporation'.[150] On their return, Ashwell chaired the United Suffragists' first public meeting and commented on her experience in an America sympathetic to the women's movement. 'There was not one sign of the attitude which, believe me, is driving mad the women of this country. There was nothing but interest, respect, and politeness.' The American press appeared to deal fairly with the suffrage movement, while English newspapers 'misrepresented Suffragists and suppressed news of their constitutional efforts. In America women had constitutional rights even without possession of the vote. In this country women's constitutional rights would have to be searched for with a microscope.'[151] Ashwell became impassioned when speaker Olive Schreiner, who had just witnessed the break-up by police of a women's deputation outside Buckingham Palace, was too distressed to continue. Ashwell, no longer ambivalent, declared:

> When you realise what is going on day by day and hour by hour, then you know what it is that is making militants. [Applause] Whatever your feeling is, whether you approve or disapprove of militancy, whether you are angry or bitter against it, or whether you are only indifferent, believe me, militancy and acts of violence do not arise of themselves, they are the result of other actions, and the whole thing is the result of the position which women are not only in, but kept in.[152]

The meeting gave a clear indication of increasing anger at the government's intransigence. Many were now compelled to acknowledge reasons for militant action. In mid-June, the *Era* quoted Ashwell's exchange with Yvette Guilbert,[153] who would only speak at a United Suffragists' meeting on 7 July provided 'you pledge your militant sisters to call a truce and to abstain from any act of violence or hostile demonstration up to that date'. Ashwell's response was:

> I do not belong to a militant society, and have no control over my militant sisters. I hold a strong belief active efforts on the part of every non militant Suffragist to obtain suffrage rights for women will eventually force those prejudiced or obtusely indifferent to realise the vital necessity for reform. Only the courageous can put an end to militancy by publicly asserting their belief in women's suffrage, and taking active steps to redress the evils of which militancy is the hideous result.[154]

Guilbert did speak at the 'How to Stop Militancy!' meeting, chaired by Ashwell, held during a week in which women from British overseas dominions visited London to see the suffragist movement in action.

Apart from a 'peaceful' event for the Poetry Society on 7 June, when Ashwell read poems to celebrate 100 years of peace between England and America, her energies at this time were fully focused on the suffragist cause.[155] On 22 June her letter on 'Woman Suffrage and the Referendum' was published. Protesting at Lord Murray's referendum suggestion, Ashwell declared: 'Our claim is not based on opinion, but on principles of liberty and justice. Woman suffrage is an immediate political necessity ... We are an inarticulate half of the community – workers, wage earners and taxpayers – and not only have a right to, but need the vote.'[156] Maintaining her links with things theatrical, in early July she addressed the Bristol Playgoers' Club. She praised Theatre Royal director Muriel Pratt, who was working to achieve a serious repertory programme, and declared 'there were two forces now striking her with equal power – the theatre and the cause of women throughout the world'.[157] Ashwell had found her voice, determination and stamina, necessary resources for the next phase of her life.

Then worst fears were realised: war was declared on Germany on 4 August 1914 and on Austria-Hungary on 10 August. With amazing rapidity, Ashwell, Decima and Eva Moore and Eve Haverfield formed what Ashwell later described as a 'really wonderful and most comic organization', the Women's Emergency Corps (WEC).[158] A temporary office was set up in Robert Street, Adelphi; letters, dated 7 August, were sent to the press and a public meeting convened at the Shaftesbury that day. The Corps' first task was to create a register, for use by any authority requiring such services, of all women, with their particular skills, who could help the war effort. The list included cooks, interpreters, crèche and mother carers, stores' distributors, clothing collectors and distributors, carers of horses and riders, motor drivers and 'all women trained in any capacity'.[159] Immediately, many hundreds of women offered their services and women's suffrage took a back seat while Britons adjusted to a changed world.

Many suffrage workers quickly devoted their energy to the Corps, whose major concern was increasing unemployment amongst young women. Businesses were closing or operating at reduced levels while men enlisted in the armed forces and women were not always considered as possible replacements. Over 3,000 offers of help from women were received within a few weeks and over half of these were classified and registered on a card index. 'We are making a special point of so organising and controlling voluntary service that there shall be no interference with the paid labour market.'[160] Nor did the Corps intend to interfere with or supersede relief work undertaken by existing societies. Co-operation was sought, and the Corps aimed to be representative of all women. On 4 September, the *Bristol Evening News* reported that the WEC had 10,000 women registered and government departments, railway companies and business houses had been informed of competent unemployed women available for work previously done by men. Ashwell also established the Three Arts Club Emergency Relief Fund, recognising female arts workers would be particularly hard hit by the war's impact on employment: 'We have to face a financial upheaval such as has never been known ... and even in homes of prosperous business men there will have to be a rigid cutting down of luxuries, of which amusement is one of the chief.'[161] August was traditionally a time when many London theatres were closed for summer (with productions moving to provincial theatres), and suggestions were made to halve admission prices and actors' salaries; already many were on the breadline. In co-operation with organisations including the Actors' Benevolent Fund, Ashwell hoped to help those in urgent need to obtain paid employment; to give training for such employment and maintenance when required; and to obtain and administer grants from existing funds for the relief of such cases. For extreme needs, money and food were also available. The fund called for donations, offers of work and help in kind. By mid-August, variety theatre managers and artistes had arranged a co-operative scheme, dividing receipts equally between them; and theatregoers were asked to support their theatres as companies devised ways to maintain work.

On 2 September the *Era* announced its War Distress Fund to provide immediate help for those in the profession. Theatres and well-known actors began donating performance proceeds. Ashwell chaired the committee established to determine recipients of support; any application had to have a reference from a theatre manager. 'Distress in the theatrical profession'[162] was not included in the scope of the National Relief Fund and there were calls for public support for such activities as the Woman's Theatre variety week in November at the Coronet.

Lena Ashwell was one of the first to suggest artists be gainfully employed to boost troop morale by providing entertainment. In October 1914 she tried very hard

to get the entertainment of troops put on national lines, and was interviewed several times on the scheme of 'every camp its own theatre', and the organising of work by professional actors, but there was little interest shown. This effort ... was followed by the formation of a Representative Committee – which I invited to organise an appeal to the War Office – a gathering of noted musicians and actors, with representatives ... of the Church as a guarantee of our respectability and good faith. An appeal was formulated and sent to the War Office that recreation should be organised, that the movement should be national, as national as the Red Cross, but our offer was refused.[163]

'Sad and disheartened' by this, she 'threw more energy than ever into the Women's Emergency Corps', writing later that when she read the first six months' report, it took her breath away: 'the tremendous amount of work that was done, and the way it gave birth to many greater efforts – the National Food Fund, the Women's Legion, the Women's Volunteer Reserve, amongst many others'.[164] Once the Corps was operational in London, Ashwell and Eva Moore initiated provincial branches in Bristol and Newcastle. On 27 March 1915 *Ladies' Field* reported that there were fifteen branches across the country, dealing with local conditions but working closely with London headquarters.

Then, 'on one never-to-be-forgotten day, when I had quite lost hope of the drama and music of the country being regarded as anything but useless, Lady Rodney called on behalf of the Women's Auxiliary Committee of the YMCA. She had returned from France, and came from Her Highness Princess Helena Victoria, Committee Chairman, to ask if it was possible for a concert party to go to Havre.'[165] Ashwell had close connections with the royal family, particularly Marie Louise, and no doubt she told the princess of her despair and desire to help troops and artists. A request from Her Highness was less easy for officials to ignore. Ashwell obtained support from a friend to cover expenses for the first concert party while Helena Victoria and her committee made arrangements with the War Office: 'owing to the very suffering state of men at Base Camps who had passed through a very difficult period of fighting, and were to be at the Base for rest and further training, this experiment of sending recreation should be made'.[166] At this time it was only a tentative experiment: conditions included no advertisement or making use of the situation to aggrandise one's professional popularity. All artists had to be known by Ashwell and to become known to Her Highness who was personally responsible for them and their conduct.

> They were to work with the Y.M.C.A., who would look after the billeting arrangements in France, and places, times, etc., for the concerts … There were grave doubts on the part of the Y.M.C.A. … I think some expected us to land in France in tights, with peroxided hair, and altogether to be a difficult thing for a religious organisation to camouflage. Some good things did come to us through the war, and one of them was the breaking down of barriers due to misunderstanding.[167]

So, as Britain embarked on a destructive war which was to last for over four years, the many recent 'battles' fought by Ashwell and her colleagues had prepared them for major physical and mental challenges to which they rose with exceptional energy and determination. As a theatre manager, actress, suffragist, spokesperson and fighter for recognition of the full capabilities of women in society, Lena Ashwell had emerged a leader. The conditions of war shifted many previously male responsibilities onto women – responsibilities which she embraced. Priorities were identified and pursued very quickly by these women: militant suffragettes became committed war workers and many women set about to change forever attitudes which had relegated women to a secondary, and often merely domestic, role in society.

Notes

1   Arthur St John Adcock, 'The Moan of a Theatre-Manager' (1903), in J. Field and M. Field (eds), *The Methuen Book of Theatre Verse* (London, 1991), 37–8.

2   The Theatrical Managers' Association was founded in 1894, with Henry Irving as the first president. Its first woman president was Prue Skene, elected in 1991. The Society of West End Theatre Managers still exists, working closely with the TMA and dealing specifically with London's theatre district.

3   This was a view expressed by Beerbohm Tree and George Alexander at the Carl Henschel dinner, 19 January 1908 (*Era*, 25 January 1908).

4   M. Borsa, *The English Stage of Today*, tr. S. Brinton (London, 1908), 39–40.

5   *Ibid.*, 46.

6   *Nation*, 7 March 1908.

7   *Era*, 21 March 1908.

8   *Era*, 7 March 1908. The Actors' Association, formed in 1891, aimed to improve work conditions. The suggestion that it should become a trade union was made in 1906 and it took on a more active role in pursuing better salaries and conditions. It was not until December 1929 that the British Actors' Equity Association was formed as a trade union for professional actors (*Oxford Companion to the Theatre*, 107).

9   The *Era*, for example, included three paragraphs on Ashwell's dresses in *The Sway Boat*: 'The gown donned by Miss Ashwell in the last act is a beautiful mixture of deep Bordeaux coloured satin of the richest and softest tint, covered with dark plum-coloured chiffon' (24 October 1908). The *Bystander*, 26 February 1908, noted that in *Diana of Dobson's*, Ashwell, while 'not one of the most notoriously good dressers', triumphed with her second act costume, whose 'glorious embroidery of shaded dahlias [was] … a sure predication of the next spring fashions'.

10 Ashwell, *Myself A Player*, 122.

11 'The Play Actors' Society, founded May 1907, for the production of original works by English authors, Shakespearean plays, and other classical works, including translations, and to benefit the position of the working actor and actress.' *Era Annual* (1918), 115.

12 C. Hamilton, *Diana of Dobson's*, Act I, in L. Fitzsimmons and V. Gardner (eds), *New Woman Plays* (London, 1991), 39.

13 Ashwell, *Myself a Player*, 152.

14 S. Stowell, in *A Stage of Their Own: Feminist Playwrights of the Suffrage Era* (Manchester, 1992), Chapter 3, gives a detailed account and analysis of the writing of *Diana of Dobson's*. Hamilton subsequently published a serious and lengthy statement in *Marriage as a Trade* (London, 1909).

15 Hamilton, *Diana of Dobson's*, Act III, 69.

16 *Sunday Times*, 16 February 1908.

17 *Ibid.*

18 London: British Library: Maud Arncliffe Sennett collection, Women's Suffrage in England 1906–36, vol. 2: unidentified newspaper, 11 January 1908.

19 *Public Opinion*, 15 May 1908.

20 *London Opinion*, 30 May 1908.

21 The Actors' Orphanage was founded in 1896 'to board, clothe and educate destitute children of actors, actresses, and members of the vaudeville profession, and to fit them for useful positions in after-life.' *Stage Year Book* (1926, 109).

22 Other productions were *Miss Hook of Holland* (462), *Brewster's Millions* (323), *The Girls of Gottenburg* (307), *The Gay Gordons* (229), *The Earl of Pawtucket* (223), *The Thief* (186). *Daily Chronicle*, 25 June 1908.

23 *Daily Express*, 9 April 1908.

24 In the Public Records Office, London, (GLC AR/BR/19/433) plans show the theatre layout in January 1898, with a narrow frontage in Great Queen Street and the depth of the stage and auditorium running along the parallel Parker Street at the back, together with Ashwell's request, submitted by E.W. Temple on 26 September 1908, to install a hot water boiler and connections.

25 *Bolton Evening News*, 21 September 1908, from programme for *The Sway Boat*, Kingsway Theatre, October 1908 (author's collection).

26 Programme for *The Sway Boat*, Kingsway Theatre.

27 *Manchester Courier*, 15 October 1908.

28 Ashwell, *Myself a Player*, 160.

29 There is a bust of Ashwell in the Chairman's office of the National Theatre, London, which proclaims her one of its founders. However, she was never considered by the later architects of the National Theatre, led by Sir Laurence Olivier, to be a key figure in this movement, and, true to her style, she was more concerned to investigate the practical application of a National Theatre idea, which she pursued after WWI with her Players.

30 Moral Re-Armament Archives: transcript.

31 *Westminster Gazette*, 10 June 1908.

32 *Daily Chronicle*, 1 May 1908.

33 *Era*, 20 June 1908.

34 C. Hamilton, *Life Errant* (London, 1935), 62.

35 The production played in Buxton, Harrogate, Bristol, Liverpool, Southport, Newcastle, Glasgow, Dublin and Birmingham.

36 Ashwell, *Myself a Player*, 153–4.

37 *Penny Illustrated Paper*, 30 October 1908.

38 *Daily Mail*, 10 October 1908.

39 Unrelated to Ashwell's decision, but timely, the *Era*'s editorial, 'Actor-Managers as Advisers', describes an incident where an audience member at Martin Harvey's *The Lost Heir* at the Adelphi sought Harvey's help. The *Era*, 17 October 1908, observed that 'the responsibilities of our actor-managers are already very onerous and numerous … it appears there is now to be added that of setting straight the crooked ways of the world as they affect the lives of individual play-goers … Miss Ashwell may receive missives from ladies who have fallen victims to the "drug habit", deploring their weakness and asking her to suggest, if not supply, the means of a cure.'

40 *Onlooker*, 5 December 1908.

41 Programme for *Grit* by H. Herman Chilton, Kingsway Theatre, November 1908 (author's collection).

42 *Daily Telegraph*, 25 November 1908.

43 *Era*, 2 January 1909.

44 *Birmingham Daily Mail*, 16 June 1909.

45 Quoted in J. Vere, 'The Playwright's Progress', intro. to E. Knoblock, *Kismet and Other Plays*, ed. J. Vere (London, 1957), 9.

46 *Liverpool Daily Post*, 12 February 1909.

47 *World*, 16 February 1909.

48 *Daily Chronicle* and *Era*, 10 April 1909.

49 Programme for *The Sway Boat*, Kingsway Theatre.

50   *Truth*, 17 February 1909.
51   Ashwell, *Myself a Player*, 154.
52   *Ibid.*, 157.
53   *Standard*, 10 April 1909.
54   Ashwell, *Myself a Player*, 156.
55   J.B. Fagan, *The Earth* (London, 1909), 16.
56   *Ibid.*, 19.
57   *Ibid.*, 29.
58   *Pall Mall Gazette*, 19 April 1909.
59   *Times*, 29 May 1909.
60   *Times*, 30 May 1909.
61   *Era*, 9 January 1909.
62   Shaw's preface to *The Shewing-Up of Blanco Posnet* (London, 1927) gives a full account of Shaw's view of the Censorship enquiry, and in 1955 the Shaw Society published a Shavian Tract, no. 3, a transcript of his evidence to the committee.
63   Ashwell, *Myself a Player*, 107–8.
64   *Report from the Joint Select Committee of the House of Lords and the House of Commons on the Stage Plays (Censorship) together with the Proceedings of the Committee, Minutes of Evidence, and Appendices*, Bluebook 214 (London, 1909), 210–14.
65   *Era*, 19 December 1908.
66   On 13 May 1909 Ashwell used the *Times* to appeal for funds to save the existence of that 'splendid corps the Legion of Frontiersmen' who, without support during three years, had grown to a force of over 3,000 men. 'They belong to the class which made the Empire, and are trying to organise for its defence.' Ashwell's brother, Roger Pocock, following his travels in the wilds of Canada, had founded the Legion in 1904 as a gung-ho association of adventurers. Meanwhile, Hilda Pocock had established the New Frances Club in the Strand, initially for theatrical women only, but in June 1909 membership and facilities were widened to include women engaged in business or literary work. On 11 December 1909 Ashwell gave recitations accompanied by Hawley at a fund-raising concert for the Club.
67   *Express*, 18 June 1909.
68   *Express Star*, 26 June 1909.
69   *Licensed Victuallers' Gazette*, 26 June 1909.
70   *Daily News*, 17 June 1909.
71   *Lloyd's Weekly News*, 10 July 1909.
72   Ashwell, *Myself a Player*, 163.
73   *Era*, 4 September 1909.
74   L. Ashwell, *The Stage* (London, 1929), 20.
75   *Era*, 13 November 1909.
76   Ashwell wrote after working with Charles Frohman, 'I still had the long lease of the Kingsway and had to do many hateful things to pay for it until, after the War, I was able to sell the lease' (*Myself a Player*, 157).
77   Two actresses of Ashwell's generation, well known for their strong personalities and stage presence and better known over time – perhaps due to their stage and personal partnerships with actor-managers Harley Granville-Barker (McCarthy) and Dion (Dot) Boucicault (Vanbrugh).
78   *Era*, 26 February 1910.
79   *Era*, 5 March 1910.
80   *Era*, 14 May 1910.

81 Ashwell, *Myself a Player*, 168.

82 *Daily Express*, 25 July 1910.

83 Ashwell, *Myself a Player*, 164.

84 Charles M.S. McLellan (1865–1916) was a New York journalist and playwright. His early work was written under the name of 'Hugh Morton'. His biggest success was *The Belle of New York*, which ran in London for two years from April 1898. He was the author of *Leah Kleschna*, which Ashwell played in London in 1905.

85 *Era*, 26 November 1910.

86 *Era*, 14 January 1911.

87 *New York Times*, 17 January 1911.

88 *Votes for Women*, 10 March 1911.

89 *Era*, 15 April 1911.

90 *Evening Standard*, 5 May 1911.

91 This play depicts a dream experienced by the pioneer of professional actresses, Margaret Hughes, in 1661, in which she has visions of future celebrated actresses, up to the present day represented by Ashwell.

92 The Pioneer Players continued until 1921, presenting a serious and not very popular repertoire which was increasingly out of tune with the post-war atmosphere: 'no-one would have gone to see their plays for light relief'. J. Melville, *Ellen and Edy* (London, 1987), 227.

93 *Star*, 28 June 1911.

94 *Referee*, 24 September 1911.

95 *Daily Chronicle*, 23 September 1911. Reproduced in *Encore* and the *Stage*, 28 September 1911.

96 *Era*, 7 September 1911.

97 Letter from Ashwell to Shaw, 1 November 1911 (London: British Library: GB Shaw Papers: MSS 50528). It is noteworthy, given her style, that Ashwell played very few of Shaw's women and none of Ibsen's. In the case of Shaw, friendship may have been an obstacle, as well as a lack of time and opportunity. Even though Ashwell may have aspired to Candida, at the time of writing this letter to Shaw the play was over ten years old and unlikely to be revived in the West End, even as a vehicle for Ashwell. This reference to the play may have been an unexplained shared joke between them.

98 *Daily Chronicle*, October 1911. Subsequently quoted in the *Era*, 4 November 1911.

99 *Era*, 4 November 1911.

100 First introduced by Asquith in November 1911 to extend male franchise, the Manhood Suffrage Bill effectively 'torpedoed' (in the words of Lloyd George) the amended Conciliation Bill which proposed female suffrage limited by age and property qualifications. Both bills had amendments suggested but eventually did not proceed – in the case of the Manhood Suffrage Bill, it was finally rejected in May 1913. See D. Crow, *The Edwardian Woman* (London, 1978), 206–10.

101 *Daily News* and *Times*, 18 November 1911.

102 Ashwell, *Myself a Player*, 165.

103 *Woman at Home*, December 1911/January 1912.

104 *Cork Constitution*, 20 December 1911.

105 *Liverpool Courier*, 3 January 1912.

106 *Pall Mall Gazette*, 2 January 1912.

107 In *Innocent Flowers: Women in the Edwardian Theatre* (London, 1981), 129, J. Holledge writes that Ashwell 'played to perfection' Queen Caroline in Laurence Housman's *Pains and Penalties*, presented at the Savoy Theatre by the Pioneer Players, 26 November 1911. Gertrude Kingston actually played the role (see *Times*, 27 November 1911). Ashwell had

previously shown, with *Waste*, her 'respect' for the Censor's decision. It would have been uncharacteristic for her to appear in this play (banned because 'it made hostile reference upon the stage to the great-grand uncle of our present sovereign' quoted Holledge, 128), given her ongoing responsibility as a theatre manager.

108 *Era*, 2 March 1912.
109 *Era*, 9 March 1912.
110 *Era*, 16 March 1912.
111 *Standard*, 30 March 1912.
112 *Era*, 25 May 1912.
113 Trewin, *All On Stage*, 187.
114 Ashwell, *Myself a Player*, 122.
115 Melba visited on 24 June 1913 (*Era*, 28 June 1913).
116 *Daily Herald*, 9 July 1912.
117 *Era*, 2 November 1912.
118 *Westminster Gazette*, 23 January 1913.
119 *Standard*, 6 February 1913.
120 *Globe*, 3 May 1913.
121 Vanbrugh, *To Tell My Story*, 83–4.
122 *Era*, 10 May 1913. The programme/platform layout leaflet for this event included an advertisement for Adola Ltd of 21 South Molton Street, London, for the Lena Pocket Beauty Case, a makeup bag with contents, designed and used by Lena Ashwell (Maud Arncliffe Sennett collection, vol. 22). From a later point of view, Ashwell's involvement in the promotion of beauty products is in conflict with her views on equality for women and her statements made over time that actresses should not be regarded as only worthy of notice if beautiful; however, the 'Lena' pocket case was intended as a practical item for 'travelling and motoring' and at the time would not have appeared out of character.
123 *Bristol Evening News*, 7 February 1913.
124 The *Era*, 17 May 1913, reported in detail on the meeting and followed this with an angry editorial on 24 May 1913 criticising an apparent lack of serious commitment to the project.
125 See C. Rover, *Women's Suffrage and Party Politics in Britain, 1866–1914* (London, 1967), 31.
126 *Westminster Gazette*, 10 June 1913.
127 *Votes for Women*, 4 July 1913.
128 *Votes for Women*, 23 May 1913.
129 *Era*, 12 November 1913.
130 *Manchester Guardian*, 13 November 1913.
131 *Flair*, 14 November 1913.
132 E.J. Morley (ed.), *Women Workers in Seven Professions: A Survey of their Economic Conditions and Prospects*, The Studies Committee, Fabian Women's Group (London, 1914). Other professions included teaching; medicine and nursing; law; municipal and parish work; national government employment; and commerce.
133 *Ibid.*, 300.
134 *Era*, 19 November 1913.
135 The venue had changed from the no longer available Court Theatre.
136 *Times*, 9 December 1913.
137 *Daily Chronicle*, 11 December 1913.
138 *Votes for Women*, 12 December 1913.
139 This furniture shop in South Molton Street, London, in which Ashwell had a share, was attempting to encourage the appreciation and purchase of furniture created by living

craftsmen (*Standard*, 31 December 1913). There is very little surviving information on Ashwell's business initiatives and interests.

140 *Daily Sketch*, 11 December 1913.

141 The heading was 'Why should women who beat men in intellect or service be passed over in Honours list just because they are women?'

142 *Votes for Women*, 27 February 1914. There appear to be no surviving copies of this journal; none were included in Ashwell's scrapbooks.

143 *Ibid.*

144 Maud Arncliffe Sennett collection, vol. 25.

145 In an attempt to prevent hunger striking, the government introduced forcible feeding, subjecting weak prisoners to cruel and injurious enforced feeding. The 'Cat and Mouse' Act was, officially, the Prisoners (Temporary Discharge for Ill Health) Act of 1913.

146 Tree played Higgins and Mrs Pat Campbell was Eliza. Tree apparently gave an overstated performance which made the production a hit, 'grossing more than £2000 a week', but Shaw gave Tree 'curt advice to stop playing for laughs and to never again play Higgins once the current run ended'. S. Weintraub, *Bernard Shaw, 1914–1918: Journey to Heartbreak* (London, 1973), 14.

147 J. Dunbar, *Mrs G.B.S.: A Biographical Portrait of Charlotte Shaw* (New York, 1963), 219.

148 Published in 1914 by A.C. Fifield, it was 'a remarkable little metaphysical treatise … an introduction to the science of self-conscious existence' (*Lady*, 29 January 1914).

149 Ashwell, *Myself a Player*, 191–2.

150 *Ibid.*, 169. She implies it took place a few months after the march in London in 1910, but Charlotte Shaw was not with her in America in late 1910/early 1911, when Ashwell performed in *Judith Zaraine*. In light of her observations given when she chaired the United Suffragists' first public meeting at the Portman Rooms at the end of May 1914, it is assumed the Boston march took place in the previous month.

151 *Votes for Women*, 29 May 1914.

152 *Ibid.*

153 Yvette Guilbert (1865–1944), a well-known music hall singer, was immortalised by Toulouse-Lautrec in many paintings and sketches. She gave lecture recitals of *chansons* on tour between 1901 and 1914 and was in England at the time (*Oxford Companion to the Theatre*, 360). She and Ashwell became friends as well as colleagues.

154 *Era*, 17 June 1914.

155 Ashwell was an active member and a vice-president of the Poetry Society between 1909 and 1928. Throughout her career Ashwell gave many recitals, usually of poetry rather than theatrical excerpts.

156 As a footnote to Ashwell's letter, the *Daily Chronicle*, 22 June 1914, stated: 'The Referendum as applied to woman suffrage has been considered by Liberals several times, and rejected, and Lord Murray would not have revived the suggestion had not his absence in Colombia and elsewhere left him out of touch with the progress of political events in England.'

157 *Era*, 8 July 1914.

158 Ashwell, *Myself a Player*, 182. The Hon. Eve Haverfield died in Serbia working for the Scottish Women's Hospital. She was the originator of the Green Cross transport service (*ibid.*).

159 *Morning Post*, 8 August 1914.

160 Circular letter, August 1914 (Maud Arncliffe Sennett collection), vol. 26.

161 *Era*, 12 August 1914.

162 *Leicester Daily Post*, 27 October 1914.

163 L. Ashwell, *Modern Troubadours* (London, 1922), 5.
164 *Ibid.*
165 *Ibid.*, 6.
166 *Ibid.*
167 *Ibid.*, 7.

4

Patriot, 1915 to 1919

In January 1915 Ashwell prepared the first Concert Party's first visit to France, while rehearsing the role of Margaret in the Granville-Barker/McCarthy Kingsway revival of *Fanny's First Play*, which opened on 13 February to mixed reviews. The world had changed since the 1911 premiere: some still found it amusing and well played, but others, including the *Times*, felt 'it may seem to the judicious the moment is not happily chosen for resuming the old Shavian capers, which were among the strangest by-products of a long peace. The fun of travestied facts and lopsided judgments then agreeably stimulated a languid world … But today we have to be at grips with facts.'[1] Ashwell was praised: 'she may not look eighteen, but she looks every inch the rebel and she employs all that nervous force of hers, all her passionate intensity, all those bursts of feminine indignation and all those quick changes of mood she has always at her service to render the scenes in which the girl figures natural and charming.'[2]

Two days later the Concert Party departed, comprising, as would be the future pattern, a soprano, contralto, tenor, baritone/bass, instrumentalist and entertainer. Theodore Flint, musical director and accompanist, had gone ahead to stay in France for the duration, arranging transport and accommodation and joining each Party on its arrival. The first Concert at the Front took place on 18 February at No. 15 Camp, Harfleur Valley.[3] In fifteen days thirty-eight concerts and a benefit performance in Rouen, for the widow of a Belgian killed in a British lorry accident, were presented.

Overseen by a committee acceptable to the YMCA, Ashwell began the enormous task of auditioning and selecting artists, promoting awareness of the concerts and raising money to continue them. She was anxious to learn how the artists were faring, and Flint's letter, written from Le Havre on 21 February, was heartening.

You asked me to let you know about each individual. It is very difficult to answer, as they are all so excellent in their way, and are all so obliging and charming, and don't mind a bit how much they sing or what they do … During the songs, or whatever it is, you could hear a pin drop, but when it is all over the roars and yells are simply thrilling … The high boots have been an enormous success; I don't know what they would have done without them, as the mud has been too awful.[4]

Y. M. C. A.

(WITH HIS MAJESTY'S FORCES)

Miss LENA ASHWELL'S

CONCERT PARTY

(From London)

WILL GIVE A CONCERT

IN THE

Théâtre Folies-Bergère

ON

WEDNESDAY, 24ᵗʰ FEB.

At 7.30 p. m.

The proceeds will be given to the widow of a Belgian, killed accidentally by a British motor lorry.

ADMISSION : 2 fr. -:- 1 fr. -:- 50 cent.

DOORS OPENED AT 7 O'CLOCK

ROUEN. — IMP. GIRIEUD

4.1 Concert Party Poster, Rouen, February 1915
(Mander and Mitchenson Theatre Collection, Bristol)

YMCA head L.G. Pilkington wrote thanking Ashwell on behalf of soldiers and workers for 'a magnificent Concert Party', whose 'success has been perfect in every way'.[5] Early newspaper articles, mostly quoting her press releases, made much of the soldiers' responses. One army doctor found the 'concert did wounded men more good than a month's nursing'.[6]

For the first major fund-raising event – 'a Great Matinee Performance at London Coliseum on Thursday 25 March, in the gracious presence of Her Majesty Queen Mary and in aid of Princess Victoria's Auxiliary Committee of the YMCA for providing Funds for Concerts for troops at Hospitals and Recreation Huts in England and France' – manager Oswald Stoll secured a company of generous star artists, whose usual rates would have amounted to over £5,000.[7] The long programme sold out in advance, raising £1,450 towards each Party's weekly travel and out-of-pocket expenses of £25. The first ensemble had returned; a second was currently in France; and a third, with pianist and composer Ivor Novello, whose 'Keep the Home Fires Burning' became an instant hit, departed in early April. Concurrently, many concerts were presented at hospitals, bases and training camps in England.

As part of her campaign, Ashwell published many articles explaining progress to date and the work of the Three Arts Club Employment Committee, through which artists were identified and contacted.[8] This committee also ran workshops for women making soft toys, greeting cards and novelties for sale, as well as Army contract knitting. There was a celebratory 'house warming' on 30 March. Ashwell's promotional material described the success of the concerts:

> The warmth of our reception shows how great a help music is, and, being a help, that it ought to be used. In the matter of recruiting, the authorities have been slow to recognise an appeal could be made to people through bands ... it is such a splendid thing that artists should be of use in wartime. We ought to be used ... [and] treated as just as important a part of the community as any other.[9]

She developed this argument in 'Laughing to Hide Our Tears', defending the instinct to seek 'gaiety, joy and laughter', to deal sanely with the terrible pain of war and to face hardships again, being 'invigorated, refreshed, and stronger for the mere change of outlook'.[10]

Fanny's First Play closed on 27 March. After only four years, the Granville-Barkers' Kingsway tenancy ended. Ashwell negotiated a new sub-lease with Vedrenne and Eadie and was then free to travel to France, during which brief visit she recited at eighteen concerts. Recounting the experience, she had 'never felt so proud of being an Englishwoman and I never longed so ardently to be an Englishman. Oh! if I could make the laggards at home see, in their mind's eye, something of what I have seen!' She returned home convinced 'we are the most music-loving people in the world'.[11] The *Musical News* gave Concert Party member William Robinson a supply of mouth organs, and after playing one in each hut or ward, he left it with the best player, or soldier most in need of cheering up. Ashwell was very moved by letters describing the receipt of this simple, comforting instrument.[12]

After an overnight journey from Le Havre, she went straight into rehearsals for Coleby's short melodramatic play *The Debt*, in which she made her debut on the Coliseum's variety bill on 19 April. She played a Secret Service woman who takes revenge, following the loss of her brother, by hunting down and disabling a German gun set up to destroy Admiralty House and the British Cabinet. She abandoned 'her usual hurried manner of speaking … and bravely dispensing with other precious Ashwellisms unfitted to melodrama, held her audience in an unrelaxing grip throughout the piece'.[13] Considering the subject matter positive and morale-boosting, she used this opportunity to promote her war work while her many articles about the Concert Parties and the Three Arts Club Women's Employment Fund, with pleas for financial contributions, were being published in regional newspapers.

With royal encouragement, retailer George Selfridge had lent a Baker Street shop to sell goods made by Three Arts workers. Ashwell appeared in support of the Belgian and Serbian Relief Fund, the Russian Flag Day and, accompanied by Hawley, recited at the Haymarket for the Women's League of Service. The theatrical profession made an extraordinary contribution to war-torn England: the imagination, energy and sense of purpose shown by AFL members made an impact on the awareness of other women who, until recently, had led comparatively easy lives. The press, lacking news on men in other than war roles, ran articles on women behind the scenes in theatres. As Cecil Chisholm observed, 'At the present time the majority of repertory playhouses are under the guidance of women. And that guidance is not merely nominal; it is active, practical, complete.'[14]

Ashwell travelled overnight to France on 4 June to join the Concert Parties. Her parting words were: 'Do believe, all of you who can get amusement and change whenever you wish, that the men who are working for Britain live in grey monotony and need the recreation we are giving them.'[15] While Ashwell was somewhere in France, Elizabeth Asquith sent letters to newspapers seeking further funds to cover Concert Party weekly costs now put at £50. Once a fortnight, a Party left for France, giving three concerts a day for up to three weeks at large base depots. Over 300 events employing some 250 artists had already been given and Ashwell calculated that some 300,000 troops had been entertained.[16]

On her return, her impressions, including 'Our Concerts in France, The "Good Night" Match Line', describing the lighting of matches by men, in pitch darkness, to show artists to their vehicles,[17] were published. Ashwell rose 'at four o'clock in the morning so as to ensure some complete quiet' to put an account of her experiences in writing. The outcome was nearly £1,000 in donations.[18] Inspired, she wrote about the impact music had on the men and on involving women, otherwise 'unemployable' through lack of skills or mobility, in doll-making workshops. Many toys and donated memorabilia were sold or auctioned at Savoy Hotel events in July.

4.2 Concert Party performance, France, 1915
(press photo, reproduced in *Stage Year Book*, 1919)

We are very proud of the excellent work … by our workers, who were entirely unused to machining and toy making. The most fascinating products – the penguins and 'cuddley' dolls – not only win everybody's hearts, but they won professional congratulation at the Board of Trade's British Industries' Fair … our workrooms are not yet self supporting … the training we give the unskilled is the most valuable part [but] it is expensive, as we pay a living minimum wage, while the inexperienced beginner is learning – and learning a handicraft means spoiling material steadily for some weeks … At present we have 83 women and girls … the failure of the Russian Opera Season at the end of one week after six weeks' rehearsals brought many singers to us in distress.[19]

Recognised as a positive force with first-hand experience of difficulties faced by soldiers and war workers, she spoke at the London Regiment's 4th Battalion patriotic recruiting meeting in early July. Her willingness to give time and energy to many causes saw her supporting Paderewski's Polish appeal, and in July she hosted Grein's Independent War Players at the Kingsway, before their tour of French and Belgian bases in England.

After announcing that 400 concerts in 11 French centres had been presented, she declared that the eighth Party, which was on its way, could, without more support, be the last. The decision was made to concentrate work in 'France with an eye on the Dardanelles'.[20] Lena Ashwell Concert Parties continued performing in England for fund-raising, but these were organised by others. From her Grosvenor Street home she personally acknowledged all donations and wrote of the impact of her programmes: 'Talks with the Wounded Tommies in Hospital in Flanders – Look

Y.M.C.A.

GRAND CONCERTS

22-27 March 1915

Miss LENA ASHWELL'S, Second Concert Party

Monday	No 1. —	Stationary Hospital	3	p. m
	Y. M. C. A. —	Hut Bruyères Camp	6-30	p. m
Tuesday	No 9. —	General Hospital	3	p. m
	Y. M. C. A. —	Hut Cavalry Camp.......	5-30	p. m
	" "	" "	7-0	p. m
Wednesday .	Folies-Bergère Theatre..................		7-0	p. m
Thursday.....	No 11. —	Stationary Hospital.......	3-30	p. m.
	Y. M. C. A. —	Territorial Camp	5-30	p. m.
	"	" "	7-0	p. m.
Friday........	No 12. —	General Hospital	3-0	p. m.
	Y. M. C. A. —	Hut 28th Division.......	5-30	p. m.
	"	" 27th "	7-0	p. m.
Saturday.....	No 8. —	General Hospital	3-0	p. m.
	M. T. —	Dépôt Bapeaume	7-0	p. m.

ARTISTES

Soprano . . .	Miss Alice de la BELLANDIERE.
Contralto. . .	Miss Paola RIVERS.
Violinist . . .	Miss Gwendolyn TEAGLE.
Tenor	Mr. Ivor NOVELLO.
Bass-Baritone ·	Sergeant G. Rowland MORFITT. R. A. M. C.
Entertainer . .	Mr. W. ROBINSON.
Accompanist. .	Mr. Theodore FLINT.

Admission Free.   Troops Only.

4.3 YMCA Grand Concert Poster, 1915
(Mander and Mitchenson Theatre Collection, Bristol)

4.4 Concert Party audience, France, 1915 (press photo, reproduced in *Stage Year Book*, 1919)

forward to a Concert as eagerly as Children. "Loch Lomond" the Favourite Song.'[21] She lamented the tendency to regard music as a luxury and artists as useless, declaring 'it is artists who preserve and express the genius of the race, or the cry of a nation's soul'. Parties visited service camps for tending horses, transport maintenance workers, forage camps, hospitals, and bases from which men left for the trenches.

She writes of the atmosphere in hospitals being 'so impregnated with concentrated pain at first we are almost afraid to begin', and of being made aware not only of the suffering of war, but also of dullness and monotony in the lives of the men.

> The violin is what the men like most. Handel's *Largo*, Schubert, dances representing national fêtes and folk-songs, and big simple airs, are more appreciated than any chorus-song … Perhaps in the future good music and good plays will be part of our national scheme of education. In the meantime it seems possible that our national love of the beautiful has been under-estimated.[22]

Using anecdotes and quotations from the military, she effectively conveys the purpose of, and response to, the Parties. A friend, Ruth Wright, returning from London to her New York home, wrote:

> It is a beautiful article, which compels tears and smiles – and a great deal of faith in British mankind … if you would write [an] article, say 1500 or 2000 words, and send it to me … I should see that whatever profits there are would be paid to you for your fund … if you would develop the theme of the New Spiritual Significance of Suffrage, and the idea that we little people, as you so well put it,

are too myopic to see the great purposes of the universe which perhaps initiated the entire suffrage movement for one of the forces of this war, I am sure the article would be of great interest and would present both suffrage and war in a somewhat novel light. You might perhaps tell a little of actresses and girls of the chorus who are making woolly toys ... [and] that all thought of suffrage had long ago been unselfishly postponed until England should be out of danger, that these women who had worked and struggled for women's political power were now placing their experience in organisation and routine-work on the altar of patriotism.[23]

Exhausted, Ashwell was not well enough to attend a fund-raising 'Café Chantant' concert in Dover, but recovered to travel to Torquay on 5 September for Pavilion Theatre manager A.M. Wilshere's benefit, performing material from her repertoire in France and explaining the work of the Parties, which by now had given approximately 2,000 concerts to troops and war workers.[24]

Undaunted by lack of facilities, some Concert Parties were now performing one-act plays at base camps, and in September 1915 playwright Gertrude Jennings reported on their success and work conditions:

Never was audacity better rewarded. True ... there were no curtains, footlights, dressing rooms or furniture. We dressed in small dark crevices at the side of the stage, our light two guttering candles on a packing case. We had for stage properties three wooden chairs and a scent bottle ... What did it matter when we had audiences who thronged to the halls, climbed upon benches and on each other's shoulders, pressed in at the doors, looked in at the windows and laughed and cheered as audiences have never done before! ... We gave two performances every night, often in the same camp, the second audience coming in as soon as the first went out ... We often gave our first evening performance outdoors ... it was not so fearfully hot and [the men] had more room.[25]

Jennings refers to a talkative donkey spoiling a love scene, but, like Ashwell, was inspired and spent most of the war in France. While her colleagues competed with the unexpected, Ashwell revived her role of Kate in *The Twelve Pound Look*, playing the Coliseum variety bill for two weeks. 'A masterpiece in miniature ... a great actress in what is probably the best playlet in the language' declared the *Evening Standard*.[26] An indefatigable example, Ashwell spoke to the Women's Freedom League National Service Organisation, alluding 'to the power of fatigue resistance shown by women workers ... [making] a special appeal to women to make themselves efficient for some kind of work', and expressing 'hope that a better understanding would grow out of the ghastly tragedy of war'.[27]

'Among all the ladies who are so excellently serving the cause of the relief of suffering and distress, none is more popular in every sphere of benevolence than Miss Ashwell, the celebrated actress. [She] is not only enthusiastic, she is thorough and practical, and a tower of strength to all organisations with which she is connected.'[28]

This eulogistic piece appeared the same day *Our Home* announced the AFL would turn its energies to establishing the British Women's Hospital. The Hospital Committee, including Ashwell, offered to raise £50,000 to establish a permanent home for disabled British soldiers and sailors. Incredibly, at the same time Ashwell was preparing to return to the Kingsway as actress-manager. Her explanation was,

> I will confess not only am I looking forward to returning to the Kingsway, but this time I hope to stay a long time if the public will allow me. I have been devoting most of my time lately to War Funds and other charities. Who can refrain from such splendid work at such a 'calling' time? Still, naturally, there comes, also, a 'call' to do what I can in my own profession.[29]

Necessity also played its part. The Kingsway lease and overheads gave her little alternative. Maintaining her previous artistic policy, she chose a new play by 23-year-old 'soldier/ dramatist' John Hastings Turner, who was standing by for active service.[30] *Iris Intervenes*, described by Turner as 'An Arabian Night in the Suburbs' and with Ashwell in the title role, was eagerly anticipated, as was her 'experiment' of employing mostly women to run the show:

> There will be a woman stage manager, a woman assistant stage manager and a woman property 'man'. The limelights will be worked by women … coached by the electrician, and there will be women scene shifters and an orchestra composed of women. There will still be some men employed, mainly upon heavy work; but there will not be one man [who is] eligible for military service.[31]

The *Glasgow News* printed an unaccredited little verse:

> To a playhouse of masculine influence void
> Our Miss Ashwell is pointing the way –
> Where only a feminine cast is employed
> To interpret a feminine play.[32]

In response, Ashwell declared: 'Distinctions between "men's and women's work" are apt to turn out, on experiment, to be purely conventional.' She hoped 'the new solidarity between men and women at work will continue after the war'.[33] These preparations did not cause her to ease up on charity work or new ideas. She spoke at a YMCA fund-raising concert, and as well as writing a *Red Triangle* article, 'Concerts for the Army: Music has a Vocation in Modern Warfare',[34] she gave newspaper interviews articulating many of her concerns:

> It is for us women to wage unremitting and strenuous war against all conditions of poverty and disease and misery that weaken the Empire at its heart. It is for us women to fight in dead earnest against the spirit of social apathy, indifference

and despair; to stand by those who have lost their economic weapons, and to save them from the defeat that comes from loss of independence.[35]

Thus she described the WEC's motivation: to help, in co-operation with Government Labour Exchanges, women find satisfying work. She described the diversity of schemes: wooden toy-making; training for market gardening, poultry-keeping and other land activities; and co-operation with organisations such as the Red Cross.

Just twelve months into the war, Ashwell outlined a novel scheme anticipating her work in the 1920s. She called for the creation of ensembles to provide regular work for performers, and access to plays and musical events for every training camp and military base around the country. Having calculated expenses and minimum fees acceptable to professional artists, she considered that, while some costs could be covered by small admission charges, it should be a government responsibility to fund it, in recognition of support already given by artists to the community, and to ensure that specialist skills were not wasted, especially in light of their potential educational role. Personnel and resources of existing organisations could be utilised. This was advanced thinking for a country with no experience of public funding for arts, and where co-operation and sharing of resources were inhibited by commercial pressures, yet Ashwell raised these issues like a seasoned campaigner.

Turner's romantic comedy opened on 16 October 1915. Ashwell played Iris Olga Iranovna, a bohemian Russian with an unconventional past, who moves into suburbia next door to churchwarden and businessman Henry Cumbers. The clash of lifestyles and personalities is immediate and ferocious, especially when Iris – who says of herself, 'My assets are the fact that I am a darling; my liabilities are the fact that I am a woman'[36] – allows Henry's son to flirt with her. In pursuit of a business rival who supposedly stole papers from Henry, he and Iris are forced to spend the night in a broken-down car on Dover road. During what many considered the play's best scene, they come to understand each other and reconcile differences without being compromised. The *Referee* was enthusiastic: 'A bright, clever, hopeful young play and all that a happy audience and a happy and able company could do to make Miss Ashwell's return to her own stage a memorably joyous one … [She] liked Iris immensely … and so did we.'[37] There was a warm welcome, due not only to her personal popularity, but because the play thoroughly deserved the laughter and applause it received. It has 'many witty lines that are the result of genuinely natural situations and it also possesses a fantastic charm of idea and a sense of character that make it worth while not only as a play but as a production'.[38] Ashwell's versatility was evident. Apart from Diana of Dobson's, her most successful roles had been serious, but now it seemed she had a predilection for comedy:

[Ashwell] has obviously found a personality in which she revels. Iris is a temperamental whirlwind … Her tantrums, her repentances, her love, her beguilements, her childlike imaginings are beautifully outlined by the author and filled in by Miss Ashwell, who has not played with more spirit and vivacity for a long time.[39]

She had found an interesting new dramatist and had the knack of selecting entertaining plays. Her article 'How Not to Write a Play' came from this experience. *Iris Intervenes* inspired many would-be authors to submit manuscripts to her. Writing some 'winged words … for authors of bad plays', Ashwell recognised that 'there was no receipt for writing a good play … but there are, apart from obvious rules of the stage, so many pitfalls and mistakes into which would-be playwrights walk'. She suggested the technically and imaginatively impossible should not be required of stage managers, actors or audiences, and stressed:

> A play must be worth writing if it is to be worth acting and seeing, and some plays, quite well constructed and well written, make one wonder … Apparently there are … people who sit down to write a play without having any particular play to write. If … they produce anything with three acts, they are too pleased to criticise it. There are also people who embark on the perilous project of writing historical plays, apparently without any knowledge … except a vague theory that in the good old days … nobody had much common sense. [40]

Iris Intervenes closed on 20 November while plans to tour it early in 1916 were initiated. The Concerts at the Front bandwagon rolled on, momentum helped by many articles and letters written from a variety of perspectives: 'The work may be tiring, but for sheer inspiration and love of one's job it is hard indeed to beat.'[41] The YMCA was happy, now, to allow artistes an element of 'self promotion' for the sake of the greater cause. Music critic Robin H. Legge read 'a huge mass of letters … from soldiers of every degree in France', before appealing on behalf of the work. Flint calculated that 'on average he plays about fifty songs per day' and since the work began had played 'nearly 25,000 songs and pieces'.[42] By now, fifteen Parties had been to France, with more ready to depart. A supporter from Aberdeen, Reverend John Gordon, described his experience in camps: 'the least we at home can do is to see that plenty of guineas are at hand to enable these delightful concerts to continue'.[43] Local newspapers featured the contributions of returning home-grown talent, illustrated with photographs capturing the environment for performers and audiences. As winter approached, Ashwell's appeal was headed 'A Great Want – First Food, then Raiment, then Shelter, then Music'.[44]

Ashwell identified the war as the time when her ambition for personal success gave way to a greater ambition for the success of greater causes. As Britons faced a second war-torn Christmas, she addressed the Student Christian Movement, exhorting listeners, 'in the state of destruction which we are going through', to seek the right standards, particularly in education, and away from the acquisitive and personal. She declared: 'now was the time for builders' of a better world. 'In history the people who really were of importance were teachers and artists', from whom people could take an example. She explained her own realisation: 'What we are here for is not to conform to what has been done before, but to make something new and better.' Her ambition was for better theatre; it was everyone's responsibility to demand

CONCERTS AT THE FRONT:

Organised by Miss LENA ASHWELL in co-operation with the Ladies' Auxiliary
Committee of the Y.M.C.A.

President : H.H. PRINCESS VICTORIA OF SCHLESWIG-HOLSTEIN.

WHY MORE CONCERT PARTIES MUST GO TO THE FRONT.

¶ BECAUSE the plea for "more Concerts" comes from every Base, from every Camp, from every Hospital, from the armies entrenched in the firing-line, from Malta and from Egypt.

BECAUSE Generals, Commanding Officers, Doctors and Chaplains of all denominations, say that the Concert Parties are accomplishing work of "great military value."

HOW MUSIC IS HELPING TO WIN THE WAR.

¶ The War will be won by the spirit and nerves of our armies, and it is the experience of the military and medical authorities, both in the camps, trenches and hospitals, that beautiful music, happiness and laughter in the midst of so much pain and desolation, nerve-racking noise and ugliness, has a psychical and physio-logical value out of all proportion to the simplicity of the expedient, and almost beyond the imagination of those who have not actually experienced the conditions of life at the Front.

THE COST OF THE CONCERTS.

¶ Over 4,000 Concerts have been given in France alone, in the camps, hospitals, and behind the trenches, often under shell-fire.

Concert Parties have also visited and are visiting Malta and Egypt and the ships of the Adriatic Fleet.

The audiences sometimes number 2,500 and even 5,000 men. Hundreds of thousands of men are thus reached every month and millions during a year.

The cost of each Concert is only £2—or on an average less than one penny for each man in the audience.

WILL YOU HELP TO KEEP THE ARMIES SUPPLIED WITH CONCERTS UNTIL THE END OF THE WAR?

¶ The armies are enduring manifold privations, dangers and suffering, and they ask for the happiness and inspiration that the music gives them.

All donations gratefully received and acknowledged by the Hon Organiser, Miss LENA ASHWELL, at 101, New Bond Street, London, W.

Cheques may be crossed "London County and Westminster Bank."

All Accounts audited by the Y.M.C.A. Auditors.

Registered under the War Charities Act, 1916.

4.5 Concerts at the Front pamphlet, 1916
(Concerts at the Front scrapbook Volume 1, Department of Collections Access,
Imperial War Museum, Lena Ashwell Collection, 09/771)

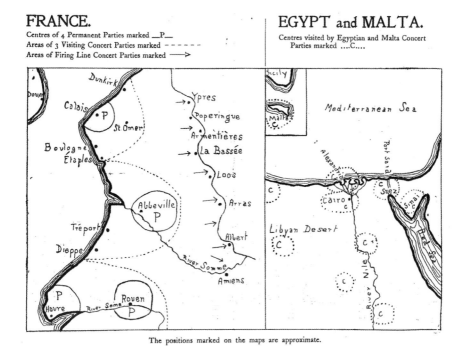

FRANCE.

Centres of 4 Permanent Parties marked __P__
Areas of 3 Visiting Concert Parties marked - - - - -
Areas of Firing Line Concert Parties marked ——>

EGYPT and MALTA.

Centres visited by Egyptian and Malta Concert
Parties marked ....C....

The positions marked on the maps are approximate.

4.6 Concert Party maps France, Egypt and Malta
(Concerts at the Front scrapbook Volume 1, Department of Collections Access,
Imperial War Museum, Lena Ashwell Collection, 09/771)

the best of 'the most powerful thing a nation can have to use in opening up doors of knowledge'. She hoped her listeners would welcome the challenge of a changed post-war world, believing 'we shall have a very much finer Church after the war ... The whole Army vibrates with a desire to have religious conviction, a sureness that what they are fighting for is really worthwhile, that there is something invisible, and therefore, indestructible, behind us'.[45] Throughout her life, Ashwell was motivated by deep religious belief, and sometimes she was carried away by her own eloquence.

It seems she first considered producing the stage version of Algernon Blackwood's novel *The Prisoner of Fairyland*, which he and Violet Pearn made into *The Starlight Express*, when Muriel Pratt was cast in *Iris Intervenes*. Pratt was obliged to give up plans to stage it, with Clive Carey's music, at the outbreak of war. Both Carey and director Basil Dean enlisted and Pratt sought work in London. Having decided to produce 'a piece of Red Cross work for the mind during the first agony of the war',[46] Ashwell engaged Henry Wilson, Arts & Crafts Society president, as designer, although he had no previous stage design experience. He was assisted by Stanley North, creator of the production 'logo', a stylised comet, used on the programme and publicity. Ralph Phillipson, in memory of his wife, provided financial backing and Arthur Penley was engaged as business manager. Considering herself to be a 'dreamer of dreams',[47] she sought suggestions for a composer. Through Robin Legge, Edward Elgar was approached on 9 November, seven weeks prior to the opening. Ashwell, already known to Elgar, wrote:

> Very dear Sir Edward. Robin Legge has encouraged me to ask if you would consider writing music for a play I hope to do at Christmas by Algernon Blackwood. The play is half reality and half fairyland & it is your help in fairyland I want so much. There is a great mystic quality in the play which I am sure will help people to bear the sorrows of war, & the end is really wonderful in its beauty.[48]

The next day, as Alice Elgar recorded in her diary, Ashwell 'showed E. the play. She longs for his music to go with it.'[49] On 11 November the Elgars were guests at *Iris Intervenes* and two days later Elgar agreed to do the music, some of it adapted from his earlier *The Wand of Youth*. Ashwell, Blackwood, soprano Clytie Hine and baritone Charles Mott became regular visitors to Elgar's home or he attended Kingsway rehearsals. It was a frantic few weeks, during which Elgar produced his largest work for the stage (300 pages of score containing more than an hour of music), and the first major piece he recorded on gramophone, with the augmented Kingsway Orchestra, in February 1916.

It was not a happy time. Ashwell was under pressure and made some inappropriate choices which alienated people: Pratt, hoping to play Jane Anne, was not cast. Despite the musical's premise that 'misunderstanding due to lack of sympathy could be changed through star-dust (sympathy)', Blackwood and Elgar, who became firm friends, heard Wilson had designed 'the Sprites in the spirit of Greek fantasy ... a false and ghastly idea. There is nothing pagan in our little Childhood Play. It is an alien symbolism altogether',[50] and began to anticipate disaster. Ashwell asked Blackwood to stay away from rehearsals and he wrote to Elgar: 'Can we do anything? I have, of course, right of veto. That means getting a new artist, postponement of opening, heavy loss of money to Miss Ashwell, and so forth. You know better than I do what a sweeping veto would involve. That our really big chance should be ruined by her strange belief in a mediocre artist is cruel.'[51] O.B. Clarence, who played Daddy, wrote: 'During rehearsals there was constant bickerings and difficulties ... There were disagreements about the symbolism of the decor, which was all rather highbrow and obscured the beauty of the story. There were even dissensions among the orchestra.'[52] Financial concerns created pressure; dancers had to be engaged and accommodated; child actors needed chaperones; and the design placed heavy demands on technical resources. Responding to Elgar's instrumentation, Ashwell agreed to a virtual doubling of musicians from her usual ensemble, to include wind, brass, harp, percussion, cow bells and a wind machine. Then she was summoned at Bow-Street Police Court for non-payment of the Kingsway's rates, amounting to £83 6s 6d. Her solicitor advised that the Vedrenne/Eadie venture had been unsuccessful; the theatre was closed for six months; and soon after its re-opening, an air raid forced re-closure. In the hope that *Starlight Express* would be successful, she was given a further month to pay.

Between 14 and 26 December Elgar and his wife worked hard on the music. On 21 December their nephew and godson, William, died. Although postponement was averted, it was a stressful time. Ashwell wrote to Elgar before the opening matinee on 29 December: 'I can't do the play without you, & it is really life or extinction for me to get the play right & it can't be right without you.'[53] The manuscript (without music) was licensed by the Lord Chamberlain on 11 December 1915, more than two weeks before the opening. Many changes were made and the final script has not survived. Ernest Bendall described the work as 'a daintily didactic little fairy play of the school of *The Blue Bird* but less dramatic in its motive and plot ... seems rather lacking in lucidity ... perhaps through its super abundance of subordinate characters ... the last Act ... has many passages of tender beauty'.[54] The story involved a poor, 'wumbled' (worried and jumbled) English writer, his tired wife and three children, who, through their Secret Star Society and the Starlight Express, find understanding, inspiration and joy to share with everyone, through sympathy, symbolised by stardust.

Apparently, the work was enjoyed by audiences and there was unanimous praise for Elgar's 'entrancing incidental music',[55] although he missed the first performance, which he had intended to conduct, after Lady Elgar had an accident. He attended many performances in January, until the production closed on 20 January, and Ashwell abandoned West End management for good. Neither the full score nor the original play was published, and there have been no staged performances since, although the music has been recorded and presented in a radio version.[56] Desmond MacCarthy's unsympathetic critique, in the *New Statesman* on 15 January 1916, bluntly declaring his dislike for the play, did not help; and the short run must be attributed as much to wartime circumstances as to the problem summarised by Northrop Moore: 'Behind all [the critics'] comments stood the silent contrast of [J.M Barrie's] *Peter Pan*', which had been presented annually at Christmas since 1904.[57]

At the start of 1916 the die was cast. After a year of juggling administration, fund-raising and performance, Ashwell achieved official acknowledgement for her Concert Parties. She wrote enthusiastically: 'There is no doubt the War Office regarded our work as important since they made an exception on our behalf with regard to permits. Few permits at that time were issued for less than three or four months, but we were given short permits for the touring parties.'[58] The YMCA now promoted them as part of its war work and used them to open new huts in France. After a year of hard work and over 1,500 concerts in France,

we seemed to be spreading widely in all directions; the number of visiting parties was increased from two to four and even five in a month. Permanent concert parties and repertory companies were established in the different Bases. More parties were asked for [at] ... the firing line, and we began arrangements for sending artists to Malta and Egypt, with the possibility of Salonica.[59]

This meant constantly renewed appeals for donations: official financial support did not follow official recognition, although an all-male Party was permitted to go right

4.7 The Lena Ashwell YMCA Concert Party, Malta, 1916
(photographer unknown, courtesy of Stuart Gough)

up behind the firing line. Officialdom had placed many obstacles in the way of this long-term aim; Ashwell's breakthrough was due as much to persistent eloquence as to the success of base camp concerts. She had influential supporters, including Ellen Terry, whose epigram 'Comfort for the mind is often more important than comfort for the body; and monotony, that deadly enemy of the soldier in the trenches, is more afraid of music than of a muffler' was reported after a press conference to announce the Concert Party's advance into Malta.[60]

There was no let-up in letters to the press, fund-raising concerts and appeals as Ashwell began an extensive tour with *Iris Intervenes*, playing at Wimbledon, HMS Crystal Palace naval training unit, Hammersmith and Eastbourne. Before leaving London, Ashwell did not seek re-election to the United Suffragists' Committee; lack of time was a big factor in her decision. Not turning her back on the women's cause, she took on a bastion of male control by proposing the Actors' Benevolent Fund committee include women. Lady Tree opposed this ('at present it would be unwise to disturb existing conditions'[61]), while George Alexander and others agreed with Ashwell, although no immediate action was taken.[62] During her tour Ashwell made important contacts with local government representatives. As a matter of civic duty and pride, they engaged in fund-raising events and provided municipal facilities, official sanction and identifiable collection points. Acknowledging support was essential and her 'thank you' letter to the people of Skipton was typical: 'I am quite sure everyone would feel amply repaid could they only see the pleasure the concerts give to our gallant troops.'[63] Much was made of stories demonstrating the benefits for soldiers and their sophisticated tastes in seeking good tunes and 'classical' pieces.

On 28 February 1916, the *Daily Malta Chronicle* reported on the Malta Concert Party's first appearance in Valletta Gymnasium. Although a formal affair attended by the Governor, it received the same enthusiastic response as witnessed in France. While relishing the experience of performing on troop and battle ships and for fishermen mine-sweepers, the Party was very aware of its vulnerability. Away from England for twenty-one weeks, this group also performed in Italy, and in September 1916 travelled to Egypt, where it remained for two years. From July 1918, four of this Party were based in Palestine. Ashwell relied on local representatives of the Crown and military to overcome obstacles, and on artists' reports, which she eagerly received. Two further Parties went to Malta in 1917 and 1918, under Red Cross auspices, as most concerts there took place in hospitals.

While those in England read her account of 'A Year's Music at the Front',[64] she was giving nightly performances in *Iris Intervenes* in Croydon and Stratford. No doubt envious of their experience, she received a report from the first firing-line Party which contains a brief account of its movements:

Feb.5th – Locre Hospital – Big Gun during Cello solo; Feb.8th – Caisse d'Epargne – packed, men had marched in with rifles & smoke helmets, ready to start for trenches at a moment's notice if necessary; Feb.10th – 2nd C.C. Hospital – Guns going all the time – windows rattling – audience greatly amused by our surprised faces; Feb.12th. Walked up Monte Rouge and watched bombardment; Feb.15th – ... within a mile of the trenches; Feb.19th – Canada Huts. Very heavy firing.[65]

Ashwell understood what her Parties were exposed to. In 'Along the Firing Line, Adventures with a Piano', she described travelling conditions, especially with a piano that was 'not the most handy item of luggage to travel with by road, even when just a five octavo pianette without legs [nicknamed 'Peter'] – the piano that never grew up',[66] and the rats who joined the audience in a dark barn in the middle of nowhere. Artistes were issued with gas helmets, 'a fearful head-dress',[67] and quickly acquired soldiers' vocabulary, including 'Blighty', a term of affection for 'dear old England', apparently of Hindustani origin. Ashwell's articles usually concluded with an appeal: at this time for a small motor-van to transport artists and piano to the firing line.

On 7 March Stoll generously opened the Coliseum again for another Great Matinee performance, which raised £700. An amusing new fantasy by J.M. Barrie, *The Real Thing at Last*, was premiered: 'a happy skit on some of the peculiarities native to kinema theatre', including the rejection of stage actors as unsuitable. Irene Vanbrugh was depicted 'releasing a film' which curled snake-like out of a cage, 'looking like a boa-constrictor ... It is quite in the Barrie vein to see, in that now familiar phrase ... a sinuous monster let loose on the public.'[68] Although Barrie was in jest, there were many, like Ashwell, who saw cinema as a mostly insidious, unwelcome innovation.

Ashwell then travelled extensively, auditioning local singers in an effective ploy to get active regional participation and to inspire local fund-raising events. In the evenings she played Iris in cities between Edinburgh and Brighton until early May. While her Concert Party was experiencing firing-line big guns, the company had its own siege experiences. 'The night before the production of *Iris Intervenes*, there was a big Zeppelin raid which did much damage to the Kingsway. On tour I hardly went anywhere without being preceded by a raid, or having one during the week.'[69] During four nights of raids in Newcastle, audiences were not deterred. Iris was the last sustained major role that Ashwell, an actress for only twenty-four years, played. While most considered she had reached the top of her profession in her portrayal of difficult and unconventional contemporary women, she was never fully tested as an actress: she played a limited range of characters, with only rare opportunities to play Shakespeare, and then not in roles through which reputations are made. She did not play many of Shaw's women or characters from Ibsen, Chekhov or Wilde, which might have given her a place in rolls of honour associated with the 'classics'.[70]

At the end of the tour, Ashwell returned to France. In mid-June Stanley Hawley died, aged 49. It was a sad time for her. Unable to attend her friend's funeral, she paid tribute in October 1917, at a Wigmore Hall memorial concert. Accompanied by Sir Henry Wood, she performed a number of recitations that Hawley had set to music. The proceeds were devoted to the publication of a work by a British composer.

The *Iris Intervenes* tour concluded just as theatres were facing new challenges. Ostensibly a wartime necessity, the Entertainments Tax on all places of amusement was introduced in May 1916. Initially it was generally accepted, although it created more work for managers and box office staff. There were some charity performance and children's entertainment exemptions, but by August it was clear that those seeking entertainment were buying cheaper seats or attending less. When the 1916 Military Service Bills became Acts, managers were obliged to rethink plans. Already most young male performers had enlisted and wartime entertainment groups were using older men. 'Naturally, that fine actress and manageress and most liberal and cultured of Suffragists, Miss Lena Ashwell was among the first to realise women's potential usefulness in a theatre. Did she not have them trained and employed as scene shifters?'[71] Ashwell found it encouraging that managers were not seeking government exemption for male workers. Instead 'the war has heightened their [women's] influence, and endowed their purpose with a wider sympathy',[72] creating virtually whole orchestras of women musicians and giving a wartime boost to older male and lesser-known female variety acts and music hall entertainers.

While London theatres tried to balance demands for economy ('If we cannot have peace, we must have retrenchment in our expenditure and reform of our social customs'[73]), with their audience's desire for glamour (and perhaps to call on the imagination of the 'more intellectual class of playgoer'[74]), this was not a problem in French camps. Troops welcomed and enjoyed Shakespearean excerpts and popular musical comedy without any trappings. Ashwell did not miss the opportunity to turn a general request into a specific when she asked a YMCA event audience 'to give me all you have got, and then more ... your new hat; your new carpet ... everything you thought you were going to buy next week ... give it me for the sake of boys at the front'.[75] Now introducing her as 'one of their greatest assets', the YMCA was selling Ashwell's illustrated booklet about Concert Party experiences. She continued to cast the net wide for support, even enlisting an old school friend who collected donations in Canada after her four sons joined the forces in Europe. One was killed in action while another, twice wounded, wrote from the Front, affectionately expressing appreciation for a concert in his camp.[76]

Ashwell returned in the first week of July with a 'Firing-Line' Party which became a 'new turn' at the Coliseum for a month.[77] The performers recreated their programme as presented to troops, using 'Peter' the piano and sharing something of the experience described by sons, brothers and husbands in their letters home. In early August, one Party was on Manchester Hippodrome's variety bill and another began a week-long series of twice-nightly entertainment for 12,000 women munitions workers at Woolwich Arsenal.

On 19 August Ashwell went back to France for a month, playing Lady Macbeth in scenes from the play in army bases and theatres in Rouen and Le Havre. With fourteen performers, some of whom were permanently based in France, the programme included musical items, Gertrude Jennings' *The Bathroom Door*, and *The Twelve Pound Look* with Ashwell as Kate. Individual male performers, under Concert Party auspices, entertained firing-line troops where there were no facilities for ensembles. Ashwell had a great personal and critical success with Lady Macbeth, although she never played the role in a complete production. When young, she had

> dreamt of playing Lady Macbeth to kings and queens in vast London theatres ... But I never dreamt ... I should play the part to thousands and thousands of men, far away from their homes and from everyone and everything they care for, in the midst of the greatest war that has ever been known ... Those audiences in khaki listened breathlessly to Shakespeare's great play rendered without scenery ... there was no illusion in the surroundings, no accessories, nothing but the beauty of real poetry with its instantaneous and deep appeal to the hearts of men.[78]

When this programme was presented at the Nottingham Arts Fair in November 1916, the *Stage* was effusive, describing in detail her portrayal and its impact on the audience: 'Miss Ashwell has done many fine things before, but she has done nothing finer or more moving than Lady Macbeth.'[79]

Not all comments were favourable. While Ashwell was still in France, John Raphael, a Paris-based commentator, published 'Entertaining Tommy' after talking with soldiers in a café. He reported that some considered entertainment at the camps too 'straight-laced' and 'patronising'.[80] Compared to Parisian entertainment for off-duty soldiers, it may indeed have been so. Some resented that officers had the best seats and priority over ordinary soldiers in meeting artistes. Ashwell never addressed this situation; she preferred to remain positive and go with the majority.

She also consciously ignored any inverted snobbery directed at the 'high arts'. Always at pains to break down barriers, she later observed: 'There is a tendency of the superior person, or there was before the war (there aren't so many superior persons about now), to imagine the best in literature, art, music and drama was rather above the heads of the people, and that an expensively cultivated mind was necessary for real appreciation. There never was a greater mistake.'[81]

Ashwell returned home to launch an appeal for the first Egyptian Concert Party and to publish her account of 'Shakespeare at the Front, Plays presented Under Strange Conditions, Blankets for Scenery':

> I dare assert the audiences he [Shakespeare] would have loved best were those ... who listened spell-bound to his wonderful words ... on the very scene where he has drawn for the world the armies of our ancestors, equally gallant, equally gay ... if we could foster and provide ... national and municipal theatres and concert halls ... it would be one of the simpler ways of adjusting the machinery of our civilization.[82]

She also returned to a stoush with producer Harold Neilson, who was promoting a tour of *Iris Intervenes* with the 'special engagement of Miss Ashwell in her original part', together with a revival of the Kingsway's *Diana of Dobson's* 'by arrangement with Miss Ashwell'.[83] She responded tersely in the same edition of the *Era*: 'Miss Ashwell asks us to announce she is in no way connected with the company now touring *Diana of Dobson's*. The company is not under [her] auspices, and she is in no way responsible for the production.' The next week the *Diana of Dobson's* tour was advertised with no mention of *Iris Intervenes*. Two weeks later the *Era* published a formal letter from Neilson's representatives, stating he 'acquired the touring rights [of *Diana*] in 1912, since which date he has revived it on four occasions. Miss Ashwell's connection ... is of a very material nature ... she has been, and still is, in receipt of a certain portion of weekly takings.'[84] She made no further comment.

On 12 October she began an exhausting round of speeches across the country, mostly presided over by local mayors. Her Bristol audience learnt that it cost £100 a week to maintain three Parties in France, one in Malta and another in Alexandria, and on 24 October she recounted her experiences in Huddersfield. While she was raising funds in Bromley, Granville-Barker was speaking in London, 'laying emphasis on the intelligence and eagerness of the British soldiers' welcome of the best art these much-needed concert parties can provide'.[85] She auditioned singers in Glasgow, joined the Concert Party in Nottingham, then visited Coal and Shipping Exchange workers at Cardiff Docks, auditioning singers and reciting at the Empire during a gala concert. This visit raised more than £1,500. For Ashwell, Cardiff's response was 'far ahead of any city except London'.[86]

North of the English border trouble was brewing. Edinburgh, most particularly *The Thistle*, had taken an irrational exception to the stipulation that Ashwell have

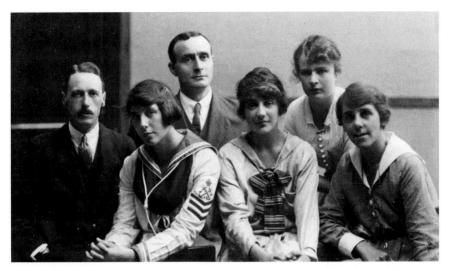

4.8 The Lena Ashwell YMCA Concert Party, Egypt, 1916
(photographer unknown, courtesy of Stuart Gough)

final say on selection of artists. This 'Scandalous Insult to Scotland' had more to do with traditionally parochial and ostensibly patriotic stances in relation to southern initiatives, than with Ashwell. The rest of Scotland was supportive, but *The Thistle* launched a savage attack on Ashwell, 'a theatrical damsel of a very aggressive type', scathingly referred to as 'a London actress', and on her German patron, Princess Victoria of Schleswig-Holstein.[87] Ashwell avoided going into print over this, leaving the letter-writing to the YMCA. Having identified herself to the Lord Provost of Edinburgh as a Scot, at least by marriage, she was amused by the description of her as one 'who comes on the stage alone and pirouettes as an English heroine, who has at last subdued Scotland and placed it under her heel', although she regretted that Edinburgh 'remained angry, at any rate unsympathetic, to the end'.[88]

In contrast, the *Times* paid tribute to the stage's generosity: 'It is safe to say no profession has thrown itself so wholeheartedly into working for good causes … it would be a worse day for charities than is suspected if the Stage were suddenly to turn crusty and refuse to lend the aid of its enormous influence and attraction.' The frequent patronage of the royal family was cited as a clear indication that the war effort of performers was recognised and they were valued. Not wanting to mention names, the article referred to Ashwell as 'an eminent actress' working in conjunction with the YMCA to organise entertainment for soldiers. 'The task is enormous and the efforts to accomplish it are more successful than ever seemed possible.'[89] This was placed in her scrapbook beside a review of the first Egyptian Concert Party.[90]

In early December, 2,000 soldiers filled Cairo's Ezbekieh Soldiers' Club and many more attended the Sultanieh Opera House Gala performance in the presence of the

Sultan, the British High Commissioner and high-ranking military men. Theodore Flint,[91] leading the ensemble, was described as 'the chap in brown' by war poet Siegfried Sassoon:

> They were gathering round …
> Out of the twilight, over the grey-blue sand
> Shoals of low-jargoning men drift inward to the sound,
> The jangle and throb of a piano … tum-ti-tum …
> Drawn by a lamp, they come
> Out of the glimmering lines of their tents, over the shuffling sand.
> O, sing us the songs, the songs of our own land,
> You warbling ladies in white.
> Dimness conceals the hunger in our faces,
> This wall of faces risen out of the night,
> These eyes that keep their memories of the places
> So long beyond their sight.
>
> Jaded and gay, the ladies sing; and the chap in brown
> Tilts his grey hat; jaunty and lean and pale,
> He rattles the keys … some actor-bloke from town …
> 'God send you home'; and then 'A long, long trail',
> 'I hear you calling me'; and 'Dixieland' …
> Sing slowly … now the chorus … one by one,
> We hear them, drink them; till the concert's done.
> Silent I watch the shadowy mass of soldiers stand.
> Silent they drift away over the glimmering sand.[92]

After three weeks in Cairo, the group performed along the Suez Canal zone. On Christmas Day they joined a soldiers' choir and 'sang carols in different wards of the hospital … At one place in the desert Royal Engineers laid telephone wires so troops ten miles farther on could share the concert … we went to and from concerts by camels.' By February they had covered the length of the Canal and in Ismailia 'gave concerts to the biggest audiences of the war: Thursday, there were 3800 men, the next concert 4000 men, and on Saturday, 6000.'[93] One Party member wrote it was generally only possible to present one concert a day, as 'singing, with the temperature at 120 degrees, proved somewhat exhausting'. They found open-air work 'in the desert less exacting than they expected. The sand deadened all other sound and the atmosphere was so clear that every word could be heard by as big an audience as could possibly be got together.'[94]

Following the disastrous Battle of the Somme in 1916, Ashwell was not alone in noticing 'gradual growth in the feeling war was habitual, and nothing could end it'.[95] By late February 1917, nine firing-line Concert Parties had gone at intervals to the Front. They travelled uncomfortably in vehicles ranging from a car, donated by a Nottingham business man, to a London bus, a large target which could only travel at night, compelling artists on some occasions to walk to performances. Conditions were difficult, often appalling, and the work exhausting. Ultimately it could not continue after the party that finished its tour in March. There were no longer any men, either over age or medically unfit for fighting, to form firing-line Parties for the rest of the year. It was not until January 1918 that permission was renewed for Parties to resume work. Meanwhile she directed her energies to finding solo entertainers, including a ventriloquist and story-teller who performed everywhere from dug-outs to firing-line tents. Once the YMCA could send lecturers on short permits, Ashwell sought suitable personalities, including actor-manager John Martin Harvey. After giving lectures in French huts, he wrote to her, 'It has been one of the most memorable incidents of my life, and I cannot tell you how grateful I am to you for making it possible.'[96]

In London Ashwell drew together a team of committed women, working behind the scenes to administer, publicise and fund-raise for her scheme. Olga Hartley, suffragist, journalist and author, promoted the concerts, while Mrs C.F. Leyel, previously with Frank Benson's company and later manager of 'Culpepper Houses' herb shops, took charge of raising money: 'with the courage of an Arctic explorer [and] … a persistence which most of us have lost at the age of five, [she] pursues her way with ruthless cheerfulness'.[97] Actress Dorothy Dundas 'presided over all arrangements for the parties, the passports, travelling, settling of innumerable disputes and difficulties … with faithfulness, tact and wisdom'.[98] The first of two imaginative fund-raising events, the *Chelsea Revue*, took place at Chelsea Palace on 20 March 1917. In the spirit of the event, the programme admitted it 'was written by far too many people, under the disability of far too large a committee'.[99] Many writers, musicians, dancers and designers, and a big cast of players, were involved. Ellen Terry, as 'The Spirit of Chelsea', inducted Ashwell, as a mere Duchess, into Chelsea society. Earlier, Ashwell's family had rented a house there, where she observed 'Chelsea had always a mild gaiety in the pursuit of Art.'[100] Elgar composed new ballet music; Augustus John was a programme illustrator; and light-hearted tribute was paid to all the 'great figures in modern Chelsea life, from Carlyle and Whistler to McEvoy'.[101] Something different for jaded charity matinee-goers, it was a great success. Some of the funniest scenes were repeated in *Ellen Terry's Bouquet*, at the Lyric on 29 June, attended by the king and queen.

The second great fund-raiser was a somewhat unconventional 'bazaar', or 'Petticoat Lane' Fair, held in early December at the Royal Albert Hall. It was a major organisational feat, masterminded by Mrs Leyel. 'A lottery is illegal and yet by any other name might smell as sweet, so Mrs Leyel arranged a huge "tombola" and we both signed a paper which, if informed against, would automatically have placed us in jail.'[102] Furriers, dressmakers, hatters, jewellers and many other businesses donated prizes which included a trip to America, two acres of land in the Chiltern Hills, and livestock such as a prize bull, pedigree puppies and a pig.[103] Many stalls sold produce, arts and crafts, toys, signed books and flowers. Early evening tableaux

4.9 Petticoat Lane Poster, December 1917
(Imperial War Museum, London, PC0770 Cat. No. IWM PST 6257)

of fashion clothing provided entertainment with a fancy dress ball for munitions workers on the final night. A coloured promotional poster was designed by Mr Plank, and 'it occurred to Mrs Leyel that pillar-boxes formed admirable posting stations, and one morning London woke to find nearly every pillar-box in the West End surrounded with this delightful picture'. Officials obviously noted their impact, 'for afterwards pillar-boxes were strictly reserved for Government posters'.[104]

The Fair received extensive press coverage, with frequent reference to the many women involved in its success. An enthusiastic response from the public ensured good attendance and income. The remote *Irish Times* published the only disagreeable and pompous comment:

> Miss Lena Ashwell's 'Concerts at the Front' Fund has been doing splendid work and deserves substantial support; but I am doubtful whether the ladies who organised the Petticoat Lane Fair, which opened at the Albert Hall this afternoon, have chosen an altogether satisfactory method of helping it. No doubt, a good deal of money will be raked in, but at what a cost for preliminary expenses and with how much expenditure of labour which might surely be better employed! The craving for excitement of some fashionable dames seems insatiable. It is better they should indulge it for a good object than a bad one, but why in war-time should they want to indulge it at all?[105]

The writer did not appreciate the long-term value of this collaborative morale booster after more than three years of war. The 261 tombola prizes were announced in late January 1918, prior to which one-third of tickets were sold outside London. After £3,000 expenses, £34,000 was raised from this brave and amusing enterprise.

Meanwhile Ashwell, with 4,000 concerts having taken place in France and 1,000 elsewhere, began promoting the idea of local artists going to the Front as 'gifts' from their home towns. With the support of regional Concerts at the Front societies, antiques were donated and auctioned. J.G. Russell Harvey and Charlie Thomas, authors of an 'excellent and amusing little book', *Ollendorff Up-to-Date*, donated profits from the second edition (5,000 copies already sold),[106] and in Cairo money raised at the Grand YMCA fête, the first such large-scale event, held in May 1917, was used to ensure concerts continued there. Visiting Hull, York and Doncaster, Ashwell recited patriotic and vividly descriptive poems written at the Front, including 'Fighting Men' and 'St George of England' by C. Fox Smith, 'The Sea is His' by R.E. Vernede, and Paul Bewsher's epic 'The Bombing of Bruges'. Taking great care to announce any official recognition she received, she made promotional use of Field Marshall Haig's view that concerts were 'a source of endless pleasure and relaxation for many thousands of soldiers' and his wish that the scheme 'may not collapse through lack of funds'.[107] Haig's acknowledgement of her work was an important step forward.

Local organisers set up auditions, and in the presence of experienced musicians and 'leading members of the city' Ashwell heard many potential artists. In

Manchester she came up against a musician who considered economic necessity the most important selection criterion, but for her

> the first requisite ... was a good artist, but one had always to consider suitability for the work, which required a certain amount of stability of character, and also a desire to be of use, and sometimes one would choose a rather less efficient artist really because of the atmosphere which the singer or player created ... the most successful parties were those in which there was a great differentiation but equally great harmony ... one's decision as to suitability and artistic value had to be made very quickly ... [It was] something to be proud of that in dealing with six hundred people [the number of artists used overall], in spite of the tremendous temptations and difficulties ... we were let down in only three or four cases.[108]

During this period she made visits alone to French bases, 'to see the parties and arrange differences, for naturally there were a great number of difficulties and dissensions which some one had to smooth out'.[109] Her determination to retain a strong personal identification with Concert Parties brought strain into her relationship with the YMCA. Despite what she considered to be her own normally compliant nature, and for the following reasons, she insisted adamantly that all entertainments remain prefixed with 'Lena Ashwell':

> My whole object ... had been demonstrating that the arts were essentially and vitally necessary to human beings ... I could not see why the professional musician or actor should be submerged in the YMCA organisation ... I always considered my name merely as a label to signify that all the people ... were professionals. Undoubtedly the entertainment work became extremely powerful, and to a non-professional it must have seemed very pig-headed to insist upon the professional standing, but then Christian organisations have not been treated with the indifference and contempt that music and drama of this country have suffered under.[110]

She writes with warmth and anecdotal humour about visiting camps and being an audience member; and she writes with sadness about great losses and pain suffered by so many. She had a brief respite, meeting her brother, adventurer Roger Pocock, in Boulogne, sitting 'in the sunshine on the ramparts of the chateau, looking out across the Channel to the milky cliffs of England'.[111] An extraordinary character and author of several autobiographies, Pocock set up the Legion of Frontiersmen in 1904. Too old for active service, he was in France as a platoon commander mobilising a Labour Corps.

Back home, Ashwell began organising musical entertainment at Ciro's, a notorious and famously frivolous nightclub in London's West End, given over to the YMCA in mid-1917 to create a 'French bourgeois café' where soldiers on leave could bring women relatives and friends to a socially respectable environment. With Paget Bowman, she masterminded five hours of concert music daily, presented in the main hall, which also accommodated the 'canteen' area where on some days up to 6,000 teas and suppers were served.[112] The resident ensemble was a talented all-female quartet of piano and strings, with additional instrumentalists and singers. Roger Quilter arranged English works by Grainger, Frank Bridge, Sullivan and many classical composers. 'Invariably it is found the best is the most liked' wrote Robin Legge, praising the enterprise.[113] Folk songs, operatic arias, madrigal groups, Shakespeare readings and Sunday evening sacred concerts were also presented. Ashwell had a great short-term success as Ciro's took on the mantle of a music club, which she hoped would continue after the war. Sadly, pleas to authorities to maintain such a venue fell on deaf ears:

> It is a hideous thought that the time is very near when Ciro's and other similar institutions for the benefit of soldiers and sailors may be closed down by official command. Ciro's has proved a triumphant success ... [It] has risen to the eminence of a music school in the very best sense of that term. Concerts there are of the highest class, and what is more, it is this highest class music that has come to be demanded by frequenters of Ciro's, soldiers, sailors and their friends.[114]

After nearly two years of capacity audiences, Ciro's Concert Party gave its fare-well performance on 14 June. Bowman paid tribute to Ashwell who 'had collected £100,000 in order this work might be done, laying aside her own career as an actress, and treating her brother and sister artistes with most affectionate solicitude'.[115] She received a volume containing 300 signatures of those artists who had worked with her. Sadly, by late summer 1919 Ciro's had returned to its pre-war activity and music clubs to occasional events in local venues.

In 1917, Penelope Wheeler and Gertrude Jennings began presenting full-length plays at YMCA bases. Dependent on actresses staying permanently, they used soldiers and officers in male roles. Wheeler created a repertory company in Le Havre, which became the prototype for Cicely Hamilton in Abbeville and others: all were initially run by women and set up during 1917 and 1918, at Etaples, Calais, Dieppe, Trouville and Rouen. With soldiers and officers in her cast, any of whom could be called for duty at short notice, Wheeler always had ready three fully rehearsed, different programmes. The company performed nightly in nearby camps and some-times in local theatres. Twice weekly they performed at YMCA Central 'entirely for the men; officers were only admitted if there was room' and presented Saturday matinees for convalescent soldiers.[116] Much benefit was ascribed to the preparation and rehearsal process for shell-shocked and injured soldiers, who built sets, painted, and made props. Workshop resources in an old granary were shared with a morris dance group led by the English Folk-Dance Society's Miss D.C. Daking. A member of an early Concert Party, she remained in France to teach women and officers, who then taught and danced with soldiers for physical exercise and entertainment. The repertory companies presented Shakespeare, recent West End plays and a wide se-lection of one-act plays, often the most suitable for their simplicity in casting and staging. 'In nearly all plays there are more men than women ... We never had more than two or three professional actors (male) in any company, and had to rely upon talent to be found amongst officers and men.'[117] Undaunted, Ashwell's colleagues produced Shaw and Shakespeare as well as *The School for Scandal*, *Quality Street* and *The Mikado*. At Abbeville, Hamilton wrote and produced her miracle play *The Child in Flanders*. Shortcomings and difficulties included makeshift staging ('the presence of unnecessary furniture is not encouraged'), sudden cast changes ('needs of the Army ... come before the needs of the stage') and shortage of costumes ('Where every male lives and moves in khaki it is no good sending your actor out to borrow garments from friends').[118] On the other hand, compensation was great: an actor having to give of the utmost is very satisfying, while the audience was praised for its imagination and generosity. Subsequently, Ashwell initiated a press campaign calling for 'women's dresses and men's mufti suits ... suitable for modern comedy', items to be sent to her in London.[119]

Despite the above, Ashwell was obliged to respond to an article about canteen theatres which gave the impression no theatre work was happening in France: 'there are already ... three strong repertory companies ... [entertaining] an average of 18,000 men a month ... The work is increasing with great speed, and should run parallel to the concert work, which is now sending five visiting parties a month and has fifteen permanent base parties.'[120] Wheeler reported that thirty plays had been produced. 'The men want the best. They would not be satisfied with much of what London accepts. They come to plays alert and eager, not half asleep and inert like so many London audiences. I see in them the promise of the long hoped-for national theatre.'[121] Ashwell frequently reiterated that rewards were not financial. Her response to a claim that soldiers paid for Concert Party performances at the Front was, 'sometimes a small charge was made for events at licensed theatres and after the Armistice was signed the YCMA had made a few charges but otherwise concerts were free and she wanted those at home who had contributed so much to know this was the case.'[122]

On 25 August 1917 the *Daily Graphic* announced that Ashwell, along with the queen and eleven other women, was a recipient of the new Order of the British Empire. This was the first time women were thus recognised for their own achievements – something of a problem for the Central Chancery of the Orders of Knighthood clerk, who hand-addressed her award letter to 'Mrs Lena Simson, Sir'. Tributes flowed from the YMCA and Paget Bowman in the *Musical News*: 'Miss Ashwell has already given over 6,000 concerts in France, in Egypt, and in Malta, to say nothing of those in camps at Aldershot, Canterbury, and on Salisbury Plain, and in numerous hospitals in and around London ... she has given employment to nearly 400 artists, some of whom might have fared ill during the war but for her efforts.'[123] Performer Elsie Gough, congratulating Ashwell, wrote that she was 'very proud to think I have been connected in a small way with your great scheme ... Truly it is a wonderful work.'[124]

Former Prime Minister Asquith made another significant public tribute to women in his preface to *Women of the War*,[125] which contains narratives by thirty women,

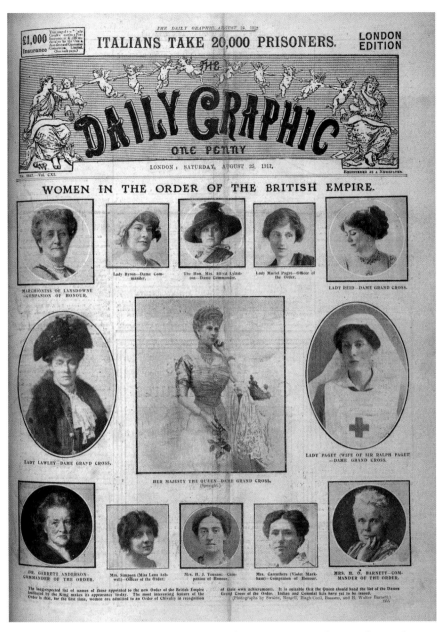

4.10 Announcement of women recipients of British Empire orders, *Daily Graphic*, 25 August 1917 (Associated Newspapers Limited and British Library Board)

including Ashwell. The man who when in government would not support votes for women, was quoted in *British Weekly* saying:

> For the first time it has taught us as a nation to realise how large and how decisive is the part that can be played in a world wide contest by those who are prevented from taking a place in the actual fighting line … Nor can it be doubted these experiences and achievements will, when the war is over, have a permanent effect upon both the statesman's and the economist's conception of the powers and functions of women in the reconstructed world.[126]

The world was certainly changing. However well these experiences were thus en-capsulated, with 'sanity and comparative absence of panegyric',[127] Ashwell's work was not yet done and as a further initiative in the provision of recreation and an extension of the repertory companies, she began a project not realised for another twelve months. Whilst in Paris she 'heard many regrets that there were no places of entertainment where troops could hear their own language',[128] so she set about to find a suitable, affordable theatre for repertory seasons. The YMCA was not able to help, making it very much her personal enterprise. The posters from June 1918 reflect this, proclaiming an 'English Season, Director: Miss Lena Ashwell, O.B.E.'.[129] As a base for companies to rehearse and perform while awaiting travel permits for France, the small Winchester Palace Theatre was rented. In the first half of 1918 troop movement increased and civilian permits were more erratic, resulting in last-minute travel cancellation. Awaiting official support, Ashwell acquired play rights and her company gave a week of trial performances, from 8 April 1918, at the Kings, Hammersmith. Subsequently, performances of repertoire for France were given in Winchester. Having difficulty obtaining permits, she sought help through Lord Beaverbrook's Ministry of Information. He was investigating the use of drama and music for propaganda purposes, as an alternative to the current ineffectual scattering of printed matter over Europe. She hoped that

> if the Comédie Française would be generous enough to invite a British Shakespear-ean company to play in their historic and world-known theatre, the company could afterwards visit neutral countries with this hall-mark of artistic excellence, and also this sign of co-operation between the two great nations would be invaluable in neutral countries. A good deal of propaganda was being done by the Germans in neutral countries through music and plays, and amongst others, Reinhardt's productions of Shakespeare's plays.[130]

While Ashwell was in Paris engaging local support, to her chagrin, Beaverbrook decided cinema, not music and drama, would be used for information and propa-ganda. She later wrote of this decision: 'There are some events in life which fill one with unspeakable rage because of their crass stupidity.'[131] It may well have been Beaverbrook's decision that left Ashwell unimpressed with cinema's ability to make a positive contribution, especially to the lives of young people. She was particularly outspoken against its influence in the 1920s.

Eventually she secured a theatre, near the Gare Saint-Lazare, which she renamed Théâtre Albert 1er. The first performance was given on 29 June 1918. Although Lord Derby and the Corps Diplomatique were present, Ashwell again felt thwarted by lack of official support and recognition. Paris was under constant bombardment, all leave to the city was cancelled and many people were departing. Not long after, the tide began to turn in favour of the Allies, and Maugham's social satire *Smith*, Haddon Chambers' *The Tyranny of Tears*, and *Mrs Gorringe's Necklace* by H.H. Davies, were given throughout that summer. The *Era* reported on this 'Theatrical Entente Cordiale', hoping it would continue.[132] At the time of the Armistice, the company was playing *The Man Who Stayed at Home* and rehearsing *Twelfth Night*. In late February 1919 the theatre, for which support had been limited, was taken over by an American cinema group. The company moved to Lille, touring surrounding towns and working in co-operation with the military.

In November 1917, the Liverpool Lord Mayor's Khaki Fund raised £7,000. Ashwell was guest at mayoral 'At Homes' and in three days 'spoke twenty-two times … when it was all over, Sir Archibald [Salvidge, Deputy Lord Mayor] almost persuaded me I might live through a General Election Campaign'.[133] She had become an articulate and respected public speaker and was assuming a more overtly political stance, recognising the need to focus on rising above war-weariness and to plan the strong involvement of women in a post-war future. She addressed women workers assembled in St James's Park: 'The spirit of womanhood of England is determined to see the war through to the end … We are not going to try to escape any of the weariness. We know we are a strength behind the armies. The army needs us.'[134] Later, she made a stern appeal to women clerical workers for the Women's Industrial Council. Seeking recognition for an equal pay for equal work principle, Ashwell stressed that no woman should work for pocket money: 'She should stand by regular women workers and insist on her proper wage or she should take voluntary work … The taking or giving employment for pocket money was a national crime that could never be forgiven nor forgotten.'[135] If more women were to be employed, she argued, help must be given to make this possible, proposing the establishment of communal kitchens, state-run crèches, education department nursery schools and training to ensure efficiency, equal pay and the removal of barriers preventing women getting to the top.[136]

In December 1917, the Representation of the People Bill, which included the vote for women, passed in the House of Commons with little opposition. Most members agreed with Asquith, who some years before had said: '"Let the women work out their own salvation." Well, Sir, they have worked it out during this war.'[137] Before reconstruction, war had to be concluded. On 24 January 1918 Chelsea Town Hall accommodated a large National Party Meeting. It was a patriotic occasion, with more than a dash of jingoism. Ashwell, seconding the motion to urge victorious conclusion, regretted that something of the horrors of war 'could not be brought home to people who lived in this feather-bed of England'. In what briefly became a controversial statement quoted out of context and against her (as 'thank God for queues'), 'she thanked God food shortages were giving the people of England a little – a very little – share of that great suffering which our men were enduring'.[138] By 1 March she was obliged, when speaking in Liverpool, to explain she had been misquoted. Ashwell's most active involvement with the National Party was before the December 1918 election. She wanted 'peace to be worthy of what the boys have done', and for 'Mr Lloyd George and Mr Bonar Law to go to the Conference with the strong support of Parliament'.[139] Supporting candidate Alfred Davies against an Asquith/Liberal opponent at Lincoln Theatre Royal, Ashwell said she did not care about politics but she did care

> a great deal for this country. There were many things women meant to have … better housing and better education, and … equal pay for equal work. They also meant to have open competition in every part of the nation's work, for which the best brains were needed, and coming into which women meant to take their part without any sex barrier whatever … They intended to have beauty and something worth living for so children of the future might not be slaves to machinery, but should have some leisure, some happiness, some beauty and some joy brought into their lives.[140]

Women could now stand for election to the House of Commons, and the entertainment profession would have benefited from parliamentary representation, but Ashwell was not inclined to stand. There were only two successful male Coalition candidates to deal with entertainment issues: Mr C. Jesson, Secretary of the Amalgamated Musicians' Union, and Walter de Frece.

Throughout the war, commentators were anticipating what theatrical fare might be sought in a changed, post-war world. Ashwell hoped her observations of the appreciation by ordinary soldiers of 'serious' music and drama would be heeded. Alfred Barnard foresaw that while 'war-worn soldiers and war-worried civilians of both sexes will need probably more entertainment and amusement than they have ever indulged in before', social reconstruction would mean 'earnest, sober and serious efforts to rebuild out of chaos a new social system, more worthy of our civilization than any hitherto contemplated'. He predicted, 'Education, habits, thought, work, eating, drinking, and legitimate pleasure will contrast strangely with all that have gone before … both Church and Theatre will have to provide fare which will be in keeping with the desire for improvement … on lines compatible with the national desire for a saner and more solid social existence.'[141] He concluded all entertainment would still meet basic human needs: those of laughter and tears. The *Era* anticipated less severe censorship on plays like Ibsen's *Ghosts* and Brieux's *Damaged Goods*,[142] (which had been banned initially), so that playwrights could deal more effectively with moral themes than had been the case before and during the war.[143] E. Temple Thurston likened wartime theatre to an anaesthetist getting a patient through an operation. Once recovered and changed, the patient would seek a greater reality:

> A thousand problems, moral and social, will arise out of the war ... [and] must be dealt with, not only by the authorities ... but by the dramatist and author, who must and will say what is in their minds. There are many things people have been thinking ... which for reasons of patriotism and the will to victory, they neither have dared nor have they wished to say ... all are to be spoken ... and [no-one] will stop their being said.[144]

Ashwell was already declaring her hand, aware that mere talk about the issues would be insufficient. There were concerns about the impact of long-term war on the drama, with the *Era* reporting on 23 January 1918 that the Actors' Benevolent and the Variety Benevolent Funds urgently needed donations to help members. The curfew, air-raids, rationing, increased prices and shortages of materials such as paper created difficulties for managements. As the nation was exhorted to 'Use Less Fuel', the *Era* suggested theatres provide warm 'communal sitting rooms', reducing individual household fuel consumption.[145] Then, in late October, the countrywide Spanish flu epidemic threatened to close all entertainment venues. In Portsmouth, near Ashwell's Winchester base, military authorities declared such venues out of bounds for troops until further notice. The Entertainments Tax had increased on 1 October and, on average, theatre, music hall and cinema takings dropped over 23 per cent.[146]

One positive outcome from war-time constraints was the strengthening of British musical resources. Local singers, composers and instrumentalists replaced imported soloists, and all-British musical programmes gained popularity for both musical and patriotic reasons. In recognition of her employment of so many in the Concert Parties, Ashwell was appointed president of the Union of Lady Musicians, formed when Stoll theatres and cinemas announced they would not displace women orchestral players when male musicians returned. In this aspect of equal employment, England remained ahead of its European neighbours, and some long-running music clubs and choral societies had their origins in this period.

For most of February 1918, Ashwell was performing with Concert Parties in France. Many soldiers ('Tommies') referred to the Parties as 'The Lenas' or, to those remaining at a base, as 'The Stationary Lenas'.[147] On her return Ashwell was upbeat:

> Our difficulties have been enormous, but we are amply repaid by the delight which the soldier boys manifest. Just picture a play being staged in a hangar inches deep in mud. An actress in evening dress has to leap from plank to plank to reach the stage. A false step and she would sink over her ankles. I have been over to France with the object of developing the theatrical side of the entertainments ... Some of our performances are given in cinemas, which hold 1500 people ... If the war lasts long enough we may see a National Repertory Theatre established in France. It may pave the way to a similar institution in England – who knows![148]

Artists had raised £79,500 for Concerts at the Front. The Parties were now presenting 14,000 concerts a year and some were providing entertainment for other charities, such as the Royal Medical Benevolent Fund Guild's garden party, one of Dr Simson's causes, in July 1918.

Ashwell was now a familiar face and often the subject of summaries of her achievements and status, such as that published by *The Truth* on 4 September:

> In South Molton Street I ran against Lena Ashwell ... I heard of her successful establishment of the English comedy theatre in Paris. On leaving her I pondered over her inaugurative power and the many big achievements which go – and remain – to her credit, the Emergency Corps, the Three Arts Club, and Concerts at the Front being the greatest of these. Assuredly she has stamped herself upon her time.

Six months later, there was further acknowledgement: 'It is lucky for England that when its accredited representatives refuse to recognise certain public work as a national duty, private enterprise always comes to the rescue.' Reference was made to all the voluntary work undertaken, which often provided the only support for many during the war. This included private hospitals, the Red Cross, the YMCA and Ashwell, 'who took the work in hand, gradually won over official prejudice and carried it through'.[149]

At the cessation of hostilities, acknowledgement was sought for the profession's major contribution: 'It has provided the antidote to national depression and has carried on in the face of much difficulty and actual danger ... it has given of its best ungrudgingly ... often in the face of vexatious restrictions and regulations ... whether the nation has been equally fair to the entertainment industry is another question.'[150] Ashwell asked more direct questions when describing theatre work performed by English inmates at Ruhleben prisoner-of-war camp, Germany:

> What is the matter with theatre in England? In Berlin Shakespeare has been played continuously during the war; in Paris two Shakespeare plays have been produced within the last few months. Even the Serbians ... before [their] great national disaster, were able to give productions of Shakespeare's plays; prisoners of war are able to play Shakespeare in camps. Why is it, then, that alone in England, with exception of the plucky enterprise at the 'Old Vic', it is impossible to see any of his works played?[151]

She appealed for help to start a British theatre at The Hague, where actors, musicians and artists released from Ruhleben were transferred before repatriation. No help was forthcoming from the Ministry for Information, although

> The Ministry is able to spend public money ... securing paintings as a record of the war. Paintings have, no doubt, a commercial as well as artistic value ... Are we convinced the only thing that counts is money? Are we prepared to give up our

inheritance in literature and to see other countries able and willing to produce our great monuments of literary art, while we sit idly by and allow, by our inertia, the use of these great works to slip out of our national life? Surely in discussing reconstruction some notice should be taken of the powerful medium of drama.[152]

When distributing awards to Incorporated London Academy of Music students, she advised them to 'always place art before monetary considerations'.[153] *Performer* considered Ashwell's concern about outside commercial interests and the dominance of 'revues and trashy forms of entertainment' to be 'hysterical'.[154] Following her YMCA speech on 'Drama and the Christian Life', the *Aldershot News* took issue with her claim that the press and theatre managers worked against serious drama, giving the example of empty seats for Terry's Shakespeare readings, suggesting Ashwell consider human nature ('the unsatisfied craving for mind recreation'[155]) and the inadequate education system.

As the end of war became a reality, Ashwell focused attention on theatre as important in helping a damaged society. On the eve of the German signing of the Armistice, the *Sunday Times* published her 'Future of the Drama'. She had seen thousands of soldiers respond positively and enthusiastically to the words and music of great creative talents, presented simply and sincerely, without condescension. She had seen such responses stimulate performers, and felt 'the nation as a whole should waken to the fact that they are the victim of a system'.[156] Pleading for money to continue her work until every soldier and war worker was home, she expressed continuing disappointment with the War Office's lack of support. She gave a stern warning to officialdom:

It has been proved – and this is a lesson of war that must not be forgotten in peace – art is not a luxury, something external that may be done without, but part of the very fibre of our national life, neglect of which is fatal. My own experience … is the health, the spirit, the morale of troops benefited enormously by the entertainments furnished; music and drama played an undeniable part in securing victory. This will not be new to those who have realised the intimate correlation between Art and Life; but may be so to others, and, I hope, will have some influence on our views when normal conditions are resumed.[157]

Performers expressed similar perceptions in their local newspapers. It would be months before all soldiers returned home and Ashwell continued to organise performances until demobilisation was complete in June 1919. Many performances were for the Allied Army of Occupation in Germany, where morale-boosting was essential. She spent Christmas and New Year in devastated areas of France, visiting the seven repertory companies whose repertoire now consisted of more than eighty plays.

Ashwell's Paris productions of *Twelfth Night* and *The Merchant of Venice* at Le Havre's Grand Theatre were current news stories, taking a back page, however, to news of Allied supremacy after more than four years of war.[158] As the theatrical profession took stock, Ashwell and Eva Moore were nominated to the Actors' Association council, hoping to take a strong lead in helping performers back into work. Elected in January, both were obliged to resign on 14 February: the Association's solicitors considered them ineligible because they were managers.

> Miss Ashwell, while accepting the decision, informed the Association it would not prevent her from taking the greatest interest in the progress which the Association would soon establish for the protection of artists, adding that the position of the artist is eminently unsatisfactory and dangerous to the national interest.[159]

Once fighting ceased and reconstruction was underway, most people had no concept of the complexity of demobilisation. It was not yet time for Ashwell to stop her tireless fund-raising and organisation of artists, although as a registered wartime charity, Concerts at the Front had to be dismantled. Her colleagues recognised the next step was support for 600 artists needing a way back into their profession. The fund moved out of the YMCA Women's Auxiliary Committee's control into 'The Lena Ashwell Demobilisation and Reconstruction Fund'. Once formally acknowledged by the Charities Commission, £3,000 was transferred to this fund.[160] Meanwhile, appeals continued, for both money and recognition of the value of the artist. The latter was Ashwell's focus in the January 1919 *Play Pictorial* supplement:

> When war took our unready nation by surprise … there were two patriotic sections of the nation … made to feel they were not of any particular use to the community at the moment – women and artists. Women were advised to stay at home and knit … members of musical and theatrical professions were told they were a peace-time luxury, only useful if famous enough to attract philanthropists and millionaires to charity matinees.

She believed that through Concerts at the Front, 'the creative, artistic life of the people was "carried on", followed the nation overseas, and proved not only the permanent primitive values of music and drama to the souls of the people, but the real value of the artist to the community'.

Charles Wyndham, one of the last great actor-managers, died in January 1919. He was very supportive of Ashwell, who felt his loss keenly. Further grief followed in February, with the drowning of two Concert Party singers after their car plunged into the dark, icy river Somme in France. Ashwell conveyed condolences to the husband of popular singer Emily Pickford and the family of young baritone Vincent Taylor. In London there were memorial services for actors killed during the war; these no doubt taking on an extra poignancy as she mourned two young artists who had set off so eagerly only a week before their untimely deaths.

While Ashwell was fund-raising in generous Cardiff, it was announced that grateful returning soldiers would help: from 'February 24 until March 1, "Concerts at the Front Week", discharged men, representing London branches of the National Federation of Discharged and Demobilised Sailors and Soldiers (NFDDSS), will canvass for Miss Ashwell's concerts at the Front'.[161] Prior to a similar week late in March, the prime minister's wife, Mrs Lloyd George, presided at a 10 Downing Street event, where Ashwell declared: 'The moment the Armistice was signed and danger was over, people closed their purses to war charities.'[162] American President Wilson's supportive letter to the NFDDSS, together with a letter from Sir Douglas Haig and a signed photograph of the prime minister, were auctioned, raising £600. Ashwell needed £20,000 to continue, until July, the work of twenty-eight Concert Parties performing away from England.

As reconstruction projects took shape, a London Shakespeare League deputation to the LCC's Education Committee argued the necessity for supporting 'acted' Shakespeare and the formation of municipal theatres or companies for this purpose.[163] Ashwell's manager Paget Bowman represented her. The idea of the actor as teacher was proposed: using Shakespeare to improve elocution in schools. Subsequently, the committee voted £350 in grants to projects, including the Old Vic, promoting Shakespeare for students. 'Unostentatiously, like many other movements pregnant with promise, the principle of giving grants of public money in support of dramatic representations has been instituted ... the power of drama as an educative force has been admitted by London's Governing Body.'[164] The *Era* suggested the Actors' Association request that a condition of a LCC grant be that actors performing in supported productions be Association members – perhaps the first thoughts on funding with 'strings attached'.

The idea of a 'Municipal Theatre' had been put forward frequently; Ashwell was alive to the possibilities and in March 1919 things began to come together. The Le Havre Repertory Company was presenting their successful *The Merchant of Venice* for the Army of Occupation in Cologne, while Hamilton's group was touring devastated French areas and performing to Labour Battalions in remote districts. The Paris/Lille 'Lena Ashwell Theatre Repertoire Company' had returned to London. An existing company, with little prospect of immediate alternative employment, was an ideal vehicle to put into action Bowman's plea for public support and recognition of good English drama, performed by companies not pursuing commercial gain. He thought 'if authorities will take the cause of recreation in hand and recognise its importance to the community today, with its extra hours of leisure, people will leap to the occasion. We may yet have a Ministry of Fine Arts.'[165]

It was clear the arts needed more official recognition. The theatrical profession emerged from the war with an increased concern for improving internal processes of management and employment conditions, as well as looking to a wider audience. Public subsidy, to alleviate financial pressures, was seen as a way drama could be improved and made accessible to all, since 'commercialism, a ruling spirit, does not make for the best interests of the community at large'.[166] This was Ashwell's next big challenge: the intertwining threads of her life were the improvement of drama (through the British Drama League and the setting up of her own repertory company) and the role of religious faith in reconstruction and particularly in the lives of women:

> The great force of theatre can ... help people to evolve an awareness of other people's conditions and lives, and to inspire the deep forces of humanity which are the source from which spring those high qualities which should be the very essence of reconstruction ... Now theatre, of all places, is the place where people go to get a change of consciousness ... [to] cast off their burden of weariness and disappointment. If the entertainment holds some inspiration of beauty and truth ... which goes with them, fixed in the mind as a seed for growth, perhaps they need not again pick up their burden.[167]

Standing at the lectern within Worcester Cathedral's chancel rails, facing a congregation of 3,000, Ashwell had given an historic recital of passages from the Scripture during Easter Week. 'It was probably the first time in the cathedral's thousand year history that Scripture passages were used, apart from the regular church service.'[168] Appearing as

> a statuesque figure at the choir screen, she declaimed with magnificent effect, and in a clear voice which sounded to the far ends of the Cathedral, some of the most moving passages of Holy Scripture, full of pathos and imagery, full of beauty, and revealing, in what to many of her hearers must have been a new sense, the sublime language of the Bible.[169]

Inevitably Ashwell became involved in current debates on women in the Church. The Dean of Durham referred to her appearance as an 'interesting experiment', calling on the Church to seek ways to draw more people to its message and advising that this should involve women.[170] The Bishop of London, however, was antagonistic to women taking part in Anglican services. For Ashwell, it was a pity 'the church still finds itself unable to make use of the power for good which women are most assuredly able to exercise'.[171] Spiritual matters informed her address to the Kent Women's Land Army: 'We women have yet to realise we are very important in the country. It is for women of the nation to uphold great spiritual standards.'[172] Such literal interpretation of Scripture should no longer be possible: 'Man' is a generic word which must include women as equal sharers in the Holy Spirit.

> It was the mental outlook of men which prevented the inspiration of women from joining with them for the furtherance of the establishment of the Kingdom of God, and since it is now possible to make use of the inspiration which is pouring through women as well as men, why should not the Church seize the opportunity? The Church has desperate need of life, of being in fuller touch with the needs and sorrows of the world, and half at least of the world is women ... But if the Church still closes its doors, we need not fret ... there is infinite opportunity outside.[173]

On 21 June 1919 the AFL reconvened briefly. Sir Frank Benson spoke on 'The Artist's Place in Reconstruction' and the meeting reasserted the League's determination for equality between men and women. The 'democratization of the arts' was an idea attracting commentators who referred to examples in Europe. Advocates for official acknowledgement that recreation for all was vital sought high-standard, accessible, British cinema free of American influence, literature available in inexpensive paperback form, music clubs such as Ciro's, and local repertory theatres. Education was important in creating interest and enthusiasm for the arts and the artist was perceived as an instrument for change. Ashwell was even more determined now to disprove a widely prevalent pre-war attitude expressed in the phrase: 'As useless as an actor, a billiard-marker, or a golf professional.'[174]

By late June 1919 most Parties were home. Ashwell distributed fifty invitations to the War Workers' Royal Garden Party as most were anxiously trying to find ways back to work; summer was not an easy time, with many theatres closed. Some artistes continued to give Concert-Party-style events in their local areas and there was considerable audience goodwill for these. Ashwell was aware of the pressures, particularly for young people, and was a signatory, along with John Drinkwater, to a letter promoting the League of Youth and Social Progress, which encouraged the active role of young people in all spheres of work.

There were many events paying tribute to wartime activities: at a special Trocadero lunch honouring all Women's War Services and to show 'Women's Appreciation of Women',[175] Ashwell, as spokeswoman for the organisers, read Alice Meynell's address praising women's wartime voluntary sacrifices. Apparently she 'was not recognised by most ... as her hair has grown perfectly grey. Most actresses would not have allowed it to do so, and I hope it is not a sign that Miss Ashwell does not intend to appear on stage any more.'[176] Grey hair notwithstanding, she was in Glasgow the next day, reciting with Myra Hess at the piano. With Carrie Tubb she gave a recital at London's Aeolian Hall on 30 October. The music was entirely works by composers killed in the war, including George Butterworth's 'A Shropshire Lad', and the poetry was written by those with direct war experience, including Rupert Brooke. A significant and fitting memorial, it 'struck at the prejudice of the moment which excludes all references to war from concert programmes ... [It] reminded us that if the war destroyed poets it also made some poetry.'[177] Two further concerts featured living and Elizabethan poets and composers. The audiences were not large and Ashwell paid costs not covered by box office income.

Before closing this chapter of her life, Ashwell wrote a detailed account, from diaries and letters of Concert Party participants, published in 1922 as *Modern Troubadours*.[178] The *Times Literary Supplement*, reviewing the book, appreciated her justifiable pride in the impact of the Parties. While acknowledging the initial opposition she faced, the reviewer thought: 'Perhaps the most interesting thing ... is its revelation of the constant relief afforded to the wounded and suffering by musical and dramatic performances.' As this led to the idea of wounded men performing, the review noted that 'at the present time there are several choirs of ex-Service men in London, who received their training as part of their medical treatment. The initiation of this movement, however indirect and unconscious, is not the least of the feathers in Miss Ashwell's cap.' While wanting to be positive, the reviewer observed that 'the information is too diffuse and ill-organized … There is also a great deal of vain repetition. Yet the book remains as a record of valuable work and untiring effort on the part of a none too-well appreciated class of the community.'[179] Cicely Hamilton described it as 'a plea for the future of spoken drama as well as a tale of work done; and of the two, the plea – though it occupies less space – is perhaps the most important … and the actual motive of the book'.[180]

On 1 November 1919 local borough council elections were held throughout London, with, for the first time, over 100 women candidates. For Ashwell, the importance of these elections could not be overestimated. 'Every man and woman in London should make it a matter of the first importance that nothing shall prevent them from taking this opportunity of establishing their power as citizens.'[181] She urged them to rise above war-weariness and previous disillusionment with local councils to support women candidates who had much to offer to ensure community well-being and the sound administration of local finance. She was delighted when women were elected and took an active role in decision-making.

The theatrical profession was voicing unease regarding the Entertainments Tax, still operating twelve months after the end of the fighting with no indication it would end. For Ashwell, planning a return to management, the tax was significant. Ten years later she identified it as one of the main reasons for her company's demise. Another shadow cast over the profession was the death, at the age of 49, of H.B. Irving, who many had predicted would assume 'the mantle left by his father as leader of the dramatic stage'.[182] Perhaps this loss focused her attention on standards in the acting profession. After attending Tolstoy's *Reparation* at St James's Theatre, she was critical – although her statements did not create a rift between them – of former protégée Athene Seyler. Giving her impressions, Ashwell quoted Irving's comment that 'the theatre was bloody sweat', and concluded: 'it is a searching, praying, agonizing effort to make reality appear in theatre. For the sake of the drama our young actresses must wake up. It is no use skating politely on the surface of life. They must dig down, and deep; and they must, above all things, work, and work with courage.'[183] At the World Christian Service Recruiting Campaign's Exhibition and Conference, in a widely reported and possibly inappropriate confrontational speech, she challenged her profession again. She declared there were many misconceptions about theatre, with people imagining lives of glamorous luxury when the reality was quite different. She claimed profits often went to exploitative managers while actors were forced to earn their living by other means. Commercial managers had more to answer for: 'There is a triviality, a licentiousness, and a sensuality connected with the stage today which is not the desire of the best artists in the profession, and which is certainly not the desire of the majority of soldiers who are accused of having clamoured for it.'[184]

Alfred Lugg, of the Actors' Association, was quick to take advantage: 'Lena Ashwell ... has done the stage a lasting service by speaking so frankly and courageously. As an association we are in accord ... In some cases actors and actresses really are expected to live on air.'[185] He gave examples of weekly wages and expenses, which included dresses, inadequate lodgings away from home, and fares: many began and finished tours in debt. He urged the public to boycott suggestive plays. The press seized on what followed: disliking Ashwell's general charge, actor-producer Oscar Asche challenged the Association to publicly name managers bringing the stage into disrepute. He offered £500 towards meeting expenses for a libel charge if they would. Shaw's response was: 'the charges are but too well grounded, and Mr Asche had better send £500 at once ... to help the battle for an economic wage for all actors and actresses'.[186] On 14 November the Association declared: 'The matter ought to be threshed out, and publicity is the best possible weapon we have',[187] but the issue petered out with formal acceptance of the 'Valentine Standard Contract' for plays and musicals for West End theatres, agreed between the Society of West End Managers and the Actors' Association.[188]

Ashwell, having raised the issue, moved on. She was overseeing rehearsals and making final arrangements for the Lena Ashwell Repertory Company's opening night, officially beginning what she later referred to as 'the third phase in my life, the experience of failure'.[189] With £3,000 and a large pool of actors and directors whose work she knew and trusted, Ashwell organised a number of hospital concerts, then rented Bethnal Green Baths on a weekly basis from the Oxford House organisation. On 12 November 1919, the *Era* announced:

Lena Ashwell's East-End Enterprise. Tonight ... Miss Ashwell, OBE, will start, at Excelsior Hall, Mansford Street, Bethnal Green, quite a new repertory theatre scheme. The play, to be given at popular prices, is *Leah Kleschna*, by the late Charles McLellan ... About Christmas Miss Ashwell and Co. will present a new Miracle play, which has been welded together, so to speak, both in dramatic and musical fashion, by Miss Christopher St John.

A playbill advertised nightly repertory (and Saturday matinees), with *Leah Kleschna* and Robert Marshall's *The Duke of Killicrankie*, directed by Cicely Hamilton, as the first two plays. Sunday concerts were performed by a quartet directed by Flint, who also played musical selections each evening.

Talk of a National Theatre and regionally based repertory theatres, and the aims of the British Drama League, had pointed the way for this project. Despite apparently auspicious circumstances, Ashwell was compelled to declare that

it would have been impossible to start such an organisation as we attempted had not the first company been composed of those who had served in the War areas. We had grown accustomed to play anywhere, under most adverse conditions, without scenery, without lighting. The war had accustomed us to

Excelsior Hall,

Mansford Street,   **Bethnal Green Road.**

(In connection with the Oxford House.)

General Manager   ...   .   EDWARD LYTTON,

Miss LENA ASHWELL

And the ARTISTS' COMMITTEE

PRESENT THEIR PLAYERS IN

REPERTORY

NIGHTLY AT 7.45.

MATINEES: SATURDAYS AT 2.30

CONCERTS: SUNDAYS: AT 2.30

BOX OFFICE OPEN FROM 10 TILL 8.
PRICES: Stalls, numbered and reserved 2/6; Tax 6d.
Area 1s.; Tax 3d.   Gallery 6d. Tax 2d.

Stage Director: R. C. HARCOURT.
Stage Manager: ALEXANDER FIELD.

In accordance with the requirements of the London County Council
. The Public may leave at the end of the Performance by all exits
and entrance doors, and such doors must at that time be open.
All gangways, passages and staircases must be kept entirely free
from chairs or any other obstructions.
The Management earnestly requests that ladies and gentlemen will
remove hats, bonnets, or any kind of head-dress.

4.11 Excelsior Hall flyer, Bethnal Green, November 1919
(Concerts at the Front scrapbook Volume 3, Department of Collections Access,
Imperial War Museum, Lena Ashwell Collection, 09/711)

a biscuit box to sit on, and army blankets for the setting. We had no dressing rooms or dressers.[190]

Even so, it was unfamiliar territory. Ashwell writes: 'it was some time before we succeeded in getting an audience, though we changed the programme every week and our charges were very small'.[191] It was here, on 23 February 1920, that the Players premiered Hamilton's *The Brave and the Fair*. Audience numbers increased but an autumn season was abandoned when Oxford House decided more money could be made hosting cinema. For a few months in spring 1920 she found a small hall in Hanwell. Except for the *Era*'s 5 May review, describing a successful season at the Park Theatre, with Esmé Church in *Diana of Dobson's*, little information remains on this venue. However, it was 'not far from the Lunatic Asylum; the lunatics did not find their way to see our plays, but the Labour Mayors did',[192] and Major Clement Attlee, mayor of Stepney, convened a meeting which agreed to help the company establish a presence in local boroughs, for performances once a week during autumn and winter months. Thus began an enterprise known initially as the Once-a-Week Players (referred to by Ashwell as 'The Roundabouts'), and subsequently as the Lena Ashwell Players, which was 'done in memory of those who fought, and the great army of those who died, and of those still with us who have come back to the bitter struggle for existence', and which lasted for ten years.[193]

Notes

1   'Untimely Shaw Revival at the Kingsway,' *Times*, 15 February 1915.
2   *Sunday Times*, 14 February 1915.
3   There were many individual and local initiatives made to entertain the troops during WWI. Ashwell's was the most wide-ranging and high profile. See L. Collins, *Theatre at War, 1914–18* (London, 1998), and J.G. Fuller, *Troop Morale and Popular Culture in the British and Dominion Armies, 1914–1918* (Oxford, 1990). This latter book makes no reference to Ashwell.
4   Concert Parties at the Front Press Cuttings, Volume 1, Imperial War Museum, Department of Collections Access, 09/771. Ashwell circulated copies to further promote the cause.
5   20 February 1915. Concert Parties at the Front Press Cuttings, Volume 1, Imperial War Museum, Department of Collections Access, 09/771.
6   *Star*, 20 March 1915.
7   *Standard*, 20 March 1915.
8   In *Modern Troubadours* Ashwell explains, 'In the storm and stress of those days, disagreements and mis-understandings grew up, which in days of peace might have been avoided. After a few months it seemed better to organise the work independently. I resigned as Governor and withdrew from the Club, and … carried on the work from the Kingsway and my own home, and afterwards at 44 South Molton Street' (110).
9   *Echo and Evening Chronicle*, 24 March 1915.
10   *Illustrated Sunday Herald*, 28 March 1915.
11   *Globe*, 7 April 1915.
12   *Musical News*, 8 April 1915. Included in Concert Parties at the Front Press Cuttings, Volume 1, Imperial War Museum, Department of Collections Access, 09/771.
13   *Daily Chronicle*, 20 April 1915.
14   'Women and the Theatre', *Lady's Pictorial*, 15 May 1915.
15   *Glasgow Evening Citizen*, 6 June 1915.
16   *Bristol Times & Mirror*, 15 June 1915.
17   *Evening News*, 29 June 1915.
18   Ashwell, *Modern Troubadours*, 34.
19   *Daily Chronicle*, 22 June 1915.
20   *Times*, 5 July 1915.
21   *Daily Sketch*, 12 July 1915.
22   L. Ashwell, 'With Captains Courageous Somewhere in France', *The Nineteenth Century*, August 1915, 344–52.
23   Letter from Wright to Ashwell, 7 August 1915 (Lena Ashwell Papers, Department of Rare Books, Special Collections and Preservation, University of Rochester, Rochester, N.Y.). No evidence has been found of an article published along the lines suggested by Wright; given Ashwell's meticulous keeping of her scrapbooks at this time, it must be assumed either the article was not written or, if written, not published. The point of view Wright and Ashwell discussed, is, however, interesting in indicating their attitudes and their perception of American response to the European situation in 1915.
24   *Daily News & Leader*, 6 September 1915.
25   *Daily Sketch*, 20 September 1915.
26   *Evening Standard*, 14 September 1915.
27   *Vote*, 17 September 1915.
28   *Loughton Advertiser*, 18 September 1915.
29   *Referee*, 10 October 1915.

30 *Evening News*, 2 October 1915.

31 *Times*, 14 October 1915.

32 *Glasgow News*, 16 October 1915.

33 *Daily Mirror*, 16 October 1915.

34 *Red Triangle*, 15 October 1915.

35 *Daily Chronicle*, 10 October 1915.

36 *Lloyd's Weekly News*, 17 October 1915.

37 *Referee*, 17 October 1915.

38 *Standard*, 18 October 1915.

39 *Ibid*.

40 *Daily Mail*, 30 October 1915.

41 Vocalist Elsie Illingworth, *Huddersfield Weekly Examiner*, 23 October 1915.

42 *Daily Telegraph*, 30 October 1915.

43 *Aberdeen Daily Journal*, 26 October 1915.

44 *Evening Standard*, 5 November 1915.

45 *Challenge*, 10 December 1915.

46 Ashwell, *The Stage*, 189. For a more detailed account of this production, see M. Leask, 'Lena Ashwell and *The Starlight Express*', *Theatre Notebook*, 63/1 (2009), 34–54.

47 Quotation from A.W.E. O'Shaughnessy's *Ode*, which, as K.E.L. Simmons points out in 'Elgar and the Wonderful Stranger: Music for *The Starlight Express*', in *Elgar Studies*, ed. Raymond Monk (Aldershot, 1990), both Elgar and Blackwood used. Ashwell was also influenced by this poem, which she quotes when referring to 'the Arts' as 'the education of the heart' in *The Stage*, 131–2. Simmons undertook extensive research into the creation of *The Starlight Express*.

48 The original of this letter of 9 November 1915 is in the archives of Novello & Co., London., quoted by Simmons, 'Wonderful Stranger', 162.

49 St Helens: Hereford & Worcester Record Office: Elgar Society archive. Quoted on the cover of the EMI Records edition of music from *The Starlight Express* (1976).

50 Quoted in J.N. Moore, *Edward Elgar: A Creative Life* (Oxford, 1984), 692 (from Novello & Co. archives).

51 Letter from Blackwood to Elgar, 25 December 1915, quoted in Simmons, 'Wonderful Stranger', 177.

52 O.B. Clarence, *No Complaints* (London, 1943), 145.

53 Quoted in Simmons, 'Wonderful Stranger', 179.

54 British Library: Lord Chamberlain's Play Collection: Letter accompanying *The Starlight Express* manuscript, 6 December 1915.

55 *Daily Telegraph*, 30 December 1915.

56 Only three of the songs and a pianoforte suite have been published, although a number of recordings were made in the 1970s. The radio version was broadcast on the BBC in 1965 and 1968. Simmons prepared an edited 'full-text' version, using Pearn's and Elgar's copies of the script, attempting to marry the words and the music (Simmons, 'Wonderful Stranger', 143, 187).

57 Moore, *Edward Elgar*, 693.

58 Ashwell, *Modern Troubadours*, 35.

59 *Ibid.*, 73.

60 *Era*, 2 February 1916.

61 *Referee*, February 1916.

62 In 1922 Ashwell commented, 'though actors have to allow the greater part of a play to be represented by women, they do not like women to represent the profession. How many years, for instance, have passed before a woman was allowed to have any power

in the Actors' Benevolent Fund? – a power so well exercised now by Lady Wyndham' (*Modern Troubadours*, 38).

63   *Craven Herald*, 26 February 1916.
64   L. Ashwell, 'A Year's Music at the Front', *Strand Magazine*, February 1916.
65   Concert Parties at the Front Press Cuttings, Volume 2, Imperial War Museum, Department of Collections Access, 09/771.
66   *Daily Chronicle*, 13 March 1916.
67   *Glasgow Bulletin*, 13 July 1916.
68   *Standard*, 8 March 1916.
69   Ashwell, *Modern Troubadours*, 111.
70   See Appendix 1 for a full list of the roles that Ashwell played.
71   *Era*, 31 May 1916.
72   *Ibid.*
73   *Era*, 14 June 1916.
74   *Ibid.*
75   *Red Triangle*, 30 June 1916.
76   December 1916. See Ashwell, *Modern Troubadours*, 152–3.
77   *Morning Post*, 18 July 1916. There is a review in the *Era*, 21 June 1916, of a Coliseum variety performance, which says Ashwell played Amina in a short play, *The Maharani of Arakan*, by George Calderon and Sir Rabindranath Tagore. This is likely to be the reviewer's error as Ashwell was most probably in France at this time and there are no reviews in her scrapbook relating to this event – or else it was a one-off event in mid-June prior to her departure for France.
78   *Pearson's Magazine*, June 1916.
79   *Stage*, 23 November 1916. At the time of writing *Modern Troubadours* in 1922, Ashwell considered that playing Lady Macbeth in France was 'my farewell to the stage as an actor' (52), but she did play a significant role with the Lena Ashwell Players in *The Ship* in 1925.
80   *Era*, 23 August 1916.
81   *Era*, 27 December 1916.
82   *North Mail* and *Daily Chronicle*, 28 September 1916.
83   *Era*, 4 October 1916.
84   *Era*, 18 October 1916.
85   *Era*, 22 November 1916.
86   *Western Mail*, 29 November 1916.
87   *Thistle*, December 1916.
88   Ashwell, *Modern Troubadours*, 112.
89   *Times*, 29 November 1916.
90   *Egyptian Gazette*, 4 December 1916.
91   Ashwell wrote that Flint 'was rejected from the Army on medical grounds, but the work he did was fairly strenuous for a delicate man' (*Modern Troubadours*, 93).
92   Originally published by Heinemann in *The War Poems of Siegfried Sassoon*, the source acknowledged by Ashwell in *Modern Troubadours*.
93   Ashwell, *Modern Troubadours*, 101–3.
94   *Halifax Daily Guardian*, 3 March 1919.
95   Ashwell, *Modern Troubadours*, 127.
96   *Ibid.*, 167.
97   Ashwell, *Myself a Player*, 204.
98   Ashwell, *Modern Troubadours*, 123.
99   *Ibid.*, 114.

100 Ashwell, *Myself a Player*, 67.
101 Quoted from the programme in Concert Parties at the Front Press Cuttings, Volume 2, Imperial War Museum, Department of Collections Access, 09/771.
102 Ashwell, *Myself a Player*, 204.
103 There is an amusing handwritten draft 'thank you' letter from Ashwell to the Irish donor of the pig (University of Bristol Theatre Collection: Mander and Mitchenson collection).
104 Ashwell, *Modern Troubadours*, 115–16.
105 *Irish Times*, 4 December 1917.
106 *Bystander*, 4 April 1917.
107 *Leeds Mercury*, 17 July 1917.
108 Ashwell, *Modern Troubadours*, 122–3.
109 *Ibid.*, 132.
110 *Ibid.*, 132–3.
111 R. Pocock, *Chorus to Adventurers* (London, 1931), 168.
112 *Daily News & Leader*, 1 October 1918.
113 *Daily Telegraph*, 9 November 1918.
114 *Daily Telegraph*, 1 February 1919.
115 *Christian World*, 19 June 1919.
116 Ashwell, *Modern Troubadours*, 177.
117 *Ibid.*, 186.
118 *Daily Chronicle*, 19 December 1917.
119 *Nottingham Express*, 2 November 1917.
120 *Referee*, 9 December 1917.
121 P. Wheeler, 'The Play at the Front, From Euripides to Shaw', unidentified newspaper, Concert Parties at the Front Press Cuttings, Volume 3, Imperial War Museum, Department of Collections Access, 09/771.
122 *Edinburgh Despatch*, 5 July 1919.
123 *Musical News*, 1 September 1917.
124 Letter from Gough to Ashwell, 26 August 1917 (Lena Ashwell Papers, Department of Rare Books, Special Collections and Preservation, University of Rochester, Rochester, N.Y.).
125 B. McLaren (ed.), *Women of the War* (London, 1917).
126 *British Weekly*, 13 September 1917.
127 *Glasgow Herald*, 6 December 1917.
128 Ashwell, *Modern Troubadours*, 187.
129 Concert Parties at the Front Press Cuttings, Volume 3, Imperial War Museum, Department of Collections Access, 09/771.
130 Ashwell, *Modern Troubadours*, 190.
131 *Ibid.*, 191.
132 *Era*, 2 and 24 July 1918.
133 Ashwell, *Modern Troubadours*, 119.
134 *Evening News*, 22 October 1917.
135 *Daily Sketch*, 2 November 1917.
136 *Daily Chronicle*, 26 November 1917.
137 Quoted in A.J.P. Taylor, *English History, 1914–1945* (London, 1970), 133.
138 *Morning Post*, 25 January 1918.
139 *Newcastle Daily Journal*, 13 December 1918.
140 Unidentified newspaper, 15 December 1918. Concert Parties at the Front Press Cuttings, Volume 3, Imperial War Museum, Department of Collections Access, 09/771.

141 *Era*, 2 August 1916.

142 *Les Avaries*, translated by John Pollock, dealing with syphilis, was staged at St Martin's Theatre, with 281 performances, from 17 March 1917.

143 *Era*, 5 June 1918.

144 *Era*, 9 October 1918.

145 *Era*, 11 September 1918.

146 *Era Annual* (1918).

147 Unidentified newspaper, 13 March 1918. Concert Parties at the Front Press Cuttings, Volume 3, Imperial War Museum, Department of Collections Access, 09/771.

148 *Sunday Chronicle*, 24 February 1918.

149 *Lady*, 13 March 1919.

150 *Era*, 13 November 1918. *The Sporting Times*, 19 November 1918, paid brief tribute to performers: 'the contribution to war funds, by means of their performances, of about three millions sterling – was probably unequalled by any other body of workers'.

151 'The Theatre and Ruhleben', *Fortnightly Review*, October 1918, 622.

152 *Ibid.*

153 *Morning Post*, 19 November 1918.

154 *Performer*, 10 October 1918.

155 *Aldershot News*, 1 November 1918.

156 *Sunday Times*, 10 November 1918.

157 L. Ashwell, 'The Artistic Growth of the Soldier', *Sunday Evening Telegraph*, 2 March 1919.

158 Undated review from *Malaceine*. The date is likely to have been 24 April 1919, as readers were advised that Shakespeare's birthday was being celebrated. Penelope Wheeler was a 'gracieuse et passionnée' Portia, H.A. Saintsbury a strong Shylock and 'L'ensemble de l'interprétation s'imposa toute de suite par la tenue et l'homogénéité, la conviction et la sincérité' (Concert Parties at the Front Press Cuttings, Volume 3, Imperial War Museum, Department of Collections Access, 09/771).

159 *Times*, 1 April 1919.

160 Papers dated 27 January and 8 July 1919 (DES Demobilisation and Reconstruction Fund F1, Vol.1, Imperial War Museum, Department of Documents).

161 *Evening Standard*, 10 February 1919.

162 *Sunday Pictorial*, 2 March 1919.

163 *Era*, 26 February 1919.

164 *Era*, 28 May 1919.

165 *Morning Post*, 18 March 1919.

166 L. Ashwell, 'Soldiers and the Drama', *Englishwoman*, September 1919, 129.

167 *Ibid.*

168 *Daily Express*, 23 April 1919.

169 *Worcester Echo*, 23 April 1919.

170 *Weekly Dispatch*, 4 May 1919.

171 *Manchester Sunday Chronicle*, 19 May 1919.

172 *National News*, 4 May 1919.

173 *Evening Standard*, 2 June 1919.

174 Ashwell, 'Soldiers and the Drama'.

175 *Morning Post*, 25 October 1919.

176 *Glasgow Bulletin*, 24 October 1919.

177 *Times*, 31 October 1919.

178 There are letters between Ashwell and the Imperial War Museum regarding the handing over of her papers. She promised her records, and on 12 February 1920 gave a brief

summary of the facts relating to the Concert Parties. She wrote on 16 April 1920 asking if the museum would like a short, interim version or would wait for the 'fair sized book' which 'may be some months, if not longer' from completion. Ashwell's scrapbooks (although apparently not individual artists' diaries) are lodged in the collection, the museum having waited until late 1922 for the material (Imperial War Museum, Concert Parties at the Front F1 BO7.8).

179 *Times Literary Supplement*, 16 November 1922.
180 *Time & Tide*, 1 December 1922.
181 *Globe*, 31 October 1919.
182 *Era*, 22 October 1919.
183 *Globe*, 4 November 1919.
184 *Evening Standard*, 6 November 1919.
185 *Daily Chronicle*, 7 November 1919.
186 *Daily Herald*, 11 November 1919.
187 *Daily Chronicle*, 15 November 1919.
188 Published in the *Era*, 10 December 1919.
189 Ashwell, *The Stage*, 153.
190 *Ibid.*, 159.
191 Ashwell, *Modern Troubadours*, 215.
192 *Ibid.*, 215.
193 *Ibid.*, 218.

5

Pioneer and patriot: the Lena Ashwell Players

Ashwell's abiding memory of her fifties was of 'years mostly spent in losing money'.[1] Her short autobiographical account of 'The Roundabouts' begins and ends with exhaustion and conveys disappointment and frustration, despite the company's many significant achievements under her determined guidance. The beginnings were hopeful, however, and by August 1920, enthused by her war work, six London boroughs were committed to performances by the Once-A-Week Players. The initial schedule included town halls in Battersea, Fulham, Greenwich and Shoreditch; the People's Palace, Mile End; the Northampton Institute; and Clerkenwell and Camberwell Baths. Mayoral support in Bethnal Green, Hackney, Islington, St Pancras, Southwark, Woolwich and Poplar meant potential visits to these areas. 'Mounting … will not be elaborate, the stage setting consisting of curtains, with just a few articles of furniture indispensable for the proper presentation of the play.'[2] Ticket prices, which did not increase over the decade, ranged from 5d to 3s 6d, including tax. The success of Lilian Baylis's Old Vic and the King's, Hammersmith, suggested there might be audiences for serious drama outside the West End, although many suburban theatres had gone over to variety or cinema in response to audience preference.

Between 1919 and 1927 Ashwell negotiated, and the Players tried out, at least fifty venues, of which only sixteen remained on their itinerary when the company closed in 1929.[3] All had unique challenges as well as commonalities. Some venues lasted one short season of three months, others a couple of years. Only five venues visited during the first three years continued until 1929. Ashwell undoubtedly approached many venues and organisations in wide-ranging efforts to sustain her company. The meetings, site visits and correspondence entailed by this process were daunting. Despite the company's performing schedule and her role auditioning actors, selecting repertoire, directing, fund-raising, public speaking and promoting, and despite sometimes indifferent health, she also ran a busy household, supporting Dr Simson's position as an eminent medical practitioner. At the same time she played a prominent role in the British Drama League, to which she was elected as one of five vice-presidents at its inaugural public meeting on 3 June 1919. The League's aim was 'to assist Development of the art of Theatre and to promote a right relation between Drama and the life of the community'.[4] Always a strong advocate for

The Aim of the Players.

Do we Starve our Higher Emotions and our Minds ?

❡ Our object is to take interesting Plays of all kinds to over seven million people, amongst whom are a number who find Plays as attractive as dancing, bridge and the cinema.

❡ We draw our repertory from the great library of successful plays and masterpieces of our national dramatic literature. We can play any play that the literary taste of the people will support. We have played and are playing plays by Henry Arthur Jones, Pinero, Galsworthy, G. B. Shaw, Sheridan and Shakespeare.

❡ We work in co-operation with the mayors and coun cillors of eight boroughs, namely, Ealing, Battersea, Canning Town, Deptford, Greenwich, Camberwell, Sutton and Hounslow. We play in these Town Halls or Public Baths during the winter months and pay a nominal fee for the hall, together with a percentage on our receipts.

❡ We hope to present to you during the forthcoming season, "As You Like It," by Shakespeare; "The Rivals," by Sheridan; "The Younger Generation," by Stanley Houghton; "Rutherford and Son," by Githa Sowerby; "Diplomacy," by Sardou; "The Silver Box," by John Galsworthy, etc., etc.

❡ At Christmas we will alternate a children's play, adapted from the delightful fairy stories of Hans Christian Anderson—which every child loves—with the beautiful Miracle Play by Cicely Hamilton, "The Child in Flanders.

5.1 The Aim of the Players, Lena Ashwell Players' pamphlet, 1923 (author's collection)

co-operation and the sharing of resources, Ashwell was an office-bearer and active participant until 1946, chairing meetings, speaking at conferences, presenting lectures and adjudicating amateur performances. In return, the League provided her with an ideal forum and continuing opportunities to speak her mind.

In most places there was little dispute about the Players' diversity, high standards and contribution to quality of life in the community, but audiences had to be chased and frequently proved elusive or fickle, turning up in large numbers for popular or familiar repertoire but unwilling to make a weekly commitment. Bad weather, elections, competing entertainments and venue discomfort were all deterrents. Pleasing all of the people all of the time was not possible. Greenwich could not get enough Shakespeare, while other places sought only light comedy and steadfastly stayed away from serious drama. Where lack of support or antagonism from local councils made effective relationships impossible or facilities were unsuitable for performance, Ashwell cut her losses and moved on quickly. Considerable time and effort were devoted to negotiating concessions and developing and maintaining communication with local authorities, community organisations and the press. The company's survival would have been possible if more initial venues, like Battersea and Greenwich, had been successful, freeing Ashwell's time and energies for more fund-raising and promotional activity.

Battersea, in the south-west, was central to Ashwell's London work and an ideal partner. One of the earliest centres visited, it was the company's most successful and long-standing commitment, hosting over 250 performances. Tuesday performances, given between late September and April every year until April 1929, began in the Grand Hall, Battersea Town Hall, on 19 October 1920. Hall bookings and other arrangements, reflecting consistent support and advocacy by successive mayors, were recorded in Council minutes from July 1920 and announced in the press. It was made clear that performances must be self-supporting: 'The expense of productions are being kept as low as possible, but it is essential ... the hall be filled at each performance, in view of the low prices charged.'[5] The local *South Western Star* encouraged Battersea to become a regular centre 'for high class music and dramatic performances', considering that 'even if a portion of the cost did fall on the rates, the improvement in the minds of people and the social uplift would ultimately tend to reduce rates. Young people would no longer be driven to low pleasures of the streets.'[6] Welcoming the Players, the *South Western Star* published Ashwell's detailed rationale:

> For the commercialisation of the drama there is no permanent remedy but municipal theatre ... The rate-payers will have nothing whatever to pay on account of these shows. At the end of the season the Mayor and Council of each borough will inspect our books, and if we have made a profit part of it is ... to be divided among them, so they share in any success we win ... the mayors and councils ... are willing to put their Town Halls at the disposal of the public on one evening each week if we provide the show. We all hope to make the enterprise self-supporting.

If we don't, there's an end to the scheme. We have a nice fit-up, easily adaptable to any hall, transported ... by an ex-service actor who has taken up road transport work. Indeed all our actors have been soldiers. I consider municipal theatre, or some such scheme as ours, leading up to it, is essential in order to get good new plays. Our aim is to give the public what it likes. My experience – I have been at this game all my life – is that it likes good stuff when it gets the chance of seeing it.[7]

Every year, bids for dates were submitted by mid-April and confirmed by the Council in late September. For some extra matinees, the hall was free or available at a reduced price. Battersea, unlike some boroughs, did not impose penalties when dates booked in error were cancelled. To help establish the company's presence, Ashwell negotiated a minimum fee, calculated on actual costs for opening the hall, and an additional end-of-season amount if box office takings were sufficient. At the end of the first six months she offered £1 1s per night, despite the Players' overall deficit. This was a very inexpensive rental and the same arrangement was recommended for the following season.[8] To promote awareness of Ashwell's accessible ticket prices, the Council successfully requested that the LCC require entertainment venues to publicly display seating plans and prices. In 1922, the nightly charge was raised to £3 3s, with agreement that Ashwell pay an additional 5 per cent if financial results made it possible.[9] Councillors were urged to promote the company to their constituents. The Players' rent did not increase again, although by 1927 local groups were charged four guineas, and non-local groups even more.

On opening night the hall was only half full. The Mayor and Ashwell urged those present to rally support to ensure continuation. Audiences built appreciably, with keen interest for *Leah Kleschna* and *Our Boys*. Shaw's *Fanny's First Play*, with Esmé Church[10] much praised as Margaret, attracted a notable audience:

the assembly was not composed exclusively or even largely of Battersea residents. The ladies who between the acts sauntered along the corridors smoking cigarettes came from some more exalted region. So, too, the many severe visaged spinsters and bob-haired adolescents – the latter eager to gain a knowledge of life. There was no lack of men, however, mostly middle-aged, regretting the goodness and the dullness of their youth.[11]

After Shaw's *Arms and the Man*, the reviewer was regretful attendance was not 'of the same Bohemian character. It was, however, fully appreciative. The leading members ... [are] established ... as favourites with local playgoers. Their personality and acting are almost the sole things that attract and entertain, there being no elaborate scenery and stage effects.'[12] For *Diana of Dobson's*, which opened the second season in late September 1921, the audience was encouragingly large. Company manager and character actress, Marion Fawcett,[13] declared their work 'more pronouncedly successful in Labour boroughs, particularly Battersea, than elsewhere',[14] and it was felt the community was appreciative of drama. Ashwell spoke about 'fighting a big fight for a little company [since] every citizen has the right to good entertainment. We want everyone to have the same advantages as those who have the money to spend on expensive seats in the City.'[15]

Acknowledgement within the profession was essential, so an *Era* review for the Players' Battersea premiere of McEvoy's *The Likes of 'Er* in January 1923 was encouraging. Ashwell's direction was praised and Battersea's appreciation was noted.[16] While the *Era* maintained interest, when the Players did not advertise locally there were only occasional references to their presence. The *South Western Star* was no exception; the reviewer giving considerable space to the fourth season opening in autumn 1923 and noting a full house for *Milestones* when advertisements were placed again after a break in 1922.[17] The reviewer took special interest in the audience, having a theory that Shaw's plays attracted a particular type from outside the borough. For *Pygmalion*, although the gallery may have contained locals, elsewhere

> Chelsea, or even Belgravia, predominated, evidenced mostly by women. Some brought their knitting, which is a great help to those who desire to look abstracted at critical moments ... the small talk was of the West End, West Endy. One heard scraps of conversation about things 'perfectly precious,' 'absolutely adorable' ... 'sweetly gracious'. It made one long for the undisguised Saxon of Mr Shaw. [When the long-awaited 'word' ('bloody') was uttered by Eliza Doolittle], the audience gave forth a mighty roar of laughter. They should have been shocked; they were delighted. Chelsea laughed loudest, but then Chelsea had the grace to pretend it had not laughed. It composed its features to a fashionable rigidity. It resumed its gracious and adorable conversation. It went on with its knitting.[18]

By the time of the mayoral/ Friends of the Players' reception after Wycherley's *The Country Wife* in mid-January 1924, Battersea's leadership and pride in its support for the company were significant. There was a determination to maintain a reputation as an area wholehearted in its embrace of people's drama. Playing on this pride, Ashwell hoped they would be there 'every year until they were too old and decrepit to play any longer'.[19]

Before the first performance in autumn 1924, and coinciding with a general election, there was a Friends' social gathering on 23 September.[20] An enthusiastic reception for *Macbeth* followed and Harold Gibson,[21] flattering the audience during the interval, declared: 'Their presence justified Miss Ashwell's contention that people wanted the best plays and would support them if they were presented. It would be quite impossible to get such a West End house for *Macbeth* during a general election. Of course, West End assemblies had not been educated up to it.' He announced, somewhat extravagantly, that next week

> *A Grain of Mustard Seed* would deal with election ideals. It was not so applicable to this district as it might be to others, because Battersea candidates were men of ideal. The Players' programme for their autumn season was printed before there

was any talk of a general election. Had it not been, it would have looked as if they had produced *A Grain of Mustard Seed* with special intent. If Parliamentary candidates made a point of seeing the play they might be encouraged to maintain ideals which they profess during the election. Electors will gain some wonderfully illuminating information about … party politics.[22]

Perhaps this approach helped: prompted by Ashwell's suggestions to councillors and appropriate officers, the Council spent money on stage improvements[23] and agreed that 'a handbill, giving particulars of entertainments … be enclosed with Rate Demand Notes', together with an advertising display board outside Municipal Buildings. From 1926, of particular help given the lack of advertising money, was a self-supporting, monthly *Diary of Events* published by the Public Amenities' Committee, with a circulation of 10,000 copies.[24] The *South Western Star* carried news and reviews, often observing the close association between the Players and this local authority, particularly in relation to audience comfort:

Battersea Town Hall on Tuesday evening was a particularly comfortable place. The heating apparatus has apparently been reinforced, with very agreeable consequences. For the improvements on stage Miss Ashwell's Players are probably entitled to the credit … the platform looked much more theatre-like than it has been wont to be.[25] Not that the 'scenery and effects' were elaborate, but they had a snug and compact appearance, which contributed greatly to the illusion of reality.[26]

The educational influence exercised by the Players was appreciated by Battersea's mayor, Councillor Young, when he spoke after a performance of *The Vagabond King*;[27] and after a performance of *The Butterfly on the Wheel*, Ashwell's guest Mrs Philip Snowdon noted that 'the Players were above the arena of party politics and ought to be supported by all shades of opinions'.[28]

Ashwell made several unsuccessful attempts to establish a base in the East End, an area of high population density, poor living conditions and low income earners. Residents in such areas were a priority for her, but they did not become her regular audience. Venues included an unsuitably large 2000-seat variety theatre, the People's Palace, in Stepney where the *East End News & London Shipping Chronicle* announced, 'Stepney Borough Council are about to try the experiment of providing the nearest approach possible in that crowded, industrial, and residential area, of the much-discussed municipal theatre.' Further to the commitment of Major Attlee, the mayor, ticket prices, including tax, were 8d, 1s 3d and 2s 4d, with season tickets for consecutive performances available from Municipal Offices or Council members. Ashwell was quoted as believing that 'a theatre worthy of its name gives its audience something to talk about as well as something to laugh about'. The plan was to provide inspiration and facilities to help local people form 'dramatic or literary circles or amateur dramatic societies … to encourage a spirit of healthy criticism, the spirit which demands and obtains good work from actor, manager and playwright'.[29]

In 1921 Ashwell tried out Canning Town Public Hall, in the heart of the Thames docklands area, with support of the vicar of Holy Trinity Church. The Council gave free use of the hall and the enterprise was assisted by the West Ham Christian Social Service Council. In early 1922 *The Taming of the Shrew*, *She Stoops to Conquer* and *Trilby* attracted large audiences but by the following February support had dwindled, losses were too great and this venue was abandoned. Many residents seemed unlikely to adopt or be able to afford a regular theatregoing habit, even if the Players' varied repertoire had appealed as entertainment. Perhaps they were daunted by a sometimes strident tone. Ashwell was well aware that the educative process and shift in attitudes would be gradual and costly, but she had neither time nor money on her side. In 1925 she attempted an East End return at the King's Hall, Hackney Baths, but the Council took a hard financial line and the decision to pull out was made after two months. Similarly, attempts at central London venues with easy access to the West End and competing entertainments were unsuccessful.

Greenwich Borough Hall, in south-east London, was a wholly successful Friday night venue from early 1921 until spring 1929. Seasons here generally began earlier, in late September, and ran longer into spring, than those at other venues. The *Kentish Mercury* reported on negotiations, audience and repertoire, and consistently reviewed performances, which immediately attracted full houses. The mayor, Alderman Lemmon, hoped Greenwich would eventually have a Council-supported municipal theatre. Ashwell agreed the Mayor's Relief Fund for Unemployed would receive any box office income after company expenses were covered. She declared: 'we are, all of us, in an extraordinary way, dependent one upon another. We are all workers … Actors, above all sections of the community, are servants of the public – to give glimpses into other people's lives.' After Ashwell had paid tribute to her hard-working company, Esmé Church responded: 'She set us an ideal, and that ideal we mean to follow, and pull it off.'[30] This ideal was difficult to pursue, particularly after a winter performance of *The Child in Flanders*, when the company's small lorry skidded into a lamp-post. Fawcett, actress Hildegard Walker and the stage carpenter were injured. Cicely Hamilton, severely hurt, required hospital treatment and a walking stick for some time. Other company members covered performances for the injured but, without the luxury of understudies or spare vehicles, such incidents added considerable pressure.

Performances in Fulham Town Hall lasted one season, between 18 October 1920 and 4 April 1921. Initially enthusiastic, the Establishment Committee thought that the 'Council would be well advised in giving its whole-hearted support to an experiment of this kind, as there is no doubt high class dramatic performances are of an educative nature and would provide healthy and enjoyable amusement for people of the borough at popular prices'.[31] It began well, if somewhat ponderously:

We feel the Council should cooperate with Miss Ashwell by granting the use of the large Hall on one evening per week subject to a proper proportion of accruing profits being given to the Council, should the undertaking prove a financial success, in payment for the hire of the hall and other expenses, and to a statement of expenses and receipts being presented at the expiration of the performances. The Council would also help by authorising a distribution of literature from the Libraries and by advertising the enterprise by means of posters in the Borough, as the success of the venture will entirely depend upon the support of the public. In the event of a financial loss the only question for Council to consider would be that of foregoing any charge for the use of the hall.[32]

Unfortunately, despite consistently full houses,[33] the Fulham project was doomed by internal Council politics, rather than any inadequacies on the Players' part. At the opening, Miss Gilliat, Public Health Committee Chair, advised that the Lady Councillors' Retiring Room had been set aside 'as a temporary nursery where children could be left and attended to by nurses while their mothers were enjoying the play'.[34] This was an unusual and significant initiative on behalf of women, but was scorned as a Labour Party indulgence in the *Fulham Chronicle*'s editorial:

> It is agreed that the municipal play … on Monday was capital, but the real delight of the evening was seen and felt in the arrangements made for the dear little babies. Mothers going to plays and meetings at Fulham Town Hall may now deposit their sucklings in a splendid apartment specially set aside for their reception. Qualified nurses are engaged to take charge of them and each tiny visitor must have a little crib quite as flowery in its way as, for instance, a speech by Mr Councillor O'Brien. The Ratepayers, of course, will be delighted to learn that the … nicely uniformed nurses … will be handsomely remunerated for their services. Everybody agrees that theatre and music hall managers who offer free accommodation for bikes are easily out done by our Labour Council's provision for every ducky deary cockaleory suchitisfitsy father was a socialist popsywopsy.[35]

Ironically, the last performance there was *The Importance of Being Earnest*, after which Ashwell 'advocated the direction of amusements by the municipal authority of the Borough. She and her friends had some hard work to do but there was real food in the theatre and it should be enjoyed further.'[36] This advocacy for Council involvement annoyed non-supportive Councillors, who voted seventeen to twelve against continuing the company's visits. Undoubtedly they knew of the Drama League's intentions to get, 'if necessary, legislation, putting theatre on the same level as public workhouses, which were partly maintained by the rates. It should be made possible for a borough council to levy, say, a farthing rate for the support of a municipal theatre.'[37] The local government *Municipal Journal*'s reaction was that ratepayers should not subsidise actors: 'if drama cannot get on without rate aid, it had better get out … it is hardly playing the game to look to the municipality to provide people with cheap amusement, even though such amusement may be classed as educational'.[38] Ashwell retorted that public baths, supported by rate payers, were not intended to subsidise bath attendants but were rather seen as a necessary part of healthy community life, and 'the Labour Mayors believe a lit-tle healthy bathing in the fine atmosphere of good dramatic literature ... may be for the good of the mentality of the race'. She knew 'municipal finances are well protected and it is unlikely a subsidy for such entertainment can be procured, but would not a halfpenny or a penny on the rates for this purpose be better spent than in the cause of maintaining prisons, hospitals, workhouses?'[39] But Fulham was a lost cause. Perhaps those who voted against it were aware of trouble brewing. As the *Era* reported:

> The Government Auditor is manifesting no sympathy with municipal drama. He has queried Shakespearean performances arranged by the LCC, on the ground that rates ought not to be devoted to such a purpose. Reporting on the accounts of Fulham Borough Council, the Auditor states he took exception to costs incurred in lighting and heating the town hall for entertainments given by Miss Ashwell and her party. No charge was made to cover expenses, but Council was to receive a payment if any profit were made. In the result Council was out of pocket, not only by the loss of hall-letting fees, but by actual costs of lighting and heating the hall. The Council had no legal authority to incur any expenditure for the purpose in question; but for this occasion he had allowed the expenditure to be put forward under the Local Authorities (Expenses) Act, and given sanction to charge it to the rate fund.[40]

This did not occur elsewhere, but such negativity made Ashwell despair.

For Ealing's Longfield Hall, not far from Hanwell, the Council required a deposit of £1 1s against hall rental of £3 3s. There were extra charges for using more than 400 seats and for additional platforms or a full-sized stage with footlights. The hall was a swimming pool, covered in winter and unavailable between April and the end of summer. The Players' relationship with Ealing was never easy. They had to apply and pay for necessary Dramatic Licences from the County Licensing Committee, and although initially the Council undertook work for licence requirements, it was reluctant when further alterations were needed. Agreement was reached to attach a promotional notice board at the Baths' entrance, but when Ashwell asked to move this to the front of the Town Hall, her request was rejected.[41] Charges were made for dates booked but not used, even when advance notice was given of changed plans. With no local newspaper coverage and insufficient support, regular visits were not viable.

As the Players' reach extended, Home County areas were identified, close enough to London not to incur touring costs. For the use of Sutton Public Hall, the Council charged a high £4 4s rent per evening and ticket prices reflected this.[42] A suitable second-hand piano was purchased and cost an extra 10s per evening. The condition that 'the hirer will give way for a better let, on good notice' meant uncertainty and occasional date changes.[43] The company was locked into a schedule with little flexibility; lost bookings meant lost income, although this was not appreciated by Council officers. Sutton was generally supportive and provided a well-established, albeit conservative audience. As elsewhere, individuals and organisations helped: Edith James, principal of the Sutton School of Music, Art and Dancing, was keen to encourage 'the artistic education of the younger generation in the district'[44] and the Rotary Club and Women's Local Government and Citizen Association cultivated general interest in drama. Shakespeare was popular with this audience, which also welcomed new plays such as Ashwell and Roger Pocock's *The Celluloid Cat* in March 1924. The play's authorship was then billed as 'anonymous', but Sutton was not easily fooled. The *Advertiser* thought it 'original in its conception', noting that: 'All kinds of surmises have been made and the general opinion seems to be the authors are well-known to patrons of these plays and had a great deal to do with the presentation of their work.'[45]

St John's Hall, Watford, proved quietly successful from the Players' first Saturday night performance on 7 October 1922 until April 1929. For Shakespeare and seasonal productions, matinees were given in St Michael's Hall and evening performances in the smaller St John's Hall, between which sets had to be dismantled and rebuilt. The *West Herts and Watford Observer* frequently noted full and enthusiastic houses. The audience catchment area was considerable, and for weekday commuters to London, a professional company visiting on Saturday evenings saved a return to the city, especially as the repertoire included recent West End successes. Shaw's *Widowers' Houses* played to

> one of the largest audiences they (LAP) have yet had. At their disposal was one backcloth, a door, some curtains ... a few sticks of furniture, but they demonstrated the fallacy sometimes held that a play's success is dependent to a great extent upon its setting. *Widowers' Houses*, played by seven actors ... proved to be the finest performance seen in the town for a long time.[46]

For *Fanny's First Play*, directed by Church, there was standing room only. Shaw's popularity in Watford may have been because he lived locally, at Ayot St Lawrence, and attended performances. Watford reviewers commented on character makeup, costumes and the use of live music (usually piano and violin), providing insight into aspects of the company's work not often mentioned elsewhere. For Ashwell's production of Stephen Phillips' *Paolo & Francesca*, readers were told the costumes, representative of the late eighteenth century, were designed by Ethel Pocock, while Kate Coates had arranged special period music.[47]

Ilford Town Hall, Essex, was an immediate and ongoing success. Three weeks before this new venue joined the itinerary, Ashwell was wounded beneath her left eye by a stray bullet from a shooting party while driving in Kent on a brief summer holiday. Although shocked, she recovered quickly and appeared in Ilford on 2 October 1923 to introduce her company. She wanted residents to say, on a weekly basis, '"tonight, I know that I shall find a play in my town hall." Whist drives and dances give way one night to the exercise of the imagination.' She wanted workers to become so interested that

> People's Theatres will be as plentiful as public libraries. Our ideas are not entirely selfish, though of course, we admit we would sooner live by our own art than exist in other capacities. We believe we can be useful to the community, more useful than the doctor of the body, because we bring health and happiness to the mind. We believe all the arts of life are a necessity, because man needs beauty as much as beef.

She concluded, 'the plays are all selected from the finest works in our dramatic literature, the scenery is scanty, and the chairs are hard, but, after all, "the play is the thing", isn't it?'[48] Summing up the company's first four visits, the *Ilford Recorder* was astonished to observe 'the all-round excellence of each member of the company, succeeding plays disclosing other sides of the actor's capacity and revealing the completing [*sic*] artist'.[49] The paper's weekly *What's On* listings included Players' dates, and regular performances were popular here, attracting residents from nearby suburbs. A successful Workers' Educational Association Modern Drama course included discussion of their performances. Participants joined the Friends of the Players, established in January 1924 with the Council's chairman as president.

Ilford was no suburban cultural backwater and the *Recorder* provided a forum for debate on municipal theatre, although not always in Ashwell's favour. Bertram Bew, of the local Mansfield House Players, perceived a general desire to have a suburban theatre, but, believing 'the ideal of a Municipal Theatre seems to frighten … by its association with rates and public monies', he considered his amateur Players could fulfil this adequately since it is 'only municipal so far as it aims at coordinating a municipality within its influence'.[50] Others recognised the potential and a need for Council commitment 'to promote healthy recreation during the winter months':

> During the summer we have our parks with facilities for cricket, tennis, bowls … in the winter, when we have fewer natural opportunities for recreation, the local authority does nothing … We have a Town Hall, but Council looks upon it merely as a means of producing revenue instead of using it for the good of the community … An enterprising Council would, for approved productions, and on condition that seats were low priced, guarantee promoters a certain revenue. If that be not possible, it could at least cut down the fee to permit a reasonable number of cheap seats, and I am sure a full house would result, and no loss be incurred.[51]

Recognition that work such as Ashwell's could not survive without a mix of public subsidy, business sponsorship or private philanthropy and box office income did not come for many years after her pioneering enterprise. In 1920s Britain, the arts were expected to manage on a commercial basis. While legislation had not changed by the end of the decade, she helped alter attitudes, making eventual changes possible. Financial support from local government would not be achieved overnight but help in kind was the first step. A varied repertoire, however, is expensive; and plays with small casts are a comparatively recent response to financial constraints. Covering overheads and actors' wages, while charging affordable ticket prices, without subsidy, relies on full-capacity, paying audiences. In Ashwell's case, shortfall meant calling on her husband's resources, which he gave of generously.[52] She also sought help from the Carnegie United Kingdom Trust, incorporated in 1917, with funds available to help community services and arts organisations such as the British Drama League. [53]

Ashwell first wrote to trustees Sir William McCormick (with whom she and her husband were friends) and Colonel J.M. Mitchell in 1919, unsuccessfully seeking support to take 'healthy entertainment to the Boroughs of East London'.[54] In July 1920 she sought £500 for a portable proscenium arch but, although Mitchell acknowledged her work, no grant was made. She responded, 'if we do not go on we can only curl ourselves up and die, with as brave a grin as possible'.[55] Mitchell was personally sorry because 'she is the kind of person who gets things done, while others stand by and do nothing'.[56] She reminded him she had received £500 for her Demobilisation Fund to help with the government's Municipal Appeal.[57] On 21 May 1921, it appears, the trustees considered Ashwell's financial methods 'unsound'. Perhaps this was because she advised them on that date that her artists were 'forming themselves into a commonwealth having a share-out ... and minimum salaries in order to keep going', prompting Mitchell to write to the London mayors 'in confidence', asking for 'the municipal point of view – were the plays of the right kind? Was the organisation sound and efficient?' In July 1921 £500 was agreed as a single contribution for capital outlay following positive responses from the mayors. In November 1922 Ashwell highlighted needy Canning Town, where 'poverty and unemployment are rife ... [and] the Players are losing ten pounds a week. Ticket prices are 5d., 8d. and 1s.3d. The Government Entertainment Tax is a very heavy item.' She received a £100 guarantee against losses for Canning Town.

Predicting a difficult winter ahead, she wrote to the Trust in late 1922, hoping 'entertainment will prove useful in allaying discontent ... if our scheme is defeated through lack of funds it will be a most discouraging precedent for anyone who tries to establish some method through which to win the cooperation of the people, with healthy entertainment. If we are successful, our example will be taken up in parts of the country.' Gratefully, she accepted a further grant towards the cost of her winter programme. By now 'the Committee felt Miss Ashwell's Players were doing most important work in these congested Metropolitan areas and unanimously agreed grant aid'.[58]

On another front, hoping to create community commitment and involvement, Ashwell sought voluntary help to build audiences and assist her company. From February 1923 Harold Gibson and business manager Hilda Pocock took responsibility for establishing and promoting local groups of 'Friends of the Players':

The annual subscription for membership of the Association is a minimum of 1/-; there is no maximum. The Benefits of Membership are, in addition to the privilege of taking part in a valuable social work: A free copy of each issue of 'The Lap' [The Lena Ashwell Players' Magazine].[59] Opportunities for meeting the Players socially and getting to know them; we are always glad to see provincial members when in London at the Century Theatre. The right to borrow plays from the Century Theatre Dramatic Library. The Obligation of Membership is to do all you can to make the best dramatic art available for everyone and to support every honest effort made in that direction. There are now nearly 2000 members of the Association scattered all over the country though the majority of members are to be found in places where the Lena Ashwell Players perform.[60]

Many speeches were made at social and seasonal events, where Friends were thanked and encouraged to recruit audiences. Ashwell rarely missed post-performance receptions; willingly reciting, greeting audiences and advocating the wider cause. Local council and Rotary representatives played an active role on Friends' committees, providing meeting facilities and other backup. Members co-ordinated volunteer programme-sellers, ushers and refreshments, arranged social events and wrote letters of support during appeals for money. They had the opportunity to suggest repertoire, which Ashwell tried to accommodate. At the end of each season, having inevitably befriended company members and taken an interest in their careers and personal lives, they exchanged gifts. Friends' membership fluctuated considerably over the years, reflecting the involvement of committed individuals, usually women.

By late 1922, having established a routine of weekly visits to a number of boroughs, Ashwell took steps to consolidate, diversify and create greater awareness of her work. Gathering momentum, and confidently supported by female colleagues as shareholders and directors, she created a new management structure and a second performing company. No longer the 'Lena Ashwell Reconstruction Fund', the Lena Ashwell Players Ltd was registered on 11 April 1923. The new company was 'to carry on the business of theatrical managers … by Lena Ashwell, Esmé Church and Marion Fawcett at 44 South Molton Street, W1. Capital: £3000 in 3000 shares of £1 each'. The directors were 'Lena Ashwell, Cicely Hamilton, Esmé Church and Marion Fawcett'.[61] Preparations began immediately for a fourth season. Two companies would make weekly visits to twelve boroughs, divided into A and B Circuits.[62] This rapid growth, which entailed selection of repertoire, directors and actors, continuous rehearsal, scheduling and promotion, led the co-directors to seek an operational base at the intimate Bijou Theatre, Notting Hill, where Ashwell had made her first amateur stage appearance more than thirty years before.[63] She acquired a lease on the building, with office space and rehearsal rooms, renamed it the Century Theatre and by April 1924 was hoping three performances a week there would provide 'surplus funds to enable performances to be given in some of the poorer parts of London, where it is impossible to cover expenses'.[64] Lacking adequate cooling facilities, performances were not possible during summer.

5.2 The Century Theatre interior, *Illustrated London News*, 23 January 1926

In early October 1924 the Players issued a confident announcement:

During the past season 112,922 people witnessed the performances of the LAP in 17 London centres … 89 plays have been produced during the four years that the work has been carried on … it has taken some time to perfect the elaborate organisation necessary for presenting a new play every week in so many different places, but with the help of the municipal and other official bodies, the Carnegie Trustees and 'The Friends of the Players' (a society which has a membership of 1400), the movement is now on the high road to success. In order to continue and develop it, a centre from which to work has been secured in the Century Theatre, Archer Street, Nottinghill Gate, but 1500 pounds is required to adapt it to conform with the requirements of the L.C.C. As the Players have no money to meet such capital expenditure, an appeal is being made for subscriptions from those who have enjoyed the benefits of performances in the past.[65]

Although money was not easy to raise, individuals responded to this appeal, encouraged by a strong line-up of distinguished supporters.[66] By late 1924 the Century was the company's showcase venue and operations base and a Drama League platform. Under its auspices, with support from the Board of Education and the BBC, Ashwell organised, in autumn 1924, a series of lectures on theatre.[67] The Century Theatre opened quietly in October 1924: while one company was performing in Ealing, Greenwich and Watford on Thursday, Friday and Saturday nights, the other was on the Century stage. John Commins was business manager and on the board of directors were Ashwell, Mrs Henry Beecham, Paget Bowman, Church, Gibson and Sir William Schooling. Gibson, also managing director and acting secretary, frequently deputised for Ashwell, and his addresses to Rotary and similar organisations had a familiar refrain.

Once the Century was up and running, Ashwell used her London premiere, on 8 January 1925, of St John Ervine's *The Ship*, to attract the national press.

Making her first stage appearance in nine years, she played the shipbuilder's octogenarian mother, Mrs Thurlow. The *Westminster Gazette* thanked her for the opportunity to see 'the strongest, and perhaps the best ... of Mr Ervine's dramatic works ... All through the play one is conscious of one's nearness to some of the big things of life, and much of that impression is due to the pervading influence of Mrs Thurlow.'[68] The *Stage* considered that her portrayal brought it to life. 'She played it exquisitely, without the slightest exertion. That our young actresses would master the technique of acting with a maximum of effect and a minimum of effort, as Miss Ashwell has done, and so save themselves from suffering disappointment and thwarted ambition.'[69] Hamilton described the play as a tense drama of father–son conflict and the audience as wondering why Lena Ashwell had been absent from the stage for so long.[70] There was speculation she would return to acting, but she declared that while 'it was a real pleasure to be on the stage again ... to receive wild applause and tributes of flowers ... this was to be the first and last time since the beginning of the war'.[71] To persistent questions, her response was: 'I have no illusions. I couldn't draw, and I don't believe there's anyone on the English stage today who can draw. The public is only drawn by a combination of circumstances.'[72] Her motivation was to promote the Players as professionals. She knew she would not be called an amateur and that only experienced actors could play continuous

The Ship

A Play in Three Acts

by

ST. JOHN G. ERVINE.

————:o:————

Old Mrs. Thurlow	LENA ASHWELL
John Thurlow (her Son a Shipbuilder)	FREDERICK LEISTER
Janet (his Wife)	KATIE JOHNSON
Jack (his Son)	ROBERT GLENNIE
Hester (his Daughter)	DAPHNE HEARD
Captain Cornelius	PHILIP REEVES
George Norwood	LAYTON HORNIMAN
Maid	MARGARET BADCOCK

Act I.
A Room in John Thurlow's country house, near the shipbuilding town of Biggport.

Act II.
The Living Room of Jack Thurlow's farm.

Act III.
Same as Act One.

Five Months elapse between Acts 1 and 2. Three Months elapse between Acts 2 and 3. Five Days elapse between Scenes 1 and 2 of Act 3, and a few hours between Scenes 2 and 3 of Act 3.

The Play produced by
FREDERICK LEISTER.

Music under the direction of	KATE COATES.
Piano	KATE COATES.
Violin	BEATRICE CHAPMAN.

The following Selections will be played :—

"Plymouth"	Ansell
"Lilac Time"	Schubert
"Tannhauser"	Wagner
"Traumerei"	Schumann
"Melodie Mignonne "	Sinding

Thursday May 5ᵗʰ 1925.

The Lena

Ashwell

Players

Century

Theatre

PRICE—TWOPENCE.

5.3 Century Theatre Programme for *The Ship*, Century Theatre, 1925
(author's collection)

repertory as the company did. While an encourager of amateur theatre and its place in the theatrical hierarchy, a few weeks later she took exception to Horace Shipp's view of Little Theatres. Not only did he suggest the British play was not as good as the foreign one, he praised the amateur over the professional. Ashwell considered the problem was a lack of encouragement for British work, and, although she did not say it, perhaps too much encouragement for the amateur. She observed that amateurs, because of the occasional nature of their productions, had opportunity to give excellent performances, but did not need to sustain this quality over time. She expressed frustration also with the difficulty of obtaining performing rights to works by Barrie and Shaw from 'the businessmen who regard such permits to us as dangerous to the commercial interests of their principals. Much of the thankless spadework of popularising the best drama is being done today by repertory companies playing in Bristol, Liverpool, Birmingham, and in my own Century Theatre. Yet Mr Shipp ignores our efforts altogether.'[73]

Another premiere followed swiftly on from *The Ship*. Michael Morton's comedy *Five Minutes Fast* opened at Sutton on 28 January and at the Century on 19 February 1925. The *Stage* noted it 'caused a deal of laughter at Miss Ashwell's interesting experimental theatre at Notting Hill'.[74] During Easter 1925, John Masefield's *Good Friday* was presented at the Century. Directed by Beatrice Wilson, extras from All Saints Dramatic Society were used for crowd scenes.[75] The audience was asked to imagine a much grander setting, but there were thrilling moments when the crowd surged through the auditorium, and praise for Kate Coates' music and the cast. Later in the year, Masefield – who had 'never seen any company ... acting together with such comradeship and keenness, with such a sense of the beauty and greatness of their work ... they are seeking to bring art back to its place by sheer spiritual endeavour'[76] – presented a clock for the Theatre foyer, inscribed with a verse of dedication:

ON THEIR COMEDY.   I tell the Time; but you within this place
                    Show to the passing Time its fleeting face.

ON THEIR TRAGEDY.   Without, the passing city roars her tides;
                    I tell the Time, you show it what abides.
                    I tell the Time; and bring a Poet's prayer
                    that Time may bless such Players everywhere.[77]

W.A. Darlington, describing Ashwell as 'not the kind of woman who sits still and trusts to voluntary contributions', advised *Daily Telegraph* readers that from 27 April the Century would be 'abandoning its repertory character and falling into line with ordinary commercial theatres ... Miss Ashwell is reviving ... *The Ship*'. She did have the power 'to draw', despite her earlier denial, and this was a way to make money in London while her other companies were touring. She played old Mrs Thurlow throughout May. Darlington noted that there were many enterprises springing up around the country offering non-commercial theatrical fare. He hoped these could be co-ordinated 'into one movement, and then perhaps even the purely commercial theatre, obeying that law of supply and demand ... will have to fall into line and cater for a thinking public also'. He considered the Players to be the best example of

> what can be done by skilful co-ordination of effort ... To Miss Ashwell must be given credit for having created a theatre public – and an educated and discrimi-nating public at that – out of nothing ... a practical woman of the theatre, [she] has catered for every taste; she has made no attempt to foist arid and austere masterpieces on minds not yet educated to appreciate them; in short she has committed none of the glaring and exasperating errors of judgment so common among those who set out to help humanity by ignoring human nature. As a result, her organisation is a success.[78]

Following the extended season of *The Ship*, Ashwell announced that from 28 September 1925 there would be nightly performances (except Sunday) and Saturday matinees at the Century, with a third company joining the existing two companies. Each would pay a weekly visit to twelve outlying halls and remain every third week at the Century. A different play would be produced every week and Notting Hill would have a permanent repertory theatre. Olive Walter and Wilfred Fletcher's company opened in Sutton with A.A. Milne's *The Dover Road*, while Mercia Cameron and Philip Reeves[79] played at Winchmore Hill in Sutro's *The Laughing Lady*. At the Century, Church and Norman V. Norman[80] presented *The Great Adventure* for a visit from the Lord Mayor and Lady Mayoress, the Sheriffs, and mayors of boroughs hosting Players' performances. Ashwell spoke of her gratitude for civic recognition. From the *Stage*'s account, it is likely the 'functionaries who swelled the crowded audience wearing full regalia with chains of office and so forth'[81] rather stole attention from the stage, where the play was presented on a set of simple drapes.

As well as providing traditional repertoire, Ashwell challenged her actors and audience, selecting stimulating plays with diverse styles and content.[82] These included the British premiere of *His Own*, by American dramatist Evelyn Greenleaf Sutherland, on 22 February 1926 at the Century. Presented as half a double bill, it was an 'effectively intense tragedietta of negro life some fifteen years after ... the American Civil War'. Although the four actors' attempts at 'the negro mannerisms of speech' had limited success, making 'some of the dialogue rather difficult to follow ... forcible and strongly emotional performances were given'.[83] Two months later, the Players premiered Mary Pakington's *The House With The Twisty Windows*. Presented along with McEvoy's *The Likes of 'Er* and directed by Irene Hentschel, this tense little drama was set in Petrograd during the Russian Revolution, and there was praise for the effective building of suspense throughout.

Ashwell did not include major works by Chekhov or from the emerging expressionist German or American drama. She encouraged women playwrights but had no funds to commission work. Only 20 plays by women, plus a handful of co-authored or adapted works, were given by the Players in their repertoire of 250 plays. Hamilton and Jennings were the female playwrights who prevailed. Hamilton was committed to the company, but 'this did not stop her deploring the fact that in 1926 they began to charge a fee to dramatists who submitted plays for consideration'.[84] Ashwell was drawn to the work of American dramatist Susan Glaspell, and the company performed her *Bernice*, premiered in 1915. At this time, Christopher St John observed, 'the company seems to be stronger in actresses than actors' – a fair assessment, no doubt motivating the search for plays by and about women.[85]

The Players attracted many young actors who went on to wider careers in theatre.[86] Early in the decade there was severe unemployment, and as Ashwell's work became better known, she was inundated with requests to join the Players. By 1923, when she presented thirty-eight plays, she was a significant employer, engaging up to fifty actors and technical personnel for each season. She relied on a strong ensemble of women, both on stage and behind the scenes, and a number of loyal, experienced actors who embraced her ideals and were prepared to make a strong commitment to the company's artistic direction. There was opportunity to play a variety of roles and to develop management and directorial skills. Everyone worked backstage during set-ups, performances and pack-ups. They were led for the most part by Esmé Church and Harold Gibson. Ashwell believed it was necessary to maintain a 'youthful purpose' and to support the pursuit of English interests in the face of foreign attempts to 'seize the centre of their intellectual and aesthetic life'. The solution 'lay in the repertory system … [and] in groups of actors co-operating with other groups of actors; not the star system, but the co-operative star system, as it might be called'.[87] She genuinely felt wartime work had changed performers' attitudes to their role in society; she was working with actors who did not all

> hanker after high salaries, and who have more ambition to be of service to the people than to be run after by them, who have an idea of giving rather than getting. These are content to make enough money to get along with, and, incidentally, it is they who make it possible for a company like the Lena Ashwell Players to be run without a serious loss.[88]

Occasionally she engaged actors for specific roles. Some helped her cause by lending their name when they were available and she was prepared to pay more for an actor with box office appeal. In 1926 Harcourt Williams appeared in his own production of G.K. Chesterton's *Magic*, and 'contributed forceful acting in the part of the mysterious "stranger", conjuror and ex-journalist'.[89] The best-known name (as his career developed) contributed the least: in autumn 1925, a young, inexperienced Laurence Olivier joined the Players, with the help of actor colleague Alan Webb,[90] who later wrote:

The pay was miserable and the conditions worse, but what was one to do? We took work where we could find it. As we were about to start the season, several of the players dropped out for better opportunities, and I got Larry in as a last-minute substitute. He didn't last, though. Much to my embarrassment he was sacked for fooling about … during a performance of *Julius Caesar* (playing Flavius) … He was a cut-up, ever seeking attention and making trouble for himself … we were all cut-ups after a fashion. None of us took what we were doing very seriously, since we were all aiming for the West End and this was as far from the West End as we could be without being in South Africa or Australia. However, most of us tried to be diligent during the actual performances. Not Larry … He was hell-bent on causing trouble, and more often than not he succeeded. I loved the boy dearly, but I can say in all honesty that I was relieved when he was given the sack.[91]

The self-absorbed Olivier did not enjoy his brief time with the Players; apparently oblivious to Ashwell's very public involvement in all company activities, he thought she 'liked to remain unseen and mystifying, just a vaguely feared figure in an upstairs office'. He paid his own fares to get to London performances 'out of £2/10/- per week, and I was back to near-starving conditions. We were always playing in boarded-over swimming-baths, plus the occasional town hall, dressing sometimes in bath cubicles or, quite often, in lavatories. I'm afraid it was I who re-christened the company, "The Lavatory Players".'[92]

Although company members accepted engagement on the financial conditions offered, Ashwell recognised, of course, that this was a cause of irritation between management and artist. She wrote later that when she tried to work on a co-operative basis, the Players' financial committee 'would vote for funds to be paid out which had not been earned … There are always those who want safety first and dread responsibility, and there are few who take on the load of responsibility, trying to cut a new road. One must consider not one side, but both sides of such problems.'[93] Clearly it was not an easy life, but many remained in the company for more than one season, acquiring skills and learning their trade under pressure and in the best tradition of 'on the job'. She relied heavily on goodwill and kept faith with her company by participating in efforts to improve conditions, gain recognition for the professional nature of the work and stamp out exploitation. After a long involvement with the Actors' Association, she was appointed to the council of the breakaway Stage Guild, established in June 1924. In July 1925 she was one of four women elected to the Guild's Managers' Section. This committee was considered to be largely responsible for introducing the Registration of Theatrical Managers' Bill. While many began to look to the example of the powerful, successful American union, Ashwell hoped the Guild's non-industrial approach would prevail, considering the theatrical profession could only succeed if it maintained sympathetic public opinion. She continued to support the Guild until the formation of Equity, by which time she was no longer running a company and illness prevented her involvement.[94]

While realistic about attitudes to be changed and the limited possibilities, given demands on ratepayers for post-war reconstruction activity, Ashwell was a clear advocate of local authority support for the arts. Some feared this would be a disaster for commercial enterprises. Their apprehensions were partly due to concerns over perceived municipal inefficiency and bureaucratic expense and over the possibility that entertainments run by municipal authorities would be in favoured positions and able to undercut competitors. Ashwell agreed that if public money was to be used, it should be to equip and facilitate existing enterprises, underway but burdened by costs and restrictions. Others welcomed the possibility of council help, pleased that attitudes were changing. Given Ashwell's five years of advocacy her role in this change should not be ignored. By this time, while local authority minutes indicate that support was rarely easily won or unanimous, she had achieved reduced rents and could call on the presence of local mayors and councils to give performances public recognition. As the *Stage* pointed out: 'To find authority not adverse, not suspicious, not even indifferent, is a gain of no little magnitude to the stage. It means – especially when authority desires to go further and become an active participator in amusements – a reversal, a complete overthrowing of policy that had nothing but bigotry and incompetence to recommend it.'[95]

The outlay on the Century and running three companies created a considerable and continuing deficit which needed funding, full houses and reduced expenditure, something Ashwell was not able to do without losing momentum. As events outside of her control began to have an impact, the balance tipped against the Players in late 1925. The queen mother's death in November meant cancellation of performances 'in conformity with the general closing of places of amusement out of respect to the Royal Family'.[96] This meant lost income, especially as the company allowed tickets to be used for another performance or to be refunded. As winter approached, Ashwell found weather conditions worked against her. Town halls and converted swimming baths were generally not warm; audiences had to be enticed from their firesides. Snow was a considerable hazard. Fog made journeys difficult, and in some cases it permeated public buildings, reducing visibility indoors. There was little time between rehearsals and performances, and Jerome's farce *Cook* started an hour late in Sutton on 12 January 1925 when heavy fog delayed actors travelling by train. The musicians were called into service 'to eke out the time' and the Friends' Chairman made a speech until the performance could finally begin.[97]

Fluctuating fortunes at Edmonton Town Hall, a regular Wednesday night north London venue from October 1923, perhaps illustrate what was happening on a larger scale. The Council, and the audience, had a somewhat ambivalent attitude. Regulations allowed a reduction for consecutive hall bookings, and £2 12s 6d was agreed, plus an extra fee for piano use, but Council members were in a quandary when offered complimentary tickets to a performance.[98] After lengthy debate, the invitation was accepted, but eleven out of twenty councillors did not vote, giving no indication whether lack of interest or reticence about accepting a 'gift' was the reason. The Council paid necessary annual stage licences and made improvements

COUNTRY LIFE

VOL. LX.—No. 1557.   SATURDAY, NOVEMBER 20th, 1926.   [POSTAGES: ISLAND 2½d., CANADA 1½d., ABROAD 5d.   PRICE ONE SHILLING.

Claude Harris.   MISS LENA ASHWELL, O.B.E. (LADY SIMSON).   *London.*

5.4 Lena Ashwell, Director of the Lena Ashwell Players, *Country Life*, 20 November 1926
(*Country Life* Picture Library)

to the facilities, including the installation of footlights, but would not assist with a booking service and cancelled performances rather than find alternative venues for election vote counting. Audience numbers fluctuated greatly: in 1924 there were 638 Edmonton Friends[99] but a year later membership dropped to 195. Ashwell and Gibson, and local councillors too, did not hesitate to keep audiences informed of company finances. Ashwell used her performance in *The Ship* at Edmonton to remind patrons that 'something more than pleasure and knowledge are required to justify the plays being continued. This is box office returns.'[100] In 1926, although the *Tottenham & Edmonton Weekly Herald* was reporting good houses, the company had overstretched its resources. Touring the suburbs (with daily set-ups and 'strikes') was not glamorous. Young, inexperienced actors struggled to remember lines and cope with the demands of weekly repertory – rehearsing during the day and per- forming every night for weeks on end. Ashwell's ideals, while perhaps embraced in theory, must have been harder in practice. In Edmonton (and elsewhere) there were hints that standards were dropping, and weekly theatregoing did not become a habit despite her encouragingly citing the area as 'an instance of a working class district where the movement was going on splendidly'.[101]

In Winchmore Hill, north London, the audience appreciated comedy, enabling the company to play 'at the proper pace', but, as Gibson reported, the venue was not entirely successful. Five other centres had paid their way but the current year's loss was £1,000, 'due partly to the fact that four new centres had opened, and the first season in a fresh district was never profitable, and partly due to the unfortu- nate circumstance that the Players' summer opening at the Prince of Wales, Rugby, coincided with the General Strike'.[102] The *Enfield Gazette & Observer* generally quoted information from press releases, which were at pains to stress commitment to the provision of theatre for educational purposes:

> The … Players are rendering a great service to education in playing each year the Shakespearean plays set for public examination … several Education Commit- tees have arranged for school matinees of their forthcoming production of *Julius Caesar*. Beatrice Wilson, who is responsible for the production, had intended to dress it in Elizabethan costume, but school authorities seemed to think it would be more useful to them if dressed in correct Roman costume, and so that has been done.[103]

Ashwell's programming reflected her endeavours to influence, and responsiveness to, the curriculum and public taste. Through the Drama League, she contributed to the Board of Education's 1921 report on *The Teaching of English in England*, which included a list of eight essentials for the study of dramatic method in train- ing colleges. She presented evidence to the Board's Adult Education Committee for its major report on *British Drama* in 1926, which considered the relationship between drama and theatre, both professional and amateur, and education. The Committee accorded full credit to the professional productions of Ashwell, the

Old Vic and the Arts League of Service, 'where avowedly educational ends are known to be served by professional means. The connexion between education and the very highest artistic standard is also recognized in the welcome allusions to the National Theatre as the keystone, as it were, of the arch of educational drama.' The outcomes of the report's many recommendations, such as the introduction of university lectureships and theatre studies courses, are still evident today. At that time, the University of London offered a dramatic art diploma, and the University of Liverpool had a lectureship in the art of theatre; otherwise, drama was studied within literature courses.

By mid-September each year, the Players' autumn repertoire was announced, while the spring programme was finalised in December. A pool of up to fifteen directors, with considerable repertoire knowledge, put in bids for plays they wanted to do. Taking into account resources, these were programmed to alternate tragedy, comedy, farce, classics and new plays, as well as to reflect seasonal activities. From extant cast lists, it is clear scripts were adapted or cut, with doubling for minor characters and gender changes for servants, young princes and children. Some of the material chosen created staging problems, required extra expense or was too daunting for audiences, despite good intentions regarding the content. Ashwell had a continuing interest in poetic drama: she had great affection for Stephen Phillips, although she had been unable to play in *Paolo & Francesca*, originally produced by George Alexander in 1902; and in 1907 Yeats had read her *Deirdre* with the view to her playing the title role. Although Alfred Noyes' 1908 blank verse *Robin Hood* was not 'ideally practicable for stage presentation',[104] she directed its Century premiere in December 1926. With only green hangings to suggest the glades of 'a very cramped' Sherwood Forest,[105] Godfrey Kenton[106] played Robin, and Church was a semi-human figure, Shadow-of-a-leaf. Despite muted response to this work, the Players presented Masefield's poetic drama *Tristan and Isolt*. For the *Times* this was 'too wildly uneven to succeed as a piece for the theatre, but it [had] a merciless quality of its own'.[107] Such productions, although not without interest and generally well received by smaller audiences, were most likely to erode company finances.

Generally, local reviewers thought the Players best at Shakespeare and light comedy. Audiences were conservative and committed to favourite actors. Given the company's weekly visits, expectation was built around the idea that the familiar would be playing the unfamiliar. New actors had to work harder for acceptance and praise. However, Nancy Price's[108] *The Merry Wives of Windsor* prompted the observation that Players' performances of Shakespeare 'are always so intrinsically satisfying, and so capably produced, it is difficult to single out any particular effort as being more cleverly realised than others'.[109] In the announcement of Ashwell's production of *King John*, playwright Lennox Robinson was quoted criticising the otherwise acclaimed *Hamlet* of John Barrymore:

Perhaps I should not have chaffed so much against the prose of Mr Barrymore's *Hamlet* if a week before I had not been listening to a performance of *The Winter's*

Tale, which was played first and foremost for its poetry. In a dismal suburb on a cramped stage, the Lena Ashwell Players presented this lovely thing. It shone like a jewel in its poor setting, catching its chief fire from Miss Esmé Church's Hermione. The play swept through like a lovely poem, like a piece of music heard in the distance on a summer's night.[110]

For *Julius Caesar*, despite Olivier's unprofessional behaviour and an unsophisticated reviewer, there was praise as well as some insight into the production's shortcomings:

Some of those present were fortunate in seeing groups of Roman patricians and plebeians making their way from the dressing rooms at one end of the building to the stage at the other. The performance itself was pageantry and impressive. During the storm the thunder was tremendous and of excellent quality; it alarmed some of the older ladies, who, if they had not paid for admission, might have gone home. Speaking and deportment were admirable except that Casca uttered his lines with an un-Romanlike simper. Great Caesar was perfectly imperial, and the cobbler was an extremely merry old soul, or sole, as he would have expressed it. The female parts were enacted with gracefulness as well as with power. Altogether it was a very enjoyable and instructive performance.[111]

Kenton, who played Ariel in Wilson's production of *The Tempest* in 1925, provided further insight into the company's productions when he described being dressed and painted completely in silver, spending most of the play between the stage and auditorium, providing a link between characters and the audience.[112] This production was apparently influenced by Colin Still's idea 'that Shakespeare, consciously or unconsciously, wrote the comedy as a mystery play'.[113]

Shakespeare was central to the company's work, and in 1922 Ashwell began lecturing on 'The Women of Shakespeare from a Woman's Point of View'. Some of these lectures were for fund-raising events and some were broadcast on BBC Radio 2LO. In 1926 she published a collection of these as *Reflections from Shakespeare*, which focused particularly on women in the tragedies, the historical context and Shakespeare's contemporary relevance. She knew serious writing about Shakespeare was a male prerogative at this time and was prepared for a degree of condescension in the response to an actress having an opinion on the subject. Indeed, this view was reinforced when critic W.L. Courtney, although recognising Ashwell had 'produced a volume full of interest and … of real importance to the theatrical public', reminded readers she was 'an actress, not a professional writer … and always strikes straight for the womanly interpretation'.[114] For Norman Marshall, the book's value lay in insights it provided for producers: 'the psychological problems are handled freshly and sanely, from an essentially modern point of view, with the clearness and firmness with which a producer learns to delineate character'. He regretted, however, that 'a book of such general interest and usefulness should cost so much [21s]'.[115]

When Ashwell, collaborating with Roger Pocock, adapted two novels, suburban critics were more enthusiastic than the national press. *Crime and Punishment* did not impress the latter: 'The dramatist's task is so obviously hopeless that there seems to be nothing to do but to wonder why it was ever attempted ... Dostoevsky did not think in terms of theatre and the theatre cannot imprison him.'[116] The *Times* reviewer found it but a thin representation of the novel, with a few good moments and some sincere acting. The siblings' version of *Dr Jekyll and Mr Hyde* did not fare any better:

There has been a fatal attempt to bring Stevenson up to date, and to lighten his tale ... by the introduction of facetious and irrelevant chatter ... The melodrama, which more dexterous treatment might have concealed, appears in violent contrast with these patches of affected modernism ... Nor is the acting of as much assistance as it might be in maintaining the seriousness appropriate to fear.[117]

Despite the familiarity of the stories, as plays they were overly ambitious for her resources. For the 1926/7 season, the Players attempted too many plays outside the popular mainstream. Marking the centenary of Ibsen's birth, his rarely performed *Lady Inger of Ostraat* was presented, but the *Times* thought it a too complicated period of Norwegian history for the audience to understand. Even so, there were performances 'of exceptional merit, and, together with the interest of an Ibsen play so rarely given',[118] a visit to the Century was recommended.

In 1926, following advice from a Drama League Advisory Committee, the Carnegie Trust focused on repertory company work, considering applications for short-term grants which encouraged future independence. Ashwell had negotiated Wednesday nights at Holloway Northern Polytechnic Institute, commencing in September 1926. Despite competing attractions including Alexandra Palace, Islington Empire Theatre, the Collins and Alhambra Music Halls, Finsbury Palais de Dance and many cinemas, Holloway attracted good audiences, to whom Ashwell endeared herself when declaring she 'had a warm spot for Islington, having made her first appearance on stage at the old Grand Theatre'.[119] To attract attention, the Players donated proceeds of a performance to the Royal Northern Hospital. Such gestures were also made elsewhere, despite the company's precarious financial position. Holloway was a venue which quickly proved eligible under Carnegie Trust policy and in 1927 the Players received £1,000 over two years for work there and in Hounslow and Streatham.

The Players were intrepid and received consistent praise for their adaptability to restricted space and limited technical facilities. When *The Ware Case*, with a Central Criminal Court setting, was presented in Hounslow, it was noted that 'Many producers would have thought twice before attempting such a scene at Trinity Hall. It was ... made fairly realistic by the Players adapting themselves to the circumstances, and, as the entire work depends on this scene, it made the play a complete success.'[120] Players' comic talents were also generally praised, but

The Northern Polytechnic, Holloway, N.7.

Every Wednesday Evening at 8 p.m.   (Doors open at 7.30).

Spring Programme, 1927.

Feb.	2.	**The Land of Promise,** by Somerset Maugham.	
Feb.	9.	**No Performance.**	
Feb.	16.	**Crime and Punishment,** adapted from the novel of Dostoevsky, by Lena Ashwell & Roger Pocock.	
Feb.	23.	**Hay Fever,** by Noel Coward.	
Mar.	2.	**The Ware Case,** by George Pleydell.	
Mar.	9.	**Tristan and Isolt,** by John Masefield.	
Mar.	16.	**Dr. Jekyll and Mr. Hyde**	
Mar.	23.	**The Marriage of Columbine,** by Harold Chapin.	
Mar.	30.	**The Fugitive,** by John Galsworthy.	

PRICES OF ADMISSION.

3/6, 2/4, 1/2 and 6d.   Season Tickets, 4 weeks, 13/6, 9/- and 4/6
(including Tax)

Booking Offices: The Northern Polytechnic, Holloway (North 4100); The Harper Piano Co. (North 1636) Ltd., 258, Holloway Road, N.7.; and Mr. John Trapp, 9, Broadway Parade, Crouch End (Mountview 0227).

The Century Theatre.

Every Evening at 8.15 p.m.   (Doors open 7.45).
Matinees, Saturday at 2.30 p.m.   (Door open 2.0).

Spring Programme, 1927.

.	31.	**Priscilla Runs Away,** by Countess von Arnim.	
b.	7.	**Crime and Punishment** adapted from the novel of Dostoevsky, by Lena Ashwell & Roger Pocock	
b.	14.	**The Land of Promise,** by Somerset Maugham.	
b.	21.	**Tristan and Isolt,** by John Masefield.	
Feb.	28.	**Hay Fever,** by Noel Coward.	
Mar.	7.	**The Ware Case,** by George Pleydell.	
Mar.	14.	**The Marriage of Columbine,** by Harold Chapin.	
Mar.	21.	**The Fugitive,** by John Galsworthy.	
Mar.	28.	**Dr. Jekyll and Mr. Hyde** Adapted by Lena Ashwell and Roger Pocock from the novel by R. L. Stevenson.	

PRICES OF ADMISSION.

5/9, 3/6, 2/4 (Reserved), and 1/2 (Unreserved)
(Including Tax).

Box Office at the Theatre, open from 10 a.m. to 9 p.m. daily.
'Phone: Park 6870.   And the usual Libraries.
enquiries should be addressed to the Business Manager, Lena Ashwell Players, Ltd., Century Theatre, Archer Street, W.11.

NORTHERN POLYTECHNIC HOLLOWAY, N.7.

Lena Ashwell Players

What shall we do on Wednesday? *(see inside)*.

THE CENTURY THEATRE,
Archer Street, Westbourne Grove, W.11.

Lena Ashwell Players

5.5 Promotional leaflets for the Century Theatre and Holloway, Spring 1927
(author's collection)

reviewer inexperience often worked against their professional status and image. Statements such as 'Miss Bacon knew her part from beginning to end' were left over from reviewing amateur productions, and pleas for larger audiences were undermined when followed by: 'It is not widely realised what a high standard these performances reach. They are carried out by trained actors and actresses, who are serving a kind of apprenticeship in the profession; and are distinctly far in advance of the average amateur dramatic society efforts.'[121] This statement highlights another problem: some assumed that companies not 'transferring' from a West End theatre with appropriate flourish must be amateur, especially given regular performances in the district and attempts to develop a genuine local association. It was a situation Ashwell never resolved, although she did 'push' the Century as their professional base.

After the formation of the third company in autumn 1925, Staines Town Hall, where the Players collaborated with Staines Brotherhood to promote their work, and Streatham Parish Hall, in south London, were added to the itinerary. Unlike poorer areas, the top ticket price at Streatham was 3s 6d, with 1s 2d the cheapest. Ashwell, determined to have a high profile here, addressed a Rotary luncheon in September 1926. The *Streatham News* accorded her speech considerable space:

> The theatre is one of the most important civic amenities ... for eight years they have been working to put theatre before the people. One of her great difficulties is not antagonism, but indifference towards theatre. Her players play every kind of play that is sound, and avoid all plays that are purely of the modern manner – sex problems. These they avoid, unless they are especially finely worked out. They have been able to give 14 of Shakespeare's plays, 15 of Shaw's, 7 or 8 of Galsworthy's and so on ... One of the great difficulties was if one was trying to do a thing not for commercial gain, people suspected that it would not be good.[122]

Rotarian S. Stephen thanked her, saying he thought 'it was a striking disgrace that arts were not encouraged by the Government'.[123] Later, when Ashwell addressed the Streatham Hill Congregational Literary Society, Reverend Rainton expressed his relief, to a crowded hall, that the Church no longer looked upon theatregoing as a sin. Ashwell spoke on drama's educational power and the need for national recognition of theatre. Before urging assistance in furthering the Players' aims, she expressed fears about the unhealthy impact of American film, stressing the need to counteract this through access to great literature: 'I would like to see plays brought so easily and simply before you that you would become accustomed to them ... and ... to know a bad play from a good one.'[124] As elsewhere, Streatham had active community amateur groups and it was usual for local papers to give their productions more detailed reviews than those of the Players. Streatham lost Ashwell money for most of the time; it had a relatively well-informed audience and she was disappointed not to make a greater impact there.

Ashwell and Gibson frequently addressed audiences after performances or at publicly convened meetings. Approaching the end of the 1927 spring season, Ashwell, with characteristic frankness, advised the Sutton audience that

> a set of curtains … cost them 30 pounds and they could not make their platforms look as nice as they could wish. Last year they lost 1200 pounds and this year their loss was about 1000 pounds. They generally made a little profit on their summer tour which went towards reducing the loss of the winter. The members of the company were all professionals … they rehearsed every day from eleven till five and then went to one of the towns on the list, reaching home late at night. They worked very hard and were not well paid. They tried to do all sorts of plays and to select the best of each kind … The mission of theatre was to make people see what life was at different angles … They were finishing their eighth season – and she hated being beaten. She wanted to give to people something that was real and true; that would raise them instead of debasing them.[125]

The company needed a guarantee of £25 a night in subscriptions from Sutton; expenses were £30. By late 1927 the deficit was £3,000 and a good week could not redress the balance of a bad one. Audiences were treated as friends and familiars: Ashwell wanted the community to take responsibility for municipal theatre, to put pressure on local councillors, and to play an active, informed role in furthering the arguments. She was not averse to emotive language, declaring she 'had come to the bitter end … because it was not fair to struggle on with all the labour and anxiety if people did not want them to succeed'.[126] The Sutton Friends worked hard, hand-delivering promotional material and ensuring relative success until the company's closure.

Ashwell often called on well-connected friends to put a positive spin on the company's status and financial needs. A letter from Lord Clarendon was used in an appeal for funds. He contended the company deserved every possible support:

> A better form of social service can, I venture to suggest, hardly be found, and I do wish to commend to the general public of this country the desirability – nay, even necessity – of supporting to the utmost of its power efforts being made by Miss Ashwell and her players to bring sunshine, fun and education into the lives of those who live outside more prosperous and comfortable centres.[127]

The Duke and Duchess of York's amazement at the high standard and inexpensive tickets, after seeing a performance at the Century, was conveyed to the press: 'They are convinced this work is of the greatest possible social and artistic value … and warmly commend it to all who are interested in social progress of any kind.'[128] She also involved colleagues, such as Marie Tempest, who participated in a fund-raising party in November 1928, while Masefield offered poetry readings and autographed copies of his *Sonnets to the Players* for sale. In December 1926 Ilford, apparently looked upon by the Players 'as their sheet anchor',[129] proudly hosted Masefield's first public lecture appearance in England, after a successful American tour. He also appeared at Greenwich, Sutton and Enfield, speaking on the decline of drama and the company's role in weaning people back to theatre.

No amount of positive talk and successful fund-raising could soften the impact of the influenza epidemic that blighted the early months of 1927. Attendances everywhere were affected and the Players suffered a blow from which recovery became increasing impossible. West End theatre manager Oswald Stoll was compelled to issue a statement attempting to dispel fears:

> The truth is that risk of infection in a modern theatre ... is actually less than in almost any other public place, while the enjoyment provided by the performance is a psychological deterrent of the utmost value – bodily health being dependent to a large extent on the state of mind. Risk is less because precautions are greater.[130]

Even after the epidemic danger passed, other factors conspired against reclaiming audiences. Many in Ashwell's audiences were Church members, who during Lent felt they must forgo theatregoing, with unfortunate box office consequences. It is unlikely a suggestion that Friends give their ticket to 'someone who would otherwise be unable to see a play', thereby still supporting the Players, was taken up in any helpful way.[131] Although there was a large Ilford audience for *Outward Bound* in September 1927, which critic H.P.J. Marshall saw as greater encouragement and inspiration to the actors than any amount of writing and talking about company ideals,[132] he did not agree with audience programme suggestions: 'if the last three plays [light comedies] ... are due to this influence, perhaps it would be better to leave the choosing to say, Miss Ashwell herself. If the public are to be educated to a higher dramatic taste ... surely it is more fitting for the educators to choose the syllabus?'[133] He also noted an unfulfilled promise of 'some wonderful scenery, in place of the usual curtains'[134] for Barrie's *The Professor's Love Story*, and questioned the Friends' activities: 'One pays a subscription, receives a little Lap every now and then, but that is all. Surely that is not the sole raison d'être of the society?' Samuel Hancock responded, saying the Friends' Ilford branch worked hard to advertise and support performances, but 'the time is now ripe when this organisation should consider and decide on action to be taken, as propagating the idea of municipal theatre was the main purpose for which they were founded'.[135] This idea felt as remote as ever and the heart had gone out of the movement. When the eighth season closed, it was clear the company was in difficulty. In Greenwich, Ashwell spoke to the audience about heavy liabilities and losses: 'It might be thought because they were a limited liability company, they made money. As a fact, we are, and we have been since the beginning, very heavily in debt.'[136]

Esmé Church's departure added to the misery. Aged 35 in 1928, and having joined Ashwell in 1916, she was loyal, long-serving and popular and had played some 150 roles. As a director, she knew the decision had been reached that, unless more

5.6 Esmé Church, *Illustrated London News*, 23 January 1926

money and support were forthcoming, by mid-1929 the company would close. The chance to work with the Old Vic Company could not be turned down. Given her later career with the Old Vic Acting School and Young Vic touring theatre, she seized the baton from Ashwell and was ready to run with the message. While it would not be true to say her departure influenced the closure decision, audiences stayed away when she was not appearing and her replacement, Nell Compton, did not fill her shoes.[137] On 21 September 1928 the *Recorder* noted that while the audience was full of familiar faces, the company was minus 'a few of their favourites of old … Esmé Church will probably be missed most of all'.

The first half of 1929 was a testing time, with another influenza epidemic, national concern over the king's health, two months of intensely cold weather and company illnesses. In a desperate attempt to put the Players on a stronger footing, and eligible for government concessions, Ashwell established The Civic Theatres Limited with a National Council and herself as President.[138] At Ilford on 19 February, hoping to explain personally, she spoke during the interval. It was apparent that

some unfortunate misunderstandings had arisen and she wanted to explain some of their difficulties. Firstly there was the choice of plays. Plays people would support were not always plays they might like themselves. They tried to make as good a collection of plays as possible … As a result of a few plays presented a certain number of people had withdrawn their support. Those plays were *Tons*

of Money, which had a fine run in London; *Eliza Comes to Stay*, which did better business at the Century than any other play; *Lady Ursula's Adventure*, which
was a very successful play a year ago, and ... *The Last of Mrs Cheyney* ... They
were a big undertaking without any capital behind them. Any losses had to be
met privately, and fell upon shoulders which could ill afford to bear them. The
difficulty of finding plays was enormous ... I understand we have lost a number
of old friends because of these plays. We have been playing 10 years and we
have brought you as many as 250 plays. Does it not seem hard on me that after
presenting all these plays exception should be taken to so few?[139]

Ashwell did not indicate why people had objected to plays by such reputable authors
as H.V. Esmond, Frederick Lonsdale and Anthony Hope. She went on:

The other grievance was that a number of old friends no longer appeared. They
could not guarantee salaries or conditions which would satisfy, for a long time,
artistes who had a great deal of ambition. Leslie Banks,[140] an old favourite,
Walter Fitzgerald and Esmé Church were all in London productions, while
Olive Walter and Kynaston Reeves were on a successful tour in Canada ... It
was not for them to detain players when they wished to go. It was for them
to release them and wish them every success. (*Applause*) Their standard was
upheld, however. If you withdraw your support, you will shoot the whole lot
... and is it worth it?[141]

This impassioned plea, familiar to theatre company managers everywhere, provides insight into why Ashwell despaired of ever winning consistent support for
her cause. Local audiences mostly displayed a very provincial, proprietary view,
which was both an advantage and a disadvantage. She was dispirited further by
the suggestion that supporters were not given sufficient information to relate their
interest to the wider movement she aspired to. It seemed the Friends needed some
inspiration and 'some informing link with the management, so ... its members
may be encouraged by the sight of a goal to strive for it'.[142] She felt like a voice in
the wilderness – for more than ten years she had advocated civic involvement in
theatre, but local initiatives were not forthcoming. It was impossible for Ashwell
and her directors, in trying to keep afloat financially and artistically, to do more
than provide examples and eloquent advocacy.

When she gave a lecture on 'Drama for the People' in 1926, the *Kentish Mercury*
correctly predicted she was destined not to realise her ambitions immediately:

Perhaps it is left to the future to realise how much [she] has ... accomplished ...
[and] the indomitable courage and enthusiasm which has triumphed over many
difficulties ... [She] has the people's interests at heart ... [This is] at the back
of her fine undertaking to meet the need as well as possible until such time as
authorities awake to a sense of their responsibility.[143]

The last years of her company were marked by changes which were too late to help her. As she began to wind up her operation, the LCC, for the first time, granted financial support towards the redevelopment of Sadler's Wells Theatre. The *Era* hoped this would begin a general move towards official help for municipal theatres. The editorial concluded:

We have municipal housing, lighting, power, water, transport, baths and libraries. Why not include municipal theatres? Surely the function of Drama in civic life is ... important enough ... to claim a certain amount of assistance from governing powers ... The type of theatre we advocate ... would no more compete with commercial managers than do public libraries ... with booksellers. In the same way municipally aided Drama might be expected to foster interest in theatre in general. Its aim should be to produce that type of play which the ordinary manager is inclined to avoid for financial reasons, and so to keep alive many treasures of our dramatic literature.[144]

By now Ashwell knew to her cost that this would remain a rhetorical question for some time to come.

After considerable success with thirteen of Shakespeare's plays in the Players' first five years, there were no other Shakespeare productions between *As You Like It* in early 1926 and *Romeo and Juliet* in March 1929. Ashwell found audiences were not sufficient to justify productions with large casts. The *Ilford Recorder* review of *Romeo and Juliet* perhaps bears this out: the play was well received but 'not quite so crowded as usual, the hall peopled by a rather more discriminating audience than usual. Is it the privilege of only a few to be able to enjoy Shakespeare?'[145] Audiences did grow over the season's last four weeks, as the weather improved. Noel Coward's *I'll Leave it to You* was presented on 2 April. During the interval, the Friends called for a large audience for the last play, *Caste*, so that a substantial petition for support could be sent to the Carnegie Trust.[146] Another case of too little, too late.

During the last week of London performances, Battersea's sophisticated audience enjoyed *Caste*, while recognising society had moved on a great deal since its premiere. During the interval Gibson announced a fund-raising raffle for a pair of Queen Victoria's silk stockings, which were 'of exquisite fineness' and had the Royal arms woven into them. It seemed fashions had moved on as well: 'Commenting in whispers some ladies remarked the stockings ... would probably be open-work ones, and therefore quite unsuitable for present wear. No Battersea lady would appear decked out in finery from even a Royal wardrobe if such finery had ceased to be fashionable.' Ashwell, apparently unaware of any social gaffe, thanked the audience for its support, adding 'if all other boroughs were as helpful and as loyal as Battersea, the Players would have no difficulty'.[147] The last mention of the Players in Council records was the cancellation of provisional dates, because 'losses last season were so great'.[148] Soon after, Battersea Council, considering their presence had been 'a great asset to the Borough', agreed to collaborate with the British

Drama League in presenting performances during the forthcoming winter, using the hall on the same terms as the Players.

From the early summer months of 1920, before giving her company well-earned holidays, Ashwell tried a number of seasons at seaside and holiday resorts, before settling into annual visits to Bath, Rugby and York where they played sustained seasons in 'real' theatres. These included two weeks at Llanelly Hippodrome on the Welsh coast in July 1920 and a season of ten plays at the Grand Opera House, Scarborough, in May 1922. There was a three-week spring season at Jersey Opera House, Channel Islands, in March 1923, and one-off visits to coastal Brighton and Eastbourne in May 1924. Competition from other summer holiday fare was too great. The Prince of Wales Theatre, Rugby, was a regular summer venue for the Players between 1923 and 1926, and in 1929, after a two-year absence, the company made a special return visit in the spring. The Players opened at York Theatre Royal on 20 April 1925, with *The Earth*, returning in late spring each year until 1929. In April 1926 the company played a fortnight's season at the Little Theatre, Leeds, en route to nearby York.

Bath's beautiful, intimate Georgian Theatre Royal hosted ten substantial spring or summer seasons between 1922 and 1929, and it is fitting that it witnessed the Players' swansong. The company's first Bath season opened on 5 June 1922 with *Diana of Dobson's*. Bath had an established audience for repertory theatre and an active Playgoers' Society. Audiences and organisations such as Rotary, on whom Ashwell depended for group bookings, were wooed assiduously. The *Bath & Wilts Chronicle* carried daily advertisements and gave comprehensive coverage of performances and social events. Ashwell made many personal appearances during the company's visits. Her speeches to local organisations and the company's presence provoked some negative views on municipal theatre. Ernest Crawford, writing a 'warning' to her, considered 'theatre should be self-supporting … if there are not playgoers enough to keep it going, it is a particularly mean form of robbery to plunder non-playgoers to pay for the amusement of the few, because the few believe drama to be "good for the education of the soul".' He referred to a pamphlet, 'Our Theatres, and why Christian people cannot go to them', pointing out religious objections, as well as financial ones if Councils charged ratepayers. He warned against official control of theatre, concluding, 'The State has already too much power over the theatre.'[149]

Initially the audience was rather thin on the ground, and two weeks after opening Marion Fawcett announced they might curtail the season. She thought the hot weather (although Theatre Royal advertisements promoted 'The Coolest Place in Bath') and trade depression might have been contributing to the disappointing result, so ticket prices were reduced.[150] Soon after, when announcing *Twelfth Night*, the company confirmed its full season. 'The services of … well-known Shakespearean actor, Balliol Holloway, have been secured to play Malvolio, his brother, George Holloway, to represent Feste, and Roy Byford is putting in a special week to impersonate Sir Toby Belch. Esmé Church … a firm favourite with local audiences, is Viola.'[151] When the visit ended, fourteen plays, with two matinees each week, had been presented. There was an elaborate farewell, with many speeches from the stage to a packed house. Actor Dan F. Roe[152] commented on Bath's beauty and inspirational surroundings;[153] indeed, after many one-night-stands in London suburbs during winter, the long season at Bath, despite morning rehearsals and the exhausting necessity of sustaining roles on and off the stage, was almost a holiday.

A short season in February 1923 included the regional premiere of local playwright Charles McEvoy's Cockney drama *The Likes of 'Er*, attended in force by the Bath Playgoers' Society. The *Bath & Wilts Chronicle* reported on the author's presence, congratulating him 'on the success with which he has depicted the inmost soul of the dwellers of this London underworld'.[154] For *The Child In Flanders*, which included many carols, another local connection was used. In what became a regular practice, the musical, and sometimes acting, resources of Bath Operatic Society supplemented the cast, stimulating local interest. Indeed, the Society's 'humorist-in-chief', Mr L.E.C. Baker, had many supporters and attracted a special review when he appeared as Snake in the Players' *The School for Scandal* in August 1922.[155] Cicely Hamilton and Shakespeare featured prominently in the ensuing eleven-week summer season, May to early August 1923. Hamilton acted in most of the productions, including her plays *The Brave and the Fair* and *The Beggar Prince*. In July there was a week of *The Merchant of Venice* and *As You Like It*, co-directed by Ashwell and Paget Bowman.[156] The company gave a special matinee of *As You Like It* in the natural amphitheatre known as Shakespeare's Dell, in Royal Victoria Park, in aid of the Mayoress's Fresh Air Fund, which provided country holidays for poor city children.[157] Another feature of the thirteen-play season was *Stolen Fruit*, a curtain-raiser by company member Cyril Twyford, which preceded performances of Sheridan's *The Rivals*, set in eighteenth-century Bath.

Audiences proved elusive for some of the five-week 1924 season, which concluded with *Diana of Dobson's* and Ashwell's tribute to Church who had worked with her the longest – 'seven years of hard labour of love'. She estimated performances had been witnessed by some 130,000 people in Greater London in the past six months.[158] She also acknowledged contributions from composer and pianist Kate Coates,[159] and violinist Joan Simson, a cousin of Henry Simson, who worked with her during the war and was now returning home to Edinburgh.

The seven-week 1925 season opened on 8 June with an early Ashwell success, Fagan's *The Earth*, attended by the mayoral party and representatives of Bath Poetry, Playgoers and Operatic Societies. To coincide with City Race Week, the 'funniest and best racing play ever written',[160] Pinero's *Dandy Dick*, was presented, and in late July *The Doctor's Dilemma* provided entertainment for British Medical Association Conference attendees. Ashwell adjudicated the British Empire Shakespeare Society's Bath branch elocution competition, hearing sixty-three entrants from whom finalists were selected for the ensuing London festival. And Masefield was guest of honour for his adaptation of H. Weirs-Jennsen's *The Witch*, originally presented at the Court Theatre. He was 'delighted with the Players' rendering of the play', and with Mercia Cameron as the witch.[161] In appreciation, he handed over the copyright of his *Sonnets to the Players*, and Bath's mayor, Alderman Chivers, had these printed in booklet form at his own expense. They were 'sold in two editions, price 1s and 2s 6d respectively, to help the Lena Ashwell repertory movement'.[162]

In 1927 the company played for thirteen weeks at the Royal, with a six-week season in February/March and seven weeks between June and August. On 17 February Masefield donated box office takings from his poetry-reading matinee to support the Players, who were bringing 'refinement and beauty into the lives of those in our cities and suburbs in the teeth of every discouragement'.[163] This discouragement, mostly in the form of apathy, was beginning to take its toll, but Ashwell continued a punishing schedule with the Bath premiere of *Crime and Punishment* on 21 February, and simultaneous premieres in Sutton and Bath on 14 March of *Dr Jekyll and Mr Hyde*. Both productions were praised by the *Bath & Wilts Chronicle*. However, on the second-last night, according to committed playgoer Fred Weatherley, while the pit, containing the cheaper seats, was full, there were only fifteen people in the dress circle. He wrote to the *Chronicle* exhorting the people of Bath to take the last opportunity that evening to see the company's work.[164]

Weatherley continued his campaign with a letter in the *Chronicle* on the first day of the Players' summer season on 20 June 1927: 'Ashwell's name in the theatrical world is an absolute guarantee of a wise selection of plays ... If you want to be stirred ... to laughter or to tears (and both are good for your digestion), if you want to see a true picture of life ... theatre will give you what you want and what you want is what you need.' Throughout the company's existence, Ashwell was not lacking in supporters such as Weatherley, but the 'it's good for you' approach was not always the most helpful. This season's repertoire included works by H.A. Jones, Pinero, Galsworthy, Maugham and du Maurier. The company travelled with multipurpose costumes and props, as evidenced by the sudden change in programme, from *The Land of Promise* to *The Whiteheaded Boy* (not included in the announced repertoire), on 22 July, when actor Kynaston Reeves was called away to his dying father.[165] Participation in local events was a feature of the company's commitment to the area, and during this season John Killner[166] directed a local production of *The Tempest* for the August Summer School of Dramatic Production.

The *Bath & Wilts Chronicle* gave an enthusiastic welcome to the four-week 1928 season: 'The return ... is like a re-union of old friends, even though we may see different faces among the company, we know the Lena Ashwell tradition of consummate artistry is there linked with an infinite capacity to play well every type of piece.' Nevertheless, Gibson announced, after the first performance, that 'previous seasons at Bath, particularly last season, had been distinct financial failures ... it would be impossible for them to come again if this season were not a success'.[167] In fact, when the company returned for its four-week season, 15 July to 10 August 1929, the decision had been made to close down. Bath, where they had staged more than seventy-five plays, was the final venue. There was surprisingly little reference made to this by the *Chronicle*: everyone was numbed into acceptance of the inevitable. Noel Coward's comedy *I'll Leave It To You* was chosen to end an era. The *Chronicle* said goodbye in its *Day by Day* gossip section:

> The ghosts of Bath make a glorious company, and it seems their number is to be increased. After Saturday, the … Players will be seen no more. The curtain will ring down on a company … who have endeared themselves to Bath audiences, for they are not, after that day, to delight another audience with their versatility and talent. One hopes … to see these distinguished actors and actresses again … but [it will] not [be] in the 'happy family' of the Lena Ashwell Players.[168]

'Auld Lang Syne' was sung, the audience linked hands with the Players 'and the curtain was rung down on a company which has suffered considerable loss, but which will always be remembered in the annals of the stage'. The next morning, company members said farewell to the manager, with Gibson 'booted and spurred … [and] mounted on a dark chestnut, looking as if he were waiting for the "gone-away" from a mythical whipper-in hollering round the stage door'.[169]

Undoubtedly Ashwell's letter announcing the Players' closure in August 1929 was sent to all local press where the company had performed, as well as to the national press, but the *Ilford Recorder* appears to have been the only newspaper to publish it in full. It was the holiday period, but the impression remains that there was little to mark the company's demise and apparently no effort to rally support for its continuation. Ashwell wrote:

> It is a very great disappointment that after ten years' work in the great London Boroughs the Lena Ashwell Players are compelled to suspend activities until such times as accumulated losses incurred on each season can be wiped out. The loss now amounts to over £5,000, which we shall gradually pay off by letting the Century, and hiring out our wardrobe and properties to amateur companies. Beginning in 1919, during the winter of each year we have performed 26 plays, making a total in all of 260 of works by the most representative dramatic authors. Each season we have brought these plays to audiences numbering over 184,000 people. The prices, which were based on cinema charges, and which were the utmost people could afford to pay, ranging from 6d. to 2s.4d., prevented the enterprise from ever being on a commercial basis – the expenses of advertisement, printing, rehearsal rooms, motor transport for the 'fit-up', authors' fees, musicians' and actors' salaries, leaving no margin for bad weather, epidemics of influenza, or other difficulties, which must always face any theatrical venture. The entertainment tax alone represents £50 a week, or approximately £1300 on a 26 week season. In all other countries in Europe there is … recognition of the needs of the great public in regard to recreation, and such enterprises as ours are subsidised so they are able to continue ministering to the needs of many people who love theatre. In our great land arts are not considered necessities, but luxuries; and, therefore, we alone in Europe insist all recreation must be purely commercial or cease to

exist. To the many who have helped us I send my grateful thanks and the sincere wish we shall be so greatly missed that public opinion may be aroused, and in the future there may be some form of cooperation between the State and the arts, especially the art of theatre.[170]

She had nothing but praise for her company's efforts. Their wartime experience made them infinitely adaptable to any venue they visited: 'It was no embarrassment to them that halls and baths should be unsuitable, platforms of different sizes, curtains often not quite hiding an organ or a rostrum quite unusual in a forest or a bedroom. Why should Town Halls be constructed to inhibit everything except a public meeting, when it would be so easy to include a proper platform and attractive lighting?'[171]

As she packed away the Players, Ashwell published her third book, *The Stage*, in November 1929. In a 'Life and Work Series', professionals wrote about their work, 'its problems, its difficulties, and its pleasures', in the hope that this would be of help to those embarking on careers.[172] Ashwell used her experience to illustrate how young actors should approach rehearsals and performance. She described the theatre of her youth and the changes it had undergone in the intervening thirty-five years. At the conclusion she gives a clear indication of her attitude: 'The machine, with its cinema, talkies, radio, gramophone, its countless and most effective instruments, may aid and support Religion and Arts, but it is still only a mechanism, cold steel, dead iron, sounding brass. It is not alive, it has not a soul, it is not human, it cannot fill the place of the divine and the human realities.'[173]

Throughout the 1920s, anxious not to squander what she saw as positive outcomes from the war, Ashwell pursued a relentless schedule of public appearances, meetings and press statements on issues that concerned her. She fought for better conditions and improved status for the theatrical profession and for women in all walks of life, and made a strong commitment to the work and ideals of the British Drama League. She worked tirelessly to establish a community-wide theatregoing habit. The Players' repertoire included mostly well-known works by established playwrights; fourteen plays by Shakespeare and fifteen by Shaw were given hundreds of performances, as well as less familiar plays, including seventeen premieres, and plays by women and non-British authors. Ashwell created a team of women directors and a repertory company providing many opportunities for imaginative work. She was most successful in middle-class areas, away from the centre of London, where people did not want to travel far for access to good theatre. She was thwarted by uncomfortable facilities for both audiences and actors, competing entertainments, the lack of a theatregoing habit, limited resources and the Entertainment Tax. She was unable to pay actors a great deal, mostly attracting the young and inexperienced, who used their time with the company to learn their craft and then moved on. She set a punishing, perhaps overly ambitious schedule, maintaining a London theatre base and three companies constantly on the road. While there was some local authority support, much of the work of promoting the company was her responsibility, coupled with artistic directorship. It is tempting to conclude that Ashwell was both before her time and attempting to do the financially impossible. Dependence on goodwill and the box office without subsidy and performing a non-commercial repertoire, in the face of fierce competition from cinema, is a tall order at any time. On a groundbreaking mission to establish municipal theatres and repertory companies throughout the country, Ashwell set herself a challenge that needed the coincidence of like-minded people, state acknowledgement of responsibility to contribute to social well-being for all members of the community, and a financial climate to make it possible. These did not come until much later. It is understandable that she was disillusioned by the outcome. By the end of 1929 she was exhausted: 'Frustration is bad for the health, and so when I sat down in the office to face the winding up and burial of so many hopes I found I was knocked out. After a short struggle I succumbed to an infuriated stomach, and the next two years had to be spent in bed.'[174] She leaves it to John Masefield to express deeper feelings associated with the company she led for nearly ten years. He 'was enchanted with their work, especially by the beauty of their speech, which had such right qualities of swiftness and rhythm'.[175]

Weary and sickened of the daily show
That moves without a banner or a creed,
I met this troop a few short years ago
And felt their courage to be art indeed.

They were like youth, flying the lonely flag
In the gay darkness where the courage shines.
While the world's hunt went by, they were the stag
Delicate in the dew, kingly with tines.

They were the artists, who, by spirit at strain,
Brought, to men's hearts, out of the conflict played,
Spirits that cannot perish, but remain
Bright in the heart with life that cannot fade.

Theirs was the living art whose splendours tower
When the dead art goes down, in the live hour. [176]

Notes

1 Ashwell, *Myself a Player*, 248.
2 *Era*, 11 August 1920.
3 See Appendix 2.
4 British Drama League, *The British Drama League, 1919–1959* (London, 1959).
5 *Era*, 4 October 1920.
6 *South Western Star*, 8 October 1920.
7 *South Western Star*, 15 October 1920.
8 The Grand Hall hire charge for a charity dance in March 1923 was set at £7 10s (Battersea: Minutes, January 1923).
9 Battersea: Minutes, 21 June 1922.
10 Esmé Church (born 1893) studied at the Guildhall School of Music and Royal Academy of Dramatic Art, and made her first stage appearance in 1913. She joined Ashwell's Concert Party in 1916. She played about 150 roles with the Players and developed skills as a director, later put to use with the Old Vic Company and Committee for the Encouragement of Music and the Arts tours. In 1936 she was appointed head of Old Vic School of Acting, performing with and directing the company, and launching the Young Vic, touring children's theatre. In the early 1960s she worked with the Royal Shakespeare Company in Stratford.
11 *South Western Star*, 28 January 1921.
12 *South Western Star*, 18 February 1921.
13 Marion Fawcett (Katherine Roger Campbell, Scottish actress-director, 1886–1957) first appeared on stage in Liverpool in 1899 and went into production and management in 1918. She was the Players' first manager and secretary. Subsequently a producer at Malta Opera House, she returned to London for many performing roles in the 1940s.
14 *South Western Star*, 30 September 1921.
15 *Ibid.*
16 *Era*, 8 February 1923.
17 *South Western Star*, 19 October 1923.
18 *South Western Star*, 2 November 1923.
19 'To drink coffee and eat sandwiches at half past 11 o'clock at night in the company of prominent actors and actresses, to be plied with chocolate creams and cigarettes by some of the actresses. There's Bohemianism for you. In such Bohemianism did burgesses of Battersea revel on Tuesday night. A little demurely at first' (*South Western Star*, 18 January 1924).
20 Ashwell's sister Ethel died in Bath on that day. The opening of the autumn season was a busy time for Ashwell, who always made personal appearances to seek renewed audience support, so this was a very distressing time for her.
21 Harold Gibson, managing director and actor, was educated at Cambridge where he controlled the Albert Institute, a working men's club. Before going on the stage and into company management, he was ordained in 1908. He was made a member of the Theatrical Artists' Club of Moscow in recognition of his work in Russia. He had a distinguished First World War record, gaining the Military Cross, and was honorary chaplain to the forces and vicar of Shirehampton and Avonmouth between 1912 and 1917.
22 *South Western Star*, 24 October 1924.
23 These improvements included new curtains for the Hall: cost £162.95 (Battersea: Minutes, 19 July 1922); a pelmet for the stage (to create a false proscenium arch) and back-stage

curtains (Minutes, 18 July 1923); 'proscenium lighting to the stage in the Grand Hall ... estimated cost £35' (Minutes, 1 October 1924); and the 're-laying with oak, a portion of the floor of the stage, Grand Hall (from back of curtains to the front of the stage) at a cost of £54/16/-' (Minutes, 22 July 1925).

24 Battersea: Minutes, 21 July 1926, 22 December 1926, 21 December 1927, 20 January 1929.

25 Most of the venues visited by the Lena Ashwell Players were multi-purpose halls (and often indoor swimming baths covered for the winter months), with only basic facilities. The works undertaken in Battersea indicate that it was still early days for such entertainments to be performed in these venues.

26 Review of Jerome's Cook, *South Western Star*, 16 January 1925.

27 *South Western Star*, 16 April 1926.

28 *South Western Star*, 25 November 1927. Philip Snowdon had the Entertainment Tax reduced in 1927 (*Era*, 4 April 1928).

29 *East End News & London Shipping Chronicle*, 8 October 1920.

30 *Kentish Mercury*, 22 April 1921.

31 *Era*, 23 June 1920.

32 Fulham: Minutes, 21 July 1920.

33 'The large hall was packed from end to end and from floor to gallery and many spectators had to sit on the radiators around the hall' (*Fulham Chronicle*, 22 October 1920). *Twelfth Night* 'was a great treat to the senior scholars of the schools ... present in large numbers. Unfortunately, a large number of people, who did not ... book their seats, had to be turned away' (*Fulham Chronicle*, 21 January 1921).

34 *Fulham Chronicle*, 22 October 1920.

35 *Ibid*.

36 *Fulham Chronicle*, 8 April 1921.

37 *Era*, 2 June 1920.

38 *Municipal Journal*, 4 June 1920.

39 *Municipal Journal*, 18 June 1920.

40 *Era*, 21 September 1921.

41 Ealing: Minute Book No.3, Minutes of meeting 25 April 1924.

42 Surrey: Minutes, 26 June 1922.

43 Surrey: Sutton Urban District Council Minutes 26 June 1922.

44 *Surrey County Herald*, 19 October 1923.

45 *Sutton Advertiser*, 27 March 1924.

46 *West Herts & Watford Observer*, 25 November 1922.

47 *West Herts & Watford Observer*, 9 December 1922.

48 *Ilford Recorder*, 19 October 1923.

49 *Ilford Recorder*, 26 October 1923.

50 *Ilford Recorder*, 16 May 1924.

51 *Ilford Recorder*, 30 May 1924.

52 Ashwell writes: 'at the end of the tenth year, I found his loss to be seventeen thousand pounds. It was then that I took my courage in both hands and cancelled everything' (*Myself a Player*, 250).

53 W. Robertson, *Welfare in Trust – A History of the Carnegie UK Trust, 1913–1963* (Dunfermline, 1964), 101.

54 I am indebted to Henry Macnicol, Ashwell's nephew, for his assistance in researching the following quoted letters and minutes from Carnegie Trust files (Scottish Records Office, Edinburgh, GD 128/41/198).

55 Letters from Mitchell to Ashwell, 4 August 1920, and Ashwell to the Carnegie United Kingdom Trust, 8 August 1920.

56 Letter from Mitchell to another trustee, Mr Alexander, 22 October 1920.
57 Letter from Ashwell to Mitchell, 22 November 1920.
58 Carnegie Trust minutes, 14 December 1923.
59 No copy of this publication has been found.
60 York: Theatre Royal Archives: programme, 1925.
61 *Era*, 2 May 1923.
62 Ealing, Winchmore Hill, Battersea, Ilford, Brockley, Lewisham, Edmonton, Deptford, Northwood, Greenwich, Sutton and Watford (*Era*, 3 October 1923). In 1925 Circuit A was Sutton, Battersea, Holloway, Beckenham, Greenwich and Watford; Circuit B was Winchmore Hill, Ilford, Edmonton, Hounslow, Streatham and Staines.
63 The Bijou saw the premiere of Wilde's *Salome* in 1905 and in January 1924 housed a successful season by the English Grand Guignol Society (*Era*, 23 January 1924).
64 *Ibid*.
65 *Kentish Mercury*, 3 October 1924.
66 Lady Astor, Stanley Baldwin, Lords Beauchamp, Burnham and Islington, J.R. Clynes, Cyril Cobb, John Galsworthy, Lloyd George, Sir John Martin Harvey, the Lord Bishop of London, John Masefield, Sir Johnston Forbes-Robertson, Fred Terry, Sybil Thorndike and Charles Trevelyan.
67 *Drama* (Drama League Annual Report), 3/3 (June 1925).
68 *Westminster Gazette*, 9 January 1925.
69 *Stage*, 15 January 1925.
70 *Time & Tide*, 23 January 1925.
71 Ashwell returned briefly to the stage in Louis Parker's *Their Business in Great Waters*, with Leslie Howard and Tallulah Bankhead, for a special Lifeboat Service fund-raising matinee at the Lyceum (*Stage*, 13 December 1928).
72 *Daily News*, 10 January 1925.
73 *Daily Telegraph*, 4 February 1925.
74 *Stage*, 26 February 1925.
75 Ashwell often used members of local schools, drama students or operatic groups as production extras. Beatrice Wilson (born in India) married actor Norman V. Norman, and first appeared on the stage in London in 1898. She toured extensively with Norman's company and Ben Greet and appeared at the Old Vic, where she later taught. She directed plays for the Players during the 1923/4 season and continued to act and direct during the 1930s.
76 *Kentish Mercury*, 25 May 1923.
77 *Era*, 12 September 1925.
78 *Daily Telegraph*, 23 April 1925.
79 Olive Walter (born 1898). Her first theatre performance was in *Grit* (Kingsway, 1908). She was a member of the Players between 1922 and 1927, subsequently touring America and Canada before becoming managing director of the Greater London Players in 1930. Wilfred Fletcher studied at Tree's Academy of Dramatic Art with Rosina Filippi. He first appeared at the Court Theatre, and toured with Frank Benson's Shakespearean company before joining Laurence Irving in *The Typhoon* and *Hamlet*. Mercia Cameron first appeared as a young girl in *Grit* at the Kingsway, having trained with Rosina Filippi and the Elizabethan Stage Society. She worked with Ashwell's Concert Parties during the war, and joined the Players in 1923. Kynaston (Philip) Reeves (born 1893) studied at the Royal Academy of Dramatic Art, and first performed in 1920. He joined the Players in 1922, remaining with them until 1928.
80 Norman V. Norman (1864–1943) made his first stage appearance in 1884, and

subsequently created and toured with his own companies as well as touring with Ben Greet and producing plays in London.

81 *Stage*, 8 October 1925.

82 See Appendix 3 for a full list of the Players' repertoire.

83 *Stage*, 25 February 1926.

84 L. Whitelaw, *The Life & Rebellious Times of Cicely Hamilton* (London, 1990), 214.

85 *Time & Tide*, 11 February 1927.

86 See Appendix 4.

87 *Stage*, 21 January 1926.

88 *Kentish Mercury*, 26 March 1926.

89 *Kentish Mercury*, 29 October 1926. Harcourt Williams (1880–1957) was appointed director of the Old Vic Theatre in 1929, where his productions were based on the theories of Granville-Barker. He married actress Jean Sterling Mackinlay, prominently associated with Children's Theatre in the UK, who presented many of her matinees for young people at the Century Theatre.

90 Alan Webb (born 1906) made his first stage appearance with the Players in 1924, remaining with them for two years. He toured extensively in repertory before joining the Old Vic–Sadler's Wells Company in 1934. He appeared in many productions of Noel Coward's plays.

91 Alan Webb, quoted in T. Kiernan, *Olivier: The Life of Laurence Olivier* (London, 1981), 34–5.

92 L. Olivier, *Confessions of an Actor* (London, 1984), 53.

93 Ashwell, *Myself a Player*, 172–4.

94 In *From Irving to Olivier: A Social History of the Acting Profession* (London, 1984), M. Sanderson provides a detailed account of the Stage Guild and the process towards the establishment of British Actors' Equity in 1930.

95 *Stage*, 27 August 1925.

96 *Kentish Mercury*, 27 November 1925.

97 *Sutton Advertiser*, 15 January 1925.

98 Edmonton: Minutes, 23 November 1923.

99 *Tottenham & Edmonton Weekly Herald*, 1 February 1924.

100 *Tottenham & Edmonton Weekly Herald*, 9 January 1925.

101 *Tottenham & Edmonton Weekly Herald*, 24 February 1928.

102 *Enfield Gazette & Observer*, 15 October 1926.

103 *Enfield Gazette & Observer*, 6 November 1925. For the Players, as a practical matter, Roman costumes would have been less expensive than Elizabethan dress.

104 *Sunday Times*, 2 January 1927.

105 *Ilford Recorder*, 28 January 1927.

106 Godfrey Kenton joined the Players in 1925, after training at the Royal Academy of Dramatic Art. He had a very successful career as a juvenile lead in the 1930s and 1940s. In the 1930s he set up the Greater London Players, with Olive Walter. Kenton was still acting in his nineties and was interviewed, aged 94, by the author in 1995 (he died in 1998). I am indebted to theatre historian and biographer Michael Kilgarriff, who put me in touch with Kenton and gave me access to his own interview notes made in 1991.

107 *Times*, 22 February 1927.

108 Nancy Price, CBE, (born 1880) was an actress-director, married to Charles Maude. She first appeared in London at the Lyceum in 1900 and had an extensive career. She founded the People's National Theatre in 1930 and subsequently the English School Theatre Movement, touring plays to schools. She wrote many books and appeared in a large number of films.

109 *Kentish Mercury*, 18 January 1924. Ten months later, Ernest Milton's *Hamlet*, directed by Beatrice Wilson, was given the same accolade (*Kentish Mercury*, 5 December 1924).

110 *Ilford Recorder*, 10 March 1925. Barrymore's *Hamlet* was performed in New York for 101 performances in 1922. He repeated this success in London in 1925 with Constance Collier and Fay Compton (*Oxford Companion to the Theatre*, 60).

111 *South Western Star*, 27 November 1925.

112 Godfrey Kenton met the author in 1995 and described his work with the Players.

113 *Kentish Mercury*, 30 October 1925. Colin Still was the author of *Shakespeare's Mystery Play* (London, 1921). Ashwell refers to Colin Still in her chapter on *The Tempest* in *Reflections from Shakespeare*, 225.

114 Quoted from an unidentified newspaper article, 22 October 1926 (Mander and Mitchenson Collection).

115 *Drama*, February 1927, 72.

116 *Times*, 8 February 1927.

117 *Times*, 29 March 1927.

118 *Times*, 1 November 1927.

119 *Islington & Holloway Press*, 30 October 1926.

120 *Middlesex Chronicle*, 5 March 1927.

121 *Middlesex Chronicle*, 28 January 1928.

122 *Streatham News*, 24 September 1926. This has continued to be an argument used against arts subsidy – if it has to be supported by public money it can't be good enough to survive in the marketplace.

123 *Ibid.*

124 *Streatham News*, 22 October 1926.

125 *Sutton Advertiser*, 31 March 1927.

126 *Sutton Advertiser*, 10 November 1927.

127 *Times*, 20 January 1926.

128 *Times*, 19 December 1927.

129 *Ilford Recorder*, 26 November 1926.

130 *Enfield Gazette & Observer*, 18 February 1927.

131 'Lent Suggestion for Playgoers', *Ilford Recorder*, 11 March 1927.

132 *Ilford Recorder*, 30 September 1927.

133 *Ilford Recorder*, 21 October 1927.

134 *Ilford Recorder*, 3 February 1928.

135 *Ilford Recorder*, 6 April 1928.

136 *Kentish Mercury*, 4 May 1928.

137 Nell Compton was the daughter of actor-manager Edward Compton and actress Virginia Bateman, and sister of novelist Compton Mackenzie.

138 *Ilford Recorder*, 8 March 1929.

139 *Ilford Recorder*, 22 February 1929.

140 Leslie J. Banks, CBE (1890–1952) first appeared with the Benson Company (1911) and joined the Players in 1921. He was president of British Actors' Equity from 1948 and appeared in many films from 1932.

141 *Ilford Recorder*, 22 February 1929.

142 *Ilford Recorder*, 1 March 1929.

143 *Kentish Mercury*, 26 March 1926.

144 *Era*, 13 March 1929.

145 *Ilford Recorder*, 8 March 1929.

146 *Ilford Recorder*, 5 April 1929.

147 *South Western Star*, 5 April 1929.

148 Battersea: Minutes, 19 June 1929.

149 *Bath & Wilts Chronicle*, 19 June 1922.

150 *Bath & Wilts Chronicle*, 21 June 1922.

151 *Bath & Wilts Chronicle*, 12 July 1922.

152 Dan F. Roe (born 1877) had early experience as a stage manager, and excelled in farce, light comedy and character roles. He performed with Sir Harry Lauder in *Three Cheers* at the Shaftesbury as well as being stage manager and comedian with the celebrated Louie Freear. He toured with the Compton Comedy Company.

153 *Bath & Wilts Chronicle*, 14 August 1922.

154 *Bath & Wilts Chronicle*, 13 February 1923.

155 *Bath & Wilts Chronicle*, 5 August 1922.

156 The first performance of *The Merchant of Venice* on 9 July was attended by members of the local branch of the British Empire Shakespeare Society.

157 The mayoress was Sarah Grand, a radical novelist of the 1880s and 1890s, the originator of the appellation 'New Woman', and a prominent suffrage worker, known to Ashwell through the Actresses' Franchise League.

158 *Bath & Wilts Chronicle*, 14 July 1924.

159 Kate Coates, pianist and composer, studied at the Royal College of Music, Manchester, and in London and Hamburg. She was a member of the first Concert Party in 1915, performing in France and Malta. She composed music for *The Beggar Prince*, *Good Friday* and the Players' Shakespearean productions. Some of her work was published by Boosey.

160 Advertisement, *Bath & Wilts Chronicle*, 9 July 1925.

161 *Bath & Wilts Chronicle*, 2 July 1926.

162 *Bath & Wilts Chronicle*, 9 August 1926.

163 *Bath & Wilts Chronicle*, 18 February 1927.

164 *Bath & Wilts Chronicle*, 19 March 1927.

165 *Bath & Wilts Chronicle*, 23 July 1927.

166 John Killner, a young light comedy actor, who worked with Annie Horniman's Halifax Repertory Co., and toured with Vedrenne & Eadie's company with 500 performances of *Milestones*. After the war he appeared in Gertrude Elliott's company and played light comedy parts with Iris Hoey. He was musical, and played the piano despite the loss of one finger from each hand.

167 *Bath & Wilts Chronicle*, 17 July 1928.

168 *Bath & Wilts Chronicle*, 8 August 1929.

169 *Bath & Wilts Chronicle*, 12 August 1929.

170 *Ilford Recorder*, 2 August 1929.

171 Ashwell, *Myself a Player*, 239.

172 The series included *The Army*, *The Architect*, *Nursing*, *Play Production* (by Basil Dean), *The Surgeon* and *The Bar*, all written by highly regarded practitioners.

173 Ashwell, *The Stage*, 192.

174 Ashwell, *Myself a Player*, 250.

175 Ashwell, *Myself a Player*, 246.

176 One of Masefield's *Sonnets of Good Cheer* (London, 1925), for the Lena Ashwell Players. Quoted by Ashwell in *Myself a Player*, 236.

6

1930 to 1957

Writing in the late 1940s, J.C. Trewin observed: 'theatre during the nineteen-twenties seemed always to be working at full and anxious stretch ... altogether the decade was a chaos of contradictions, doubts, and conflicting enthusiasms'.[1] This statement rings true for Ashwell in 1929. Aged 60, finding it impossible to continue, she abandoned the work she had undertaken 'at full and anxious stretch' for a decade. In August her company members dispersed to seek other theatre work. She wrote to the Carnegie Trust, advising that the Lena Ashwell Players' Council had resolved to sell the Century Theatre in order

> to liquidate all outstanding accounts and to provide extra capital ... in the event of the Theatre not finding a purchaser, the movement should cease altogether; and in order to pay off debts, the Theatre should be let to amateurs. Miss Ashwell expressed the opinion that it would take some time to wipe off the debt, and she did not think it would ever be possible to resume the work. The Committee regretted the action which had been found necessary, and hoped a good price could be got for the Theatre, which would provide for payment of the debt, and a balance to carry on the travelling companies.[2]

With no buyer and an accumulated deficit of some £5,000, Ashwell remained as Century leaseholder until the end of 1934.[3] From 1924 to 1933 she made annual application to the LCC Theatres and Music Halls Committee for stage-play licences. The theatre accommodated approximately 300 people, and box office income can never have been very large. The building was extensive: besides the theatre, there was a similar sized large hall beneath it, suitable for dances. The licence did not permit her to use this for public events; it might have been possible to make money if she had been able to do so. Overall, the building's facilities were attractive to hirers: she had made alterations and improvements and there were dressing rooms, rehearsal space in the lower hall, a kitchen and buffet area, workshops and storage areas, as well as two offices.[4]

After renting the Century to amateur theatre and community groups for six years, she relinquished it with relief to the Rudolf Steiner Association during 1935 when Vera Compton-Burnett became the Twentieth-Century Theatre's licensee.

6.1 Century Theatre interior, 1994 (photograph by author)

Eurhythmy performances, recitals, lectures and workshops were presented there for a number of years, after which it was sold for commercial use. From the 1960s it was an antiques warehouse with a Westbourne Grove shopfront. After receiving a Heritage listing, it was restored in the late 1990s as a theatre, conference and meeting place, retaining the name of Twentieth-Century Theatre. Ironically, the foyer now contains a display celebrating Laurence Olivier's performance here as a member of the Lena Ashwell Players!

The early 1930s were a difficult time. As well as enduring constant ill health, Ashwell suffered a great loss when Henry Simson died, aged 60, in September 1932. He had provided her with financial and emotional security to pursue her ambitions. Bereft, she was obliged to sell property (they owned two country houses and a London mews) to maintain her household. With a real sense of having failed to convince the 'great Empire leading in world affairs, a powerful people' that theatre was 'a power that might lead toward a vision without which we must perish',[5] Ashwell, while still a believer in theatre as an instrument for human good, sought a strengthening of her personal faith:

I did not succeed in anything I planned to do. This sounds very desperate and tragic, but really is quite the reverse. Trouble is the only lever God can use to wake us from the deep sleep of accepted values; hardship and pain keep us awake and striving; we fight our way through an ever-increasing awareness towards the vision of Beauty. There are many definitions of beauty, but it seems to me there is only one path to it, the active co-operation of the mind with the Creative Life itself, the effort to obtain an actual, practical experience of the Plan of the Supreme Architect, the only Artist.[6]

She continued to pursue James Porter Mills' teachings and republished his *Knowledge is the Door*, under the auspices of The Fellowship of the Way in 1937. She organised lectures and members' meetings from her home at 19 Grosvenor Place, London. She described Mills as

> a pioneer in that he brought a knowledge of methods of the East into relation with the power of revelation given to the world by the life of Jesus Christ ... Prayer was not only the appeal to a transcendent being to remove our difficulties and temptations; but through meditation, or dwelling on the words of life, the mind could be transformed into an instrument of contact with that invisible reality, the realm of the Spirit ... This is a new age with new concepts, and the emphasis is placed on the mind and its power to change our civilisation.[7]

Little is known about Mills' life, although his ideas are still of interest, mostly in America.[8] Ashwell never abandoned her quest for self-knowledge: for many years she corresponded with Claude Bragdon, the American architect, author and lecturer. Throughout his life, Bragdon spoke

> for the artistic conscience, resisting at every turn the debasing of beauty and formal values in the name of material progress, and positing as achievable goals the discoveries of the spiritual life. From two decades as a practising architect, he had turned to stage design and self-expression, merging the functionalism of Louis Sullivan and the theosophy of Annie Besant into a personal credo.[9]

Extant letters, in which she addressed Bragdon as a confidant and spiritual advisor, express her interest in the occult.[10] She posed many questions about his writings as well as expressing heartfelt concerns about the state of the world. She was also influenced by writers interested in mysticism and eastern religions, such as Count Hermann Keyserling and Sir Oliver Lodge, as well as by the Church of the Old Catholics. Her response to the outbreak of the Second World War shows a woman deeply troubled by its impact on the young.

> There is no exuberance as in 1914, no romance. Just facing the fight to the death against the forces of evil ... We are so near too to all the heartache of Poland & the torture of the Jews & the cruelty, the abnormal cruelty which confronts civilization. There are days when it is hard to breathe even though so many horrors & so much misery have blunted the capacity for feeling.[11]

After the Second World War she wholeheartedly embraced the Moral Re-Armament movement, which sought to prevent a recurrence of such horrors. Before this catastrophic event, Ashwell published *Myself a Player* in 1936. She chose her title well: her autobiography bears out her perception of herself as an active participant in life, rather than an observer or commentator. According to the *Times Literary Supplement*,

> Miss Ashwell's life has been unlike that of most players ... [She] seems never to have lost all that air of a creature wild, or wild-wood, elusive, natural, unconventionally direct ... Miss Ashwell's career as actress and actress-manager is not the principal subject of her book, nor that part of the story that most impresses the reader. All the time there is another and deeper story being told: the story of her development, through happiness and unhappiness, as a woman, and beneath that again as a living spirit. Her private life is not kept out of sight; and behind the story of the Kingsway Theatre lies a much more interesting and psychologically important story of private relations. Miss Ashwell's proper and peculiar work lay on the far side of her management of the Kingsway ... The chapters on these achievements during and after the War are enough by themselves to set this book apart from ordinary theatrical biography ... A chapter on The Changing Theatre shows a healthy dislike of the modern 'producer' by one trained under the actor-manager, and some shrewd criticism of cinema. Indeed, Miss Ashwell is no lover of modern theatre, nor of a good deal of modern life; and at the close of her candid and confiding book, she reveals her means of escape from it.[12]

Myself A Player provides considerable insight into Ashwell's personality. She writes with passion and conviction about theatre and was not afraid to express an opinion or make judgements about developments and conditions which pleased or displeased her. She is honest about her failures and disappointments and expresses her ideas, particularly in relation to the works of Shakespeare, with clarity and confidence. Unlike autobiographies by contemporaries such as Eva Moore,[13] the book has limited detail about roles she played and people she worked with, except where they impacted on her development and wider role in the community. She barely touches on social aspects of her life in theatre, preferring to convey her impressions on, and aspirations for, the role of theatre in society.

Ashwell maintained her commitment to the Drama League, continuing active involvement until its work was suspended for the duration of the Second World War. *Drama* expressed regret at the Players' disbanding, hoping it would be temporary: 'The whole enterprise has been a piece of work of which Miss Ashwell may be justly proud, and which has done much to keep alive the idea of municipal drama in this country.'[14] Ashwell chaired the League's annual meeting in 1930, when it announced it would undertake widespread National Theatre propaganda during winter. There was hope that the support of Labour prime minister, Ramsay McDonald, would help, along with BBC involvement. Ashwell 'urged every member to do as much as possible to popularise the idea ... She also urged those against the National Theatre to voice their protest so that more life might be put into the movement.'[15] She described herself 'as an old member of the theatrical profession' and expressed her admiration for the work and national importance of the League, praising Geoffrey Whitworth, 'to whose indefatigable energy and infinite trouble the success of the League was due'.[16] Much of the League's energy for the next two decades went into the National Theatre scheme. Ashwell and Whitworth were in the House of Commons in November 1929 to hear the proposal to appoint a panel to select a joint committee to draw up an agreed scheme.[17] At the same time, the *Stage* reported that there was a vote pending in the House of Commons to introduce a bill, proposed by Socialist MP for Peckham, Mr John Beckett, to enable local authorities to spend an amount up to a penny rate annually on the establishment of municipal theatres.

Ashwell did not have a high public profile during the 1930s and 1940s, although she lectured and performed in the new medium of BBC radio. The extent of this work is unknown as most broadcasts were live and not archived. In August 1926 a local London radio station, possibly 2LO, presented a British Legion programme recreating a wartime Concert Party. Ashwell recited poems and Carrie Tubb sang. In May 1934 she made her radio drama debut in *Bathsheba of Saaremaa*. Two months later, with Raymond Massey, she participated in a documentary drama on Canadian history, devised by Jack Inglis and Roger Pocock. The only known extant recording of Ashwell's voice is from a BBC radio broadcast of Shaw's *The Dark Lady of the Sonnets*, on 22 April 1938, as part of the National Theatre campaign. She played Queen Elizabeth to Robert Donat's Shakespeare. Shaw introduced the play, describing how it was written from an idea by Dame Edith Lyttelton. Ashwell was nearly 70 at the time of this recording, but her voice is strong and clear.[18]

Ashwell retained a lively interest in and awareness of the changing styles in theatre writing and performance. Noel Coward particularly impressed her:

There is one who works from inside [the theatre], the most successful ... the richest, Noel Coward. Almost anything which he turns out attracts the public. He is the voice of the age. And as in the age itself there is cause for hope and faith, and deep cause for tears. Sometimes, when praise is pouring down upon his head there is regret that one who could do much should do so trivial and stupid a thing ... then one is swept off one's feet with pure joy at seeing true theatre come back again. He has something which seemed ... to be lost, the something that is theatre, the springs of drama bubbling up from life itself without effort.[19]

Influenced and informed by Bragdon's stage designs and architectural ideas, she took an interest in technical changes taking place in the theatre at this time:

I keep working out the proscenium-less theatre & feel it is a real escape from film & television (the new encroacher). They cannot do what a ring can do showing all sides of the picture, but it will take a long time & new methods of acting. The present theatre suffers from its aloofness & the modern effort at realism makes for separateness. It was a revelation to see George Robey (do you know the old music hall star?) playing Falstaff. His asides to the audience & their response as if they were invisible friends, aiders & abettors of his secret thoughts.[20]

Ashwell assumed the mantle of a theatrical 'elder statesman', providing advice and support when called upon. Such was her involvement with the Entertainments National Service Association (ENSA), established after the outbreak of the Second World War. She was a member of ENSA's international advisory committee. Led by Basil Dean, an 'arrogant and autocratic man with a strong dislike for the freewheeling variety performer [and] not an easy man to get on with'[21], the organisation had many problems behind the scenes and was defined by comedian Tommy Trinder as 'Every Night Something Awful'.[22] Ashwell convened and chaired the Lectures Section as well as organising some Concert Parties going to the Front, but ill health prevented more active involvement.

Her niece, Fiona (Simson) Edwards, who lived with Ashwell and Hilda Pocock during the war, remembers Ashwell being in poor health after undergoing a major operation in 1943 and recuperating at their country house in Chieveley, Buckinghamshire.[23] Despite this, when the Drama League reconvened, a recovered Ashwell was present at the 1946 Birmingham conference. She was no doubt pleased that, as *Drama* reported,

> conspicuous amongst the delegates were the large number of Drama Organis-
> ers – a professional body of experts, increasing daily in number, appointed and
> paid for by Municipal and County Councils and the Carnegie Trust ... I could
> not help noticing the faces of people on the platform. Six years of war had not
> altered them much ... Miss Lena Ashwell, stalwart of the stage, founder member
> of the League, brimming with good humour and energy. (She had just proposed
> in a neatly turned and witty speech the need for more Municipal theatres.)[24]

Following Geoffrey Whitworth's death, in October 1952 Ashwell unveiled a plaque to his memory.[25] Ten days before, her own role was acknowledged when Athene Seyler unveiled a Peter Lamda bust of Ashwell at League headquarters, Fitzroy Square.[26] This was Ashwell's last official appearance on behalf of the League, which became the British Theatre Association, continuing to serve professional and amateur theatre. It could not attract sustained public funding and went into liquidation in 1990. Its demise, after seventy years, left a large gap in training and advice services as well as reducing accessibility to play scripts and other resources for amateur groups.[27]

During the Second World War, Ashwell recited at the Poetry Society's weekly matinees, which were described as 'an essential wartime service'.[28] Through her love of poetry and the spoken word, together with her religious pursuits, she was drawn to playwright Christopher Fry, who became a devoted friend and constant visitor, especially when she was too frail to leave the house. Her letters to him, written between 1952 and 1954, reveal her continuing passion for friendship and purposeful theatre.[29] She read drafts of his poetic drama *The Dark is Light Enough*. Although she was delighted Fry wanted to dedicate it to her, she wrote on 27 January 1954 saying,

> it is a really great play and may make the world here see the hopeless futility of war (and many other things besides), so someone really important *now* might help to open their eyes to what a sad world they are building. I belong to the past and have only one virtue – my profound belief in the transforming power of the spoken word in theatre, on the change of heart and mind a play creates … this moment, on our bad little planet is the moment of the power of ideas. The miracle of what our little minds might grow into. So, most wonderful friend – dedicate the play to the future and not to one who tried a little, failed much! Lena.

She wrote a few months later, anxious about the play's production. She felt that

> at this moment in civilization the theatre should be alive and real – these dreadfully stupid old plays, *A Woman of No Importance*, *The Way of the World*, are given at tremendous expense – over produced, over dressed, over expensive – seem a very poor tribute to the hope of a new world … I am … praying your play will come to show that theatre has real life and brings new hope and not these dead rays of the past.[30]

Sadly, she suffered a slight stroke soon after and did not see the Aldwych premiere on 30 April 1954 with Edith Evans as Countess Rosmarin. Fry prevailed: the published text of *The Dark is Light Enough* contains the dedication 'To Lena Ashwell with affection and admiration. Christopher Fry. Edith Evans'.[31] Ironically, just two years later, John Osborne's 'kitchen-sink' realism in *Look Back in Anger* rapidly began to displace Fry's poetic drama as the new drama – perhaps not drama that would have pleased the ailing Ashwell.

Two of Ashwell's letters to Fry make reference to Moral Re-Armament (MRA), which became the focus of her energy and commitment in the late 1940s.[32] Also known as the Oxford Group, this was 'a non-denominational revivalistic movement founded in 1922 by U.S. churchman Frank Buchman'.[33] It sought to deepen the spiritual life of individuals while encouraging them to continue as members of their own Churches. Ashwell came in contact with the movement through the Westminster Theatre, and through her nephew Henry Macnicol. From 1931 the theatre saw many productions of avant-garde drama, including plays by James Bridie and Pirandello. Between 1935 and 1938, the Group Theatre presented works by Auden, Isherwood, Spender and MacNeice, followed in 1938 by London Mask Theatre, initiated by J.B. Priestley and Ronald Jeans. In 1946 the Theatre was acquired by Westminster Memorial Trust 'as a living memorial to men and women of Moral Re-Armament who had given their lives in the fight against Hitler'.[34] Ashwell

6.2 Ashwell aged 80 (courtesy of Henry Macnicol)

attended the dedication ceremony, meeting MRA playwright and chaplain Alan Thornhill[35] and former tennis champion H.W. ('Bunny') Austin. In 1948, when Ashwell was 79, Austin invited her to MRA headquarters in Caux, Switzerland, where she worked as an advisor and producer with the group's actors and writers. Austin wrote: 'Lena was in her late seventies, but she had the vitality of a woman half her age … It was hard to keep up with her.'[36] By all accounts, she thrived on this new theatrical venture.

In his eulogy at her memorial service Alan Thornhill declared:

She had a marvellous way to see in actors, many rough and ready and many very new, some quality of unselfconsciousness and naturalness which touches with real conviction and sincerity that could be turned into artistry and power. She had the eye to see in these plays their real purpose to do again what the first plays in our theatre of the Middle Ages tried to do – to bring faith to simple men and women who at that time did not know how to read or write. And perhaps it is true in this age, when so many people are spiritually or morally illiterate, we need miracle and mystery plays of today that aim to give men some of the ABCs of faith and of a cure for ills that afflict us personally and in our nations.[37]

Held Over !

"JOTHAM VALLEY"

Directed by
HOWARD REYNOLDS
LENA ASHWELL

Featuring

LELAND HOLLAND
ILENE GODFREY   and a singing Cast of *Fifty*

"Genuine and moving." - Brooks Atkinson, *New York Times*

"Played with high and good spirits."
Robert Coleman, *New York Daily Mirror*

"No one should miss it." - - - - - - - - - Reginald Owen

PERFORMANCES DAILY THROUGH MARCH 3rd.
CORONET THEATRE . . . Tickets NOW
Evenings - 8:40 p.m. Matinees - Thursdays, Saturdays - 2:40 p.m.

6.3 Promotional leaflet for *Jotham Valley*, Coronet, New York, 1951
(Moral Re-Armament Archives)

Ashwell subsequently met Buchman and travelled regularly to Caux, speaking at conferences and advising on MRA productions such as Thornhill's *The Forgotten Factor*. When the musical revue *The Good Road*[38] was performed at His Majesty's, London, in November 1948, it was under the auspices of MRA's National Committee of Invitation, of which Ashwell was a member. She returned to the stage as Lady Arlington in Thornhill's *Annie The Valiant*, premiered during the MRA World Assembly at Caux on 14 July 1950. The following January she performed the role during a season at the Washington Lisner Auditorium. While in New York, Ashwell co-directed, with Howard Reynolds, a production of Cecil Broadhurst's musical play *Jotham Valley*, with MRA members. Her suggestion that they perform a special matinee to inform actors and actresses of the movement was taken up, and provided her with the opportunity to address the audience 'on her vision for theatre and its part in inspiring a better world'.[39] During this visit Ashwell had a fall, breaking a bone in her leg. When she returned home she was less mobile, from then on concentrating her energies, with the assistance of her sister, on the promotion of MRA ideals in London.

In March 1953 Ashwell and Hilda Pocock convened a meeting for leaders of groups such as the National Council of Women, the Anglo-American Teachers' Exchange, the Royal College of Nursing, the Colonial Office and Embassies, the Salvation Army and other co-operative organisations, to inform them of the advance of Moral Re-Armament. They acknowledged that there was prejudice against this movement, but Ashwell reminded 270 people present that she had fought as a suffragette against the perception that 'only ugly women want the vote!'[40] She considered the uniting of nations through MRA to be as worthwhile a fight as that of the suffragettes. This meeting resulted in a radio broadcast on Woman's Hour on 1 June 1953, the eve of Queen Elizabeth II's coronation, in which a housewife spoke of ways ordinary women at home and at work could back the queen in her task.

Ashwell addressed a further MRA public meeting at the Royal Festival Hall on 10 May 1953. At this, her last public appearance in England, she declared:

> As old as I am, I am aiming to be here in another 20 years. It is a great thing to be 80 and know you have found something worth living for. With all my heart, I recommend you all to look at the deep freeze in your own minds, and open and melt it, so you see the great value, the great mission and great movement of Moral Re-Armament.[41]

Six weeks later, her 'Letter to the Women of Britain', was as passionate as Ashwell's wartime pleas for support, calling on the female half of the population to see 'how very deeply materialism of the Right and of the Left is destroying the life of this country', and exhorting them to 'make it your business to know what is going on in the world and learn the answer. Pass on that answer to other women of all classes.'[42] Ashwell was seeking to involve local communities, as she had done in fund-raising for Concert Parties and the Players. Ashwell's last public gesture for MRA was at

Caux in late July 1953, when she addressed a Conference: 'I have found the great value of the effort for personal change and mind you, it is very difficult and very hard, and very painful and the awful thing is that it is always going on. It never stops ... it doesn't matter how old you are. You are still free to be changed.'[43] By now her health was extremely fragile; tributes following her death indicate she spent her last few years very quietly. She suffered a number of strokes, rendering her speechless and bedridden, but she retained enthusiasm for MRA ideals to the end. Hilda Pocock proved a devoted nurse. Bunny Austin wrote: 'These two old ladies were like sturdy oaks with their roots deep in the great traditions of Britain.'[44]

Lena Ashwell died at home at 5 Belgrave Mews West, London, on 13 March 1957, aged 87. The *Times* obituary described her as 'an actress whose emotional force and sincerity were perhaps unique in English theatre during the comparatively short time during which she played leading parts ... everything she did rang true'. Her influence 'in the theatre of her generation was always salutary',[45] a view expressed by those who paid tribute in print[46] and spoke at her memorial service at Christ Church, London W1, on 20 March 1957. Edith Evans, Athene Seyler and Reverend Thornhill recalled her life-long 'youthful voice' and passion for theatre. Buchman was unable to attend, but sent a message saying 'Lena has taken her last call. The curtain goes up for her on the new world for which she longed and fought.'[47] Violet Markham's tribute, published in the *Times* three weeks after Ashwell's death, best sums up her role in a changing world and the response, from her friends and colleagues, to her death:

> Lena Ashwell was not only a distinguished actress but a woman of wide sympathies and culture who touched other and varied sides of life. As her life went on her power of spiritual insight grew ever greater. Her interests were deeply concerned with the borderland where the practical evidence of the five senses merges into a new experience of the life of the spirit. In a material world she hoisted and kept flying a banner inscribed with her faith in the spiritual basis of the Universe. Though this aspect of her life was not known to the general public, a wide circle of friends knew her as a guide and teacher to those who sought to follow the Way under her direction. She knew by experience the power latent in silence and meditation and their healing quality in the difficulties and perplexities of life. I heard her speak with the inspiration of a prophet to the small group gathered around her. She was not concerned with creeds ... but bringing home to her class what she held to be the potent spark of the divine in the human heart and the infinite possibilities latent in it. It was a grief to her friends that sickness and ill-health laid a heavy hand on her closing years ... The order of release, now it has come, has set free a fine and tender spirit.[48]

Five years later, and two years before her death at the age of 93, Hilda Pocock presented Westminster Theatre with a sculpted head of Ashwell, unveiled by Edith Evans in May 1962. Sometime later, relatives and friends provided funds to equip

Dressing Room 2. A plaque on the door contained a dedication 'to the memory of Lena Ashwell, Lady Simson, actress, patriot, pioneer, who loved the Westminster Theatre'. Renovation works began at the theatre in 1999, but a major fire in 2002 destroyed much of the building. While attempts have been made to build another theatre on the site, at the time of writing in 2011 no progress has been made. The fate of the dressing room dedication is unknown and another tangible reminder of Ashwell appears to have vanished.

Lena Ashwell is best remembered as an actress who portrayed unconventional women and representatives of the 'New Woman' in Edwardian theatre. Her roles in *Mrs Dane's Defence* (1900) and *Diana of Dobson's* (1908) are referred to in accounts of theatre of the period, partly because these plays were considered important examples of realism in a changing social environment, and because the authors, H.A. Jones and Cicely Hamilton, were also significant for their work in the theatre of their day. Ashwell has received less recognition for her encouragement of new theatrical writing, particularly at the Kingsway, but also during the 1920s, and for her support and encouragement of women playwrights. In the short periods of her forays into theatrical management before the First World War, she presented at least fifteen new full-length or one-act plays. As a theatre and company manager she encouraged women to develop directorial and stage management skills. Her managerial innovations included the creation of repertory companies, support of young musicians and a genuine relationship with her audience and wider community. From as early as 1899 with her appearance in *Grierson's Way*, she used theatre to address the human condition, presenting and performing in such plays as *Leah Kleschna*, *The Shulamite*, *Irene Wycherley* and *The Earth*. Through the pursuit of a purposeful theatre, both as an actress and as a manager, she began to find and use her voice as an effective means to challenge the status quo both on and off the stage. Her role in the female suffrage fight has been given some acknowledgement, but accounts have failed to notice that Ashwell was one of the few AFL members who progressed quickly through the movement to emerge as an articulate spokeswoman on women's issues beyond the winning of the vote. She continued her advocacy for equality and shared responsibility until her death.

Ashwell's wartime achievements alone should have guaranteed recognition. Her swift and immediate reaction to the outbreak of war in 1914 provided hope and comfort to thousands of soldiers and hundreds of performers. Since the outbreak of the Second World War, governments have seen the need to provide comfort and morale boosters for troops in the form of entertainment, but even accounts of ENSA's creation imply that the idea was a new one in 1939.[49] Similar neglect can be found in accounts of public subsidy for the arts. Despite Ashwell's groundbreaking work with local councils during the 1920s and her consistent advocacy for government support as was being given elsewhere in Europe, historical accounts of the origins of the Arts Council of Great Britain (the principal state-supported arts funding body) consider 1930, with the creation of the Pilgrim Trust, to be the starting point.[50] No mention is made of Ashwell's initiatives, which provided practical examples

6.4 Bust of Ashwell stored at the National Theatre, 1994
(photograph by author)

of appropriate working relationships between arts and community, which are still part of the modus operandi of many regionally based arts organisations and local government authorities. These initiatives, together with her energetic involvement in the British Drama League, helped shape arts provision (now sadly much eroded by financial constraints) not only throughout Britain, but also, by example, especially after the Second World War, in Commonwealth countries as far afield as Australia. While Ashwell did not live to see the creation of either a National Theatre Company or its building, she was aware of the establishment, in 1940, of the Council for the Encouragement of Music and the Arts, which spent both charitable and public funds in support of the arts. It was not until 1948, nearly thirty years after she had shown the way, that government legislation gave local councils legal authority to encourage arts and entertainment. To this day, such funding is discretionary: arts can be supported, but such support is not a statutory requirement.[51]

Ashwell's memory has not fared well at the National Theatre. The bust stored in the Chairman's office there declares she was an 'Actress and Pioneer of a National Theatre', but she is not mentioned as such in any recent accounts of the theatre buildings and company situated on London's Southbank.[52]

It was not until many years after its completion in 1976 that the National Theatre began touring productions. More than fifty years before this, while others merely talked about it, Ashwell was on the road with her company, advocating a National Theatre as part of the provision of municipal theatre, and providing communities with access to a wide repertoire of plays. Despite her contribution, she has been neglected by social and theatre historians. Perhaps the original protagonists were embarrassed by her activity in the face of their own inertia. Similarly with arts in education: access to the arts in all forms is now an accepted part of formal education, but when Ashwell was a strong voice promoting both the credibility and the benefit of such access, there were many who resisted, either because they considered theatre lacked respectability or because it was outside of their interest or experience. Ashwell's awareness of the beneficial impact of good music and drama on the soldier heightened her determination to share this experience in the wider community, and she never missed an opportunity to promote this objective.

Ashwell was influential in changing attitudes and providing positive examples through her commitment to improving the conditions of work and status of actors. Throughout her career as an actress and manager she played an active role in professional organisations established to help members in pursuit of careers that have never provided much security or stability. Inspired by Henry Irving, she was not afraid to criticise anything she saw as working against the credibility of the profession, and she sought lively debate to ensure questions were asked and problems addressed. Even in retirement, enforced to a large extent by ill health, Ashwell advocated the presentation of drama as a way of stimulating positive attitudes and countering superficial and materialistic responses to a rapidly changing world. Throughout all her endeavours, she inspired the support of like-minded colleagues and was sustained by a close-knit family, a fulfilling marriage and strong religious beliefs.

Hers was a formidable spirit, and as John Masefield acknowledged, when dedicating his *Sonnets of Good Cheer* to the Lena Ashwell Players:

Generally, the inspiration of all little communities that are worth their salt and are doing memorable work, comes from one person … Inspiration is a vague word for several qualities; such as faith, that the work is worth doing; hope, that the world may some day know this; and courage, to keep the thing going, in the midst of adversity. It is always by such qualities of soul that the individual inspires the little band to go down into the trouble to alter the thought of the world.[53]

Notes

1   J.C. Trewin, *The Theatre Since 1900* (London, 1951), 139–41, 209.

2   Minutes, Carnegie Trust Music Sub-Committee meeting, 12 July 1929. Carnegie Trust files (Scottish Records Office, Edinburgh, GD 128/41/198).

3   London County Council minutes, 21 November 1933, indicate Ashwell was granted a licence until the end of 1934. The minutes of 10 July 1934 imply that while licences would continue to be granted, individual theatres would not be listed in the minutes, although it appears Ashwell relinquished the lease in 1935.

4   Work included the installation of a ceiling ventilation fan, a hot water system and a false proscenium on the stage.

5   Ashwell, *Myself a Player*, 277.

6   *Ibid.*, 278.

7   *Ibid.*, 278–9.

8   Haanel College and Metaphysical Seminary, Scottsdale, AZ, espousing the Universal Church of Metaphysical Practice, teaches courses using Mills' 1915 treatise, *A New Order of Meditation*.

9   *Dictionary of American Biography*, Supplement Four, 1946–1950, ed. J.A. Garraty and E.T. James (New York, 1974), 106. Bragdon wrote of his theatre experiences in *Merely Players* (New York, 1929).

10 Letters written between 28 February 1939 and 3 September 1946, shortly before his death, imply a more extensive correspondence (Lena Ashwell Papers, Department of Rare Books, Special Collections and Preservation, University of Rochester, Rochester, N.Y.).

11 Letter from Ashwell to Bragdon, 7 January 1940 (Lena Ashwell Papers, Department of Rare Books, Special Collections and Preservation, University of Rochester, Rochester, N.Y.).

12 *Times Literary Supplement*, 14 November 1936.

13 Moore, *Exits and Entrances*.

14 *Drama*, October 1929, 8.

15 *Drama*, October 1930, 11–12 (minutes of the eleventh AGM).

16 *Ibid.*

17 *Stage*, 28 November 1929.

18 London: BBC Sound Archive Collection, PB/TLO 4093; F 38/40; PF 12 FRH 93475/6, Mono Analogue.

19 Ashwell, *Myself A Player*, 266–7.

20 Letter from Ashwell to Bragdon, 28 February 1939 (Lena Ashwell Papers, Department of Rare Books, Special Collections and Preservation, University of Rochester, Rochester, N.Y.).

21 R. Fawkes, *Fighting for a Laugh* (London, 1978), 13. Dean's book, *The Theatre at War* (London, 1956), gives a detailed account of ENSA but only briefly acknowledges Ashwell's contribution.

22 *Ibid.*

23 From a conversation between Fiona Edwards and Henry Macnicol in Jamaica, March 1995, reported to the author.

24 *Drama*, Autumn 1946, 18.

25 At the Town Hall, Crayford, Kent, near to where in 1918 Whitworth had lectured and decided to establish the League.

26 This bust subsequently went to the National Theatre. A copy was displayed at the

Westminster Theatre library until 1999. It is now in the possession of Ashwell's niece, Daphne Waterston, Administration Secretary for MRA.

27 R. Hutchinson and A. Feist, *Amateur Arts in the UK* (London, 1991), 55–6.

28 *Picture Post*, 13 April 1940.

29 These letters are in the Victoria & Albert Museum – Theatre Museum. Fry's letters to Ashwell have not been located.

30 Letter from Ashwell to Fry, 6 April 1954.

31 C. Fry, *The Light is Dark Enough* (London, 1954).

32 Dated 23 September 1952 and 6 April 1954.

33 See 'Frank N.D. Buchman (1878–1961)', in *New Encyclopedia Britannica*, 15th edn (Chicago, 1998), vol. viii, 307.

34 Westminster Theatre programme for *Sentenced to Life* by Malcolm Muggeridge and Alan Thornhill, May 1978. Author's collection.

35 The Reverend Alan Thornhill's first MRA play, *The Forgotten Factor*, included Ashwell's nephew Henry in the cast for the Westminster production in 1948, and was premiered in 1943 in Washington, DC. Thornhill continued as a writer and churchman, travelling from Denmark to London in March 1957 to conduct Ashwell's memorial service.

36 H.W. (Bunny) Austin, *A Mixed Double* (London, 1969), 180.

37 Transcript, 20 March 1957 (Moral Re-Armament Archives).

38 This was written by the cast, previewed in Caux, 11 September 1947, and subsequently played in New York, Boston, Montreal, Washington, DC, Los Angeles and San Francisco, then in Switzerland, Holland, Germany and England.

39 Henry Macnicol, 'Some notes on Lena, Lady Simson and the Westminster Theatre', sent to the author in 1995.

40 From a transcript of Ashwell's speech, 25 March 1953 (Moral Re-Armament Archives).

41 From a transcript of Ashwell's speech, 10 May 1953 (Moral Re-Armament Archives).

42 Letter from Lena Ashwell and Hilda Pocock to the Women of Britain, 22 June 1953 (Moral Re-Armament Archives)

43 Transcript (Moral Re-Armament Archives).

44 Austin, *A Mixed Double*, 180.

45 *Times*, 15 March 1957.

46 Athene Seyler and Phyllis Whitworth paid tribute in *Drama*, 45 (Summer 1957), 35–6.

47 Transcripts (Moral Re-Armament Archives).

48 *Times*, 3 April 1957.

49 For example, in *The Greasepaint War* (London, 1976), J.G. Hughes writes: 'Although previous battles might well have been won without the help of troop concerts, what had been for centuries a minor inconvenience fought by hardened professionals became by the end of 1940 a universal death struggle … there developed among servicemen and war workers, in fact the whole population whose familiar world had crumbled, a longing to rediscover if only for an hour or two a magic enclave where war faded into insignificance' (56). He makes no mention of Ashwell's work in the First World War.

50 E.W. White, *The Arts Council of Great Britain* (London, 1975), Chapters 1 and 2.

51 For further information, see (Lord) J. Redcliffe-Maud, *Support for the Arts in England & Wales: A Report to the Calouste Gulbenkian Foundation* (London, 1976), 102.

52 Laurence Olivier was the first director of the National Theatre in 1963. Although late in life he could smile about the inauspicious start to his career with Ashwell's company, his and subsequent managements have not acknowledged her contribution, which seems ungenerous and neglectful.

53 Masefield, preface to *Sonnets of Good Cheer*.

Appendix 1

Ashwell as actress: plays, roles and theatres in which she appeared

Roles are in **bold**

30 March	1891	*The Pharisee* by Malcolm Watson and Mrs Ellen Lancaster-Wallis, **Martin**, Islington Grand.
June	1891	*That Dreadful Doctor* by Charles Young, **Mrs Beauchamp**, on tour Cambridge, then Opera Comique.
November	1891	*Through the Fire* by W. Lestocq & Yorke Stephens, **Dolly**; *Two in the Bush* by Murray Carson, **Nettie Carr**; *Gloriana* by James Mortimer, **understudy**, Globe.
December	1891	*The Reckoning* by Silvanus Dauncey, **Mrs Chilcot**, Globe.
Summer	1892	*Lady Windermere's Fan* by Oscar Wilde on tour.
25 March	1893	*Man and Woman* by Henry C. de Mille and David Belasco, **Dora Prescott**, Opera Comique.
30 September	1893	*Sowing the Wind* by Sydney Grundy, **understudy**; and the curtain-raiser, *In Strict Confidence* by Paul Heriot, Comedy.
December	1893	*The Piper of Hamelin* by Robert Buchanan, **Liza**, Comedy.
February	1894	*Dick Sheridan* by Robert Buchanan, **Lady Pamela**, Comedy.
March	1894	*Frou-Frou* by Henri Meilhac and Ludovic Halevy, **Pauline** and **Gilberte Brigard**, Comedy.
17 May	1894	*Marriage* by Brandon Thomas and H. Keeling, **Lady Belton**, Royal Court.
13 August	1894	*Sowing the Wind* by Sydney Grundy, **Rosamund**, Gaiety, Dublin and on tour.
12 January	1895	*King Arthur* by J. Comyns Carr, **Elaine**, Lyceum.
22 May	1895	*The Prude's Progress* by Jerome K. Jerome and Eden Phillpotts, **Nelly Morris**, Comedy.
15 June	1895	*A Practical Joker* by C.L. Hume, **Sybil**, Comedy.

September	1895	*Her Advocate* by Walter Frith, **Blanche Ferraby**, Duke of York's.
31 January	1896	*The Fool of the Family* by Fergus Hume, **Kitty Trevor**, Duke of York's.
May	1896	*A Match-maker* by Clotilde Graves and Gertrude Kingston, **Margaretta**, Shaftesbury.
6 June	1896	*Carmen* adapted by Henry Hamilton from novel by Prosper Mérimée, **Dolores**, Gaiety.
19 December	1896	*Richard III* by William Shakespeare, **Edward, Prince of Wales, Lady Anne**, Lyceum.
February	1897	*Delicate Ground* by Charles Dance, **Pauline**, Terry's.
17 August	1897	*The Sleeping Partner* by L'Arronge and Martha Morton, **Nellie Bassett**, Criterion.
18 October	1897	*The Vagabond King* by Louis N. Parker, **Stella Desmond**, Metropole and Royal Court.
January	1898	*Sweet Nancy* adapted by Robert Buchanan from novel by Rhoda Broughton, **Barbara Gray**, Avenue.
5 March	1898	*The Sea Flower* by Arthur Law, **Mrs Trafford**, Comedy.
6 November	1898	*The Broad Road* by Robert Marshall, **Cecilia Melville**, Terry's.
24 December	1898	*The Crystal Globe*, Sutton Vane's adaptation of the novel *La Joueuse D'Orgue* by Xavier de Montépin, **Claire Sollier**, Princess.
7 February	1899	*Grierson's Way* by H.V. Esmond, **Pamela**, Haymarket Royal.
March	1899	*The Mayflower* by Louis N. Parker, **Joan Mallory**, Royal Court.
23 May	1899	*Wheels Within Wheels* by R.C. Carton, **Lady Curtois**, Royal Court.
7 October	1899	*Man and His Makers* by Louis N. Parker and Wilson Barrett, **Sylvia Faber**, Lyceum.
10 March	1900	*Bonnie Dundee* by Laurence Irving, **Lady Jean Cochrane**, Adelphi.
5 May	1900	*Quo Vadis* adapted by Stanislaus Stange from Henryk Sienkiewicz's novel, **Lygia**, Adelphi.
7 September	1900	*Julius Caesar* by William Shakespeare, **Portia**, Her Majesty's.
9 October	1900	*Mrs Dane's Defence* by Henry Arthur Jones, **Mrs Dane**, Wyndham's.

10 October	1901	*The Mummy and the Humming Bird* by Isaac Henderson, **Lady Lumley**, Wyndham's.
1 March	1902	*Caesar's Wife*, trans. of *L'Enigme* by Paul Hervieu, **Leonore de Gourgiran**, Wyndham's.
5 June	1902	*Mrs Dane's Defence* revival, **Mrs Dane**, Wyndham's.
9 September	1902	*Chance the Idol* by Henry Arthur Jones, **Ellen Farndon**, Wyndham's.
12 December	1902	*Othello* by William Shakespeare, **Emilia**, Lyric.
17 February	1903	*Resurrection* adapted by Henry Bataille and Michael Morton from novel by Leo Tolstoy, **Katusha**, His Majesty's.
30 April	1903	*Dante* by M.M. Sardou and E. Moreau, trans. Laurence Irving, **Pia del Tolomei** and **Gemma**, Royal, Drury Lane.
28 December	1903	*The Darling of the Gods* by David Belasco and John Luther Long, **Yo-San**, His Majesty's.
5 September	1904	*Marguerite* adapted by Michael Morton from *La Montansier* by G.A. de Caillavet, Robert de Flers and M. Jeoffrin, **Marguerite**, Coronet and on tour.
2 May	1905	*Leah Kleschna* by C.S. McLellan, **Leah**, New.
19 April	1906	*The Bond of Ninon* by Clothilde Graves, **Ninon de L'Enclos**, Savoy.
12 May	1906	*The Shulamite* adapted by Edward Knoblock from novel by Claude and Alice Askew, **Deborah Krillet**, Savoy and American tour.
22 January	1907	*The Undercurrent* by Victor Mapes, Studebaker, Chicago.
9 October	1907	*Irene Wycherley* by A.P. Wharton, **Irene Wycherley**, Kingsway.
12 February	1908	*Diana of Dobson's* by Cicely Hamilton, **Diana Massingberd**, Kingsway.
9 October	1908	*The Sway Boat* by Wilfred T. Coleby, **Lady Kilross**, Kingsway.
24 November	1908	*Grit* by H. Herman Chilton, **Erith Winter**, Kingsway.
11 February	1909	*The Truants* by Wilfred T. Coleby, **Freda Saville**, Kingsway.
14 April	1909	*The Earth* by J.B. Fagan, **Countess of Killone**, Kingsway.
1 September	1909	*Madame X* by Alexander Bisson, **Jacqueline Fleuriot**, Globe.
8 November	1909	*The Great Mrs Alloway* by Douglas Murray, **Mrs Hartland**, Globe.

23 February	1910	*Misalliance* by George Bernard Shaw, **Lina**, Duke of York's.
1 March	1910	*The Twelve Pound Look* and *Old Friends* by J.M. Barrie, **Kate** and **Mrs Brand**, Duke of York's.
16 January	1911	*Judith Zaraine* by C.M.S. McLellan, **Judith**, Astor, New York.
10 April	1911	*The Master of Mrs Chilvers* by Jerome K. Jerome, **Annys Chilvers**, Kings, Glasgow and Royalty, London.
3 May	1911	*As You Like It* by William Shakespeare, **Rosalind**, Stratford Shakespeare Festival.
8 May	1911	*The First Actress* by Christopher St John, Kingsway.
19 May	1911	*The Hue and Cry After Cupid* by Ben Jonson, **Juno**, St James's.
27 June	1911	*The Vision of Delight* by Ben Jonson, **Phantasy**, His Majesty's.
2 October	1911	*The Man in the Stalls* by Alfred Sutro, Palace.
4 December	1911	*The Twelve Pound Look* by J. M. Barrie, **Kate**, Portman Rooms, London.
9 February	1912	*Shakespeare's Dream*, **Ophelia**, New Princess.
February	1912	*The Constant Husband* by Cicely Hamilton, Palladium.
February	1912	*A Pageant of the Stage* by Christopher St John, Royal Albert Hall.
16 May	1912	*Mrs Dane's Defence* by H.A. Jones, **Mrs Dane**, New.
8 December	1913	*Woman on Her Own*, trans. by Charlotte Shaw of Brieux's *La Femme Seule*, **Thérese**, Coronet.
13 February	1915	*Fanny's First Play* by George Bernard Shaw, **Margaret Knox**, Kingsway.
19 April	1915	*The Debt* by W.T. Coleby, Coliseum.
13 September	1915	*The Twelve Pound Look* by J.M. Barrie, **Kate**, Coliseum.
16 October	1915	*Iris Intervenes* by John Hastings Turner, **Iris Olga Iranovna**, Kingsway.
8 January	1925	*The Ship* by St. John Ervine, **Old Mrs Thurlow**, Century and on tour.
December	1928	*Their Business in Great Waters*, Lyceum.
14 July	1950	*Annie The Valiant* by Alan Thornhill, **Lady Arlington**, Caux, Switzerland.
January	1951	*Annie The Valiant* by Alan Thornhill, **Lady Arlington**, Lisner Auditorium, Washington, DC.

Appendix 2

Lena Ashwell Players: touring schedule 1919–1929

VENUE	1919	1920			1921			1922		
	AUT	SPR	SUM	AUT	SPR	SUM	AUT	SPR	SUM	AUT
Bethnall Green, Excelsior Hall	■	■								
Hanwell, Park Theatre		■								
Battersea, Town Hall				•	•		•	•		•
Stepney, People's Palace				•						
Canning Town, Public Hall							•	•		•
Clerkenwell, Northampton Institute				▲	▲					
Mary Ward Settlement, WC1							▲	▲		▲
Newington, Public Hall				▲						
Shoreditch, Town Hall				•						
Greenwich, Borough Hall					•		•	•		•
Fulham, Town Hall					•	•				
Deptford, Borough Hall							•	•		•
Camberwell, Old Kent Rd Baths							•	•		•
Camberwell, Surrey Masonic Hall										
Eltham, Parish Hall								•		
Blackheath, Concert Hall										▲
Brockley, St Cyprian's Hall										
Lewisham, Ladywell Baths										
Ealing, Longfield Hall										•
Sutton, Public Hall										•
Watford, St John's Hall										•
Watford, St Michael's Hall										▲
Harrow, Victoria Hall										•
Northwood, Central Hall										
Ilford, Town Hall										
Chiswick, Empire Theatre										▲
Westminster, Cathedral Hall										▲
Notting Hill, Century Theatre										
Hackney, King's Hall										
Edmonton, Town Hall										
Edmonton, Empire Theatre										
Enfield, Assembly Rooms										
Winchmore Hill, St Paul's Institute										
Holloway, Northern Polytech Inst.										
Hampstead Garden Suburb, Club										•
Cricklewood, St Gabriel's Hall										
Hounslow, Holy Trinity Hall										
Staines, Town Hall										
Streatham, Parish Hall										
Dulwich, Public Baths										•
Beckenham, Grand Hall Baths										
Llanelly, Hippodrome			■							
Jersey, Opera House										
Brighton, West Pier Theatre										
Eastbourne, Pier Theatre										
Rugby, Prince of Wales Theatre										
Scarborough, Grand Opera House									■	
Leeds, Little Theatre										
York, Theatre Royal										
Bath, Theatre Royal									■	

• Weekly; ■ Daily; ▲ Occasional

SPR = Spring; SUM = Summer; AUT = Autumn

1923			1924			1925			1926			1927			1928			1929	
SPR	SUM	AUT	SPR	SUM	AUT	SPR	SUM	AUT	SPR	SUM	AUT	SPR	SUM	AUT	SPR	SUM	AUT	SPR	SUM

Appendix 3

Lena Ashwell Players: repertoire

Title and genre	Author	Year written, or first performed/ published	Cast as performed by the Players Male: M Female: F	When performed by Lena Ashwell Players * Also presented by wartime Concert Parties, 1915–19
9.45 Melodrama	Owen Davis & Sewell Collins	1925	10M, 6F	January 1929
Abraham Lincoln Drama	John Drinkwater	1918	42 M&F	January 1928
Admiral Guinea Drama	R.L. Stevenson & W.E Henley	1884	3M, 2F	March 1921
The Adventures of Lady Ursula Comedy	Anthony Hope	1898	12M, 3F	October 1928
Advertisement Drama	B. MacDonald Hastings	1915	10M, 4F	October 1927
All of a Sudden Peggy Comedy	Ernest Denny	1906	6M, 5F	May 1923
Ann Farce	Lechmere Worrall	1912	3M, 3F	April 1924
Arms and the Man Comedy	G.B. Shaw	1894	4M, 3F	February 1921, April 1922
As You Like It Comedy	W. Shakespeare	1600	16M, 4F	January 1923, February 1926

Title and genre	Author	Year	Cast (M/F)	When performed
At Mrs Beam's Comedy	C.K. Munro	1923	4M, 7F	December 1928
At the Barn Romance	Anthony Wharton	1912	7M, 4F	March 1928
The Bathroom Door Farce	Gertrude Jennings	1916	3M, 3F	*April 1921, March 1922
The Beggar Prince Children's parable	Cicely Hamilton	1922	4M, 3F + children	January 1923, January 1924
Belinda Romance	A.A. Milne	1918	3M, 3F	December 1923
Bernice Drama	Susan Glaspell	1915	2M, 3F	July 1927
A Bill of Divorcement Drama	Clemence Dane	1921	5M, 4F	January 1924
The Bishop's Candlesticks Drama	Norman McKinnel	1901	3M, 2F	*April 1921
The Blindness of Virtue Romance	Cosmo Hamilton	1913	3M, 5F	January 1922
Bought and Paid For Drama	George Broadhurst	1911	4M, 3F	Summer 1923
The Brave and the Fair Drama	Cicely Hamilton	1920	3M, 3F	April 1923
Bulldog Drummond Adventure	'Sapper' (Cyril McNeile) & Gerald du Maurier	1921	14M, 2F	January 1929

Title and genre	Author	Year	Cast (M/F)	When performed
The Butterfly on the Wheel Drama	Edward Hemmerde & Francis Neilson	1911	12M, 3F	November 1927
Caesar's Wife Comedy	W.S. Maugham	1919	5M, 4F	Century Theatre, 1925/6, December 1928
Candida Mystery	G.B. Shaw	1895	4M, 2F	*January 1922
Captain Drew on Leave Comedy	Hubert Henry Davies	1905	4M, 2F	March 1922
Caroline Comedy	W.S. Maugham	1916	3M, 4F	*April 1924
The Case of Lady Camber Comedy	Horace Annesley Vachell	1915	4M, 4F	November 1921
The Case of Rebellious Susan Comedy	H.A. Jones	1894	7M, 5F	February 1928, Summer 1928
Caste Comedy	T.W. Robertson	1867	5M, 3F	March 1924, April 1929
The Celluloid Cat Drama	R. Pocock & L. Ashwell	1924	7M, 2F	March 1924
The Charity that Began at Home Comedy	St John Hankin	1906	6M, 6F	December 1925
The Child in Flanders Nativity	Cicely Hamilton	1917	4M, 3F, 1 boy	*December 1920, 1921, 1923, 1924

Title and genre	Author	Year	Cast (M/F)	When performed
A Christmas Carol	C. Dickens, adapt. Beatrice Wilson	1923		December 1923
Come Out of the Kitchen Comedy	Albert Ellsworth Thomas	1916	6M, 5F	November 1926, Summer 1927
Cook Comedy	Jerome K. Jerome	1917		January 1925
The Country Wife Comedy	W. Wycherley	1675	6M, 3F	January, July 1924, Summer 1925
Cousin Kate Comedy	Hubert Henry Davies	1903	3M, 4F	*December 1922
The Cricket on the Hearth Fairy tale	C. Dickens, adapt. Marion Fawcett	1922	4M, 6F	December 1922
Crime And Punishment Drama	Adapt. L. Ashwell & R. Pocock	1926	8M, 3F	February 1927
Cupid and Common Sense Drama	Arnold Bennett	1908	3M, 6F	April 1922
Cupid and the Styx Comedy	J. Sackville Martin	1909		*March 1921
Daddy Long Legs Romance	Jean Webster	1914	6M, 8F + children	December 1927, Summer 1928
Dandy Dick Farce	A.W. Pinero	1887	7M, 4F	December 1924, Summer 1925

Title and genre	Author	Year	Cast (M/F)	When performed
The Dark Lady of the Sonnets Interlude	G.B. Shaw	1910	2M, 2F	May 1924
David Garrick Comedy	T.W. Robertson	1864	9M, 4F	November 1922
The Death of Tintagiles Drama	Maurice Maeterlinck	1922	1M, 6F, 1 boy	February 1926
The Devil's Disciple Melodrama	G.B. Shaw	1897	10M, 3F	May 1924
Diana Of Dobson's Comedy	Cicely Hamilton	1908	4M, 7F	April 1922, April 1924
Diplomacy Romance	Victorien Sardou	1924	7M, 5F	November 1927, Summer 1928
The Doctor's Dilemma Tragedy	G.B. Shaw	1906	11M, 3F	July 1925
A Doll's House Drama	H. Ibsen	1879	3M, 3F, extras + children	December 1923
Doormats Comedy	Hubert Henry Davies	1912	3M, 3F	February 1923
The Dover Road Comedy	A.A. Milne	1922	4M, 2F	October 1925
Dr Jekyll and Mr Hyde Drama	Adapt. L. Ashwell & R. Pocock	1927	8M, 3F	March 1927
The Duke of Killiecrankie Comedy	Robert Marshall	1904	4M, 4F	October 1921

Title and genre	Author	Year	Cast (M/F)	When performed
The Earth Drama	J.B. Fagan	1909	7M, 5F	April and June 1925
The Easiest Way Drama	Eugene Walter	1908	3M, 3F	October 1922
The Education of Mr Surrage Comedy	Allan Monkhouse	1912	5M, 3F	October 1925
The Elder Miss Blossom Comedy	Ernest Hendrie & Metcalfe Wood	1898	At least 2M, 2F	November 1922
Eliza Comes to Stay Farce	H.V. Esmond	1913	5M, 4F	November 1928
The Enchanted Cottage Fable	A.W. Pinero	1921	4M, 5F	July 1929
An Enemy of the People Drama	H. Ibsen	1882	7M, 2F, 2 boys	November 1925
Everyman Mediaeval Mystery	Attributed to Peter Dorlandus	Early 16th century	17M&F	March 1921
The Fake Drama	Frederick Lonsdale	1924	7M, 5F	October 1926
Fallen Angels Drama	Michael Morton & Peter Traill	1924	4M, 3F	October 1924
Fame and the Poet Satire	Lord Dunsany		2M, 1F	August 1926
A Family Man Drama	J. Galsworthy	1921	10M, 5F	February 1925

Title and genre	Author	Year	Cast (M/F)	When performed
Fanny and the Servant Problem Comedy	Jerome K. Jerome	1909	5M, 6F	January 1926
Fanny's First Play Satire	G.B. Shaw	1911	5M, 4F	January 1921, December 1922
Five Birds in a Cage Comedy	Gertrude Jennings	1915	3M, 2F	*December 1922
Five Minutes Fast Comedy	Michael Morton	1925	2M, 6F	February 1925
French Leave Comedy	Reginald Berkeley	1920	6M, 2F	January, April 1928
The Fugitive Drama	J. Galsworthy	1913	8M, 7F	April 1927
The Gay Lord Quex Comedy	A.W. Pinero	1899	4M, 10F	March 1921, January 1929
Getting Married Comedy	G.B. Shaw	1908	8M, 5F	May 1923
Good Friday Drama	J. Masefield	1917	7M, 1F	April 1925
The Grain of Mustard Seed Drama	H.M. Harwood	1920	10M, 3F	October 1924
The Great Adventure Comedy	Arnold Bennett	1913	8M, 4F	October 1925
The Great Broxopp Satire	A.A. Milne	1923	5M, 5F	April 1928, Summer 1928

Title and genre	Author	Year	Cast (M/F)	When performed
The Green Goddess Romance	William Archer	1921	7M, 2F	February 1929
Hamlet Tragedy	W. Shakespeare	1602	20M, 2F	November 1924
Hayfever Comedy	Noel Coward	1925	4M, 5F	February 1927
Her Husband's Wife Comedy	A.E. Thomas	1916	3M, 4F	January 1925, Summer 1925
Hindle Wakes Drama	Stanley Houghton	1912	4M, 5F	October 1926
His Excellency the Governor Farce	Robert Marshall	1901	7M, 5F	*March 1922, October 1924
His House in Order Comedy	A.W. Pinero	1906	6M, 7F	November 1921
His Own Drama	Evelyn Greenleaf Sutherland	1926	2M, 1F, 1 boy	February 1926
Hobson's Choice Comedy	Harold Brighouse	1915	7M, 5F	March 1924
The House with the Twisty Windows Drama	Mary Pakington	1926	4M, 3F	April 1926
How He Lied to Her Husband Comedy	G.B. Shaw	1907	2M, 1F	February 1925
Husbands are a Problem Comedy	Harris Deans	1922	4M, 4F	February 1926

Title and genre	Author	Year	Cast (M/F)	When performed
If Four Walls Told Drama	Edward Percy	1922	5M, 5F	February 1928
I'll Leave it to You Comedy	Noel Coward	1920	4M, 6F	March 1929
The Importance of Being Earnest Comedy	O. Wilde	1895	5M, 4F	*April 1921, December 1924, Summer 1925
In the Night Melodrama	Cyril Harcourt	1919	4M, 1F	January 1925
The Invisible Foe Drama	Walter Hackett	1917	3M, 2F	April 1923
The Iron Hand Drama	H. Caine	1916	2M, 2F	June 1923
It Pays to Advertise Farce	Walter Hackett & Roi Cooper Megrue	1914	8M, 4F	February 1929
Jane Clegg Drama	St John G. Ervine	1913	3M, 2F, 2 children	November 1926
John Drayton, Millionaire Drama	Henry Mackinnon Walbrook	1925	5M, 2F	November 1925
John Glayde's Honour Drama	Alfred Sutro	1907	6M, 5F	April 1922
Julius Caesar Tragedy	W. Shakespeare	1599	13M, 4F	November 1925
Just to Get Married Drama	Cicely Hamilton	1910	4M, 5F	*February 1921, March 1925

Title and genre	Author	Year	Cast (M/F)	When performed
King John Drama	W. Shakespeare	1594	11M, 7F	March 1925
The Kiss Cure Comedy	Ronald Jeans	1914	4M, 2F	December 1924
A Kiss for Cinderella Fantasy	J.M. Barrie	1916	10M, 12F	January 1929
Lady Frederick Comedy	W. Somerset Maugham	1907	7M, 5F	December 1920
Lady Inger of Ostraat Drama	H. Ibsen	1854	7M, 2F	October 1927
Lady Patricia Comedy	Rudolf Besier	1911	6M, 3F	January 1926
Lady Windermere's Fan Comedy	O. Wilde	1892	7M, 9F	January 1923
The Land of Promise Comedy	W. Somerset Maugham	1914	7M, 6F	February 1927
The Last of Mrs Cheyney Comedy	Frederick Lonsdale	1925	8M, 6F	September 1928
The Laughing Lady Comedy	Alfred Sutro	1922	5M, 5F	October 1925
Leah Kleschna Drama	C.M.S. McLellan	1904	7M, 3F	October 1920, October 1922, October 1924
The Liars Comedy	H.A. Jones	1897	10M, 6F	November 1923

Title and genre	Author	Year	Cast (M/F)	When performed
The Likes of Her/'Er Drama	Charles McEvoy	1923	5M, 5F	February 1923, March 1926
The Lilies of the Field Comedy	John Hastings Turner	1923	4M, 7F	March 1929
The Lion and the Mouse Drama	Charles Klein	1905	10M, 8F	March 1922
The Little Minister Comedy	J.M. Barrie	1897	10M, 5F	November 1926, Summer 1927
Lord Richard in the Pantry Farce	Sydney Blow & Douglas Hoare	1919	6M, 6F	December 1927, Summer 1928
The Lost Leader Drama	Lennox Robinson	1919	11M, 2F	March 1925
Macbeth Tragedy	W. Shakespeare	1606	21M, 7F	*October 1924
Magda Drama	Hermann Suderman	1902	6M, 6F	October 1928
Magic A Fantastic Comedy	G.K. Chesterton	1913	6M, 1F	October 1926
The Magistrate Farce	A.W. Pinero	1885	10M, 4F	January 1927, Summer 1927
Man and Superman Comedy	G.B. Shaw	1903	7M, 6F	February 1924
The Man from Hong Kong Drama	Mrs Clifford Mills	1925	10M, 5F	June 1929

Title and genre	Author	Year	Cast (M/F)	When performed
The Man from Toronto Comedy	Douglas Murray	1918	3M, 6F	November 1923
The Man of Destiny Comedy	G.B. Shaw	1896	3M, 1F	January 1923
The Man Who Stayed at Home Drama	Lechmere Worrall & J.E. Harold Terry	1914	6M, 6F	March 1923
The Marriage of Columbine Comedy	Harold Chapin	1910	4M, 5F, 1 boy	March 1927
The Marriage of Kitty Comedy	Fred Gresac, F.de Croisset, adapt. Cosmo Gordon-Lennox	1902	4M, 3F	*December 1922
Mary Goes First Comedy	H.A. Jones	1913	8M, 4F	October 1927
Mary, Mary, Quite Contrary Comedy	St John G. Ervine	1923	5M, 5F	February 1928
The Master Builder Drama	H. Ibsen	1892	4M, 3F	January 1927
The Merchant of Venice Drama	W. Shakespeare	1595	13M, 4F	*April 1921, April 1923
Merely Mary Ann Comedy	Israel Zangwill	1903	8M, 11F	October 1922
The Merry Wives of Windsor Comedy	W. Shakespeare	1599	16M, 4F	January 1924

Title and genre	Author	Year	Cast (M/F)	When performed
A Message from Mars Drama	Richard Ganthony	1899	21 characters	December 1921, December 1927
Milestones Comedy	Arnold Bennett & Edward Knoblock	1912	9M, 6F	October 1923
The Mirror for Souls Mediaeval mystery	Anon.			April 1924
Misalliance Comedy	G.B. Shaw	1910	6M, 3F	December 1925
Miss Hobbs Comedy	Jerome K. Jerome	1899	5M, 4F	December 1926
The Mock Doctor Comedy	Molière, adapt. Henry Fielding	1732	8M, 3F	March 1922
The Mollusc Romance	Hubert Henry Davies	1907	2M, 2F	*March 1927
Money Doesn't Matter Comedy	Gertrude Jennings	1922	2M, 4F	February 1926
The Morals of Marcus (Ordeyne) Romance	William J. Locke	1906	2M, 3F	March 1924
Mr Abdulla Mystery	Reginald Berkeley	1926	At least 3M, 3F	February 1928
Mr Hopkinson Farce	R.C. Carton	1905	8M, 3F	December 1921
Mr Preedy and the Countess Farce	R.C. Carton	1909	9M, 4F	November 1927

Title and genre	Author	Year	Cast (M/F)	When performed
Mrs Dane's Defence Drama	H.A. Jones	1900	8M, 4F	October 1922
Mrs Dot Farce	W.S. Maugham	1908	8M, 4F	September 1927
Mrs Gorringe's Necklace Comedy	Hubert Henry Davies	1903	5M, 5F	October 1920, December 1922
Much Ado About Nothing Comedy	W. Shakespeare	1599	14M, 4F	October 1921
My Lady's Dress Drama	Edward Knoblock	1914	1M, 4F	December 1926
The Naked Truth Comedy	George Paston (Evelyn Symonds) & W.B. Maxwell	1910	7M, 6F	November 1923
The New Morality Comedy	Harold Chapin	1920	4M, 3F	January 1926
Niobe Comedy	Harry & Edward Paulton	1892	5M, 6F	February 1922
Nobody's Daughter Drama	George Paston (Evelyn Symonds)	1910	5M, 4F	March 1923
Nocturne One-act drama	A.P. Wharton	1913	2M, 3F	December 1921
O'Flaherty, VC Drama	G.B. Shaw	1915	2M, 2F	March 1921
Othello Tragedy	W. Shakespeare	1604	10M, 3F	February 1924

Title and genre	Author	Year	Cast (M/F)	When performed
Our Boys Comedy	H.J. Byron	1875	6M, 4F	November 1920
Our Flat Farce	Mrs Musgrave	1889	4M, 3F	March 1929
Outward Bound Drama	Sutton Vane	1923	6M, 3F	October 1927
A Pair of Silk Stockings Comedy	Cyril Harcourt	1914	8M, 6F	Season 1924/5
A Pair of Spectacles Comedy	Sydney Grundy	1890	8M, 3F	February 1921
Paolo & Francesca Tragedy	Stephen Phillips	1902	8M, 7F	November 1922
Passers By Drama	C. Haddon Chambers	1911	4M, 4F, 1 boy	October 1922
The Passing of the Third Floor Back Fantasy	Jerome K. Jerome	1908	6M, 6F	March 1928
The Pelican Drama	F. Tennyson Jesse & H.M. Harwood	1924	7M, 4F	December 1928
Peter's Mother Drama	Mrs Henry de la Pasture	1906	6M, 5F	February 1926
The Pigeon Fantasy	J. Galsworthy	1912	7M, 2F	October 1926
Mr Pim Passes By Comedy	A.A. Milne	1920	3M, 4F	February 1924

Title and genre	Author	Year	Cast (M/F)	When performed
Postal Orders Farce	Roland Pertwee	1916	1M, 4F	February 1922
Priscilla Runs Away Romance	Countess Elizabeth von Arnim	1910	4/5M, 4F	February 1927
The Professor's Love Story Comedy	J.M. Barrie	1894	7M, 5F	January, April 1928
The Proposal Comedy	A. Chekhov	1889	2M, 1F	January 1926
Prunella (Or Love in a Dutch Garden) Romance	Laurence Housman & H. Granville-Barker	1904	11M, 10F	October 1921
The Purse Strings Comedy	Judge Parry	1919	3M, 3F	February 1924
Pygmalion Comedy	G.B. Shaw	1914	8M, 7F	December 1921, November 1923
Quality Street Comedy	J.M. Barrie	1902	6M, 9F	December 1927
Raffles, The Amateur Cracksman Adventure	E.W. Hornung & Eugene Pressbrey	1906		March 1926
The Rat Melodrama	David Lestrange (Ivor Novello & Constance Collier)	1924	At least 2M, 3F	February 1929

Title and genre	Author	Year	Cast (M/F)	When performed
Remnant Romance	Dario Niccodemi & Michael Morton	1917	5M, 3F	June 1923
The Rest Cure Comedy	Gertrude Jennings	1914	1M, 4F	*April 1921
The Rivals Comedy	R.B. Sheridan	1775	8M, 5F	March 1923
Robin Hood Drama	Alfred Noyes	1908	10M, 11F	January 1927
The Romantic Age Romance	A.A. Milne	1920	5M, 4F	February 1925, Summer 1926
The Romantic Young Lady Romance	G.M. Sierra, trans. Helen & H. Granville-Barker	1918	5M, 6F	February 1922, March 1923
Romeo and Juliet Tragedy	W. Shakespeare	1593	17M, 4F	March 1929
Rookery Nook Farce	Ben Travers	1926	5M, 6F	November 1928
Rutherford and Son Drama	Githa Sowerby	1912	4M, 4F	January 1923
A Safety Match Drama	Ian Hay	1921	17M, 8F	April 1925
The School for Scandal Comedy	R.B. Sheridan	1777	12M, 4F	*March 1922
The Schoolmistress Farce	A.W. Pinero	1886	9M, 7F	February, July 1929

Title and genre	Author	Year	Cast (M/F)	When performed
The Second Mrs Tanqueray Drama	A.W. Pinero	1893	7M, 4F	March 1928
Sherlock Holmes Drama	Arthur Conan Doyle & William Gillette		16M, 5F	March 1928
She Stoops to Conquer Comedy	O. Goldsmith	1773	6M, 4F	*January 1922, May 1923, November 1928
The Ship Tragedy	St John G. Ervine	1925	4M, 4F	January 1925
Shortage Comedy	W.T. Coleby	1920	6M, 4F	October 1920
The Sign on the Door Drama	Channing Pollock	1921	8M, 4F	October 1928
The Silver Box Drama	J. Galsworthy	1906	11M, 6F	January 1926, Summer 1927
The Skin Game Tragicomedy	J. Galsworthy	1920	8M, 5F	February 1924
Smith Satire	W.S. Maugham	1909	4M, 4F	*February 1923
Sowing the Wind Drama	Sydney Grundy	1893	8M, 4F	November 1921
The Sport of Kings Comedy	Ian Hay	1924	8M, 6F	January 1928, Summer 1928
Stolen Fruit Drama	Cyril Twyford	1923		June 1923

Title and genre	Author	Year	Cast (M/F)	When performed
Sweet Lavender Drama	A.W. Pinero	1888	7M, 4F	December 1921
The Taming of the Shrew Comedy	W. Shakespeare	1596	12M, 3F	*January 1922, October 1923
The Tempest Drama	W. Shakespeare	1611	17M, 1F	October 1925
The Thief Drama	Henri Bernstein, adapt. Haddon Chambers	1907	5M, 2F	May 1922
The Third Degree or *Find the Woman* Melodrama	Charles Klein	1912	5M, 2F	November 1924 (*Find the Woman*), November 1928 (*The Third Degree*)
The Thirteenth Chair Mystery	Bayard Veiller	1917	10M, 7F	November 1927, Summer 1928
Three Wise Fools Comedy	Austin Strong	1919	11M, 2F	April 1926
Tilly of Bloomsbury Romance	Ian Hay	1919	8M, 7F	January 1926, Summer 1926
To Have the Honour Comedy	A.A. Milne	1924	5M, 6F	December 1926
Tons of Money Farce	Will Evans & Valentine (Archibald Thomas Pechey)	1914	6M, 4F	October 1928

Title and genre	Author	Year	Cast (M/F)	When performed
The Toymaker of Nuremburg Romance	Austin Strong	1910	12M, 3F, + children	December 1926
The Tragedy of Nan Drama	J. Masefield	1908	7M, 5F	March 1925
Trelawny of the Wells Romance	A.W. Pinero	1898	10M, 7F + children	November 1926
Trilby Drama	George du Maurier, adapt. Paul Potter	1895	9M, 5F	February 1921, February 1922, May 1923, December 1926, Summer 1927
Tristan and Isolt Tragedy	J. Masefield	1927	8M, 8F	February 1927
The Truth about Blayds Drama	A.A. Milne	1921	4M, 4F	October 1924, Summer 1925
Twelfth Night Comedy	W. Shakespeare	1600	11M, 3F	*January 1921, March 1922, November 1923
The Tyranny of Tears Comedy	C. Haddon Chambers	1899	4M, 3F	*October 1921
The Unfair Sex Farce	Eric Hudson	1925	4M, 4F	March 1929
The Vagabond King Drama	Louis N. Parker	1897	8M, 5F	March 1926
The Walls of Jericho Drama	Alfred Sutro	1904	6M, 4F	January 1921

Title and genre	Author	Year	Cast (M/F)	When performed
The Ware Case Drama	George Pleydell	1915	9M, 3F	March 1927, Summer 1927
What Every Woman Knows Drama	J.M. Barrie	1908	8M, 3F	October 1925, Summer 1926
What Might Happen Extravaganza	Henry Francis Maltby	1926	5M, 4F	November 1928
Wheels Within Wheels Comedy	R.C. Carton	1899	7M, 3F	November 1924
The Whiteheaded Boy Drama	Lennox Robinson	1916	5M, 7F	October 1926, Summer 1927
Widowers' Houses Drama	G.B. Shaw	1892	5M, 2F	November 1922
Wife to a Famous Man Drama	G.M. Sierra, trans. Helen & H. Granville-Barker	1914	8M, 6F	February 1925, Summer 1926
A Winter's Tale Drama	W. Shakespeare	1610	12M, 6F	January 1925
The Witch Drama	H. Wiers-Jenssen, trans. J. Masefield	1917	7M, 5F	March 1926, Summer 1926
Witness for the Defence Drama	A.E.W. Mason	1911	8M, 2F	April 1924
The Woman in the Case Drama	Clyde Fitch	1905	4M, 3F	February 1922

Title and genre	Author	Year	Cast (M/F)	When performed
A Woman of No Importance Drama	O. Wilde	1893	8M, 7F	March 1928
Woman to Woman Drama	Michael Morton	1921	4M, 3F, 1 boy	October 1923
You Never Can Tell Comedy	G.B. Shaw	1897	6M, 4F	*November 1921, October 1923
The Younger Generation Comedy	Stanley Houghton	1910	7M, 4F	*February 1923
The Young Idea Comedy	Noel Coward	1923	7M, 7F	December 1925
The Young Person in Pink Comedy	Gertrude Jennings	1920	2M, 12F	April 1923

Appendix 4

Members of the Lena Ashwell Players

Includes actors, musicians, production and administrative personnel. This list, compiled from reviews, extant programmes and promotional material, is not definitive. Spelling is inconsistent and it has not always been possible to identify the correct spelling.

* Member of wartime Concert Party
  Leading players and/or long-term members, directors or musicians are in *italics*

Rodney Ackland, Helen Adam, A. Davenport Adams, Janet Adie, Betty Aitken, Douglas Allen, Frederick Annerley, Gwen Anthony, William Armstrong, Walter Ashley, Marie Ault*,

Wilfred Babbage, *Jane Bacon*, *Margaret Badcock*, Hilda Baker, Iris Baker, Lawrence Baker, *Leo Baker*, Molly Balviard-Hewett, *Leslie J. Banks* CBE, Edith Barker-Bennet, Janet Barrow, Patricia Barry-Furniss, Reyner Barton, Lawrence Bascombe, Betty Beardmore, Reginald Beckwith, Charles Bennett, Edwin Bennett, Holland Bennett, George Berrell, Stanley Berry, Mary Best, Geoffrey Bevan, Richard Bird, George Blackwood, *Elizabeth Blake*, H.E. Blatch, *John Boddington*, Ann Bolt, *Arthur Boodle*, *Paget Bowman**, Gordon Boyd, Philip Brandon, Howard Brennan, Honor Bright, Diana Brook, Kathleen Burchell, Patricia Burke, Eileen Butler, John Butler, Roy Byford,

Kate Callcott, *Mercia Cameron**, Alex Campbell, Archibald Campbell, Collette Campbell, Norman B. Cannon, J.S. Carre, Leo G. Carroll, Drew Carron, Betty Carter, H.E. Carter, James Casey, Olive Castle, Beatrice Chapman, Edward Chapman, Theo Charlton, A.M. Chatterton, Harmon Cheshire, Dorothy Chevalier, *Esmé Church**, Carmen Clare, Katherine Clarke, Norman Clarke, Thelma Clarke, Violet Clarke, Douglas A. Clarke-Smith, Susan Claughton*, *Rosemary Clifford*, Dorothy Clifton, Winifred Clynes, *Kate Coates**, Cyril Cobb, Honor Cole, John Collins, Elizabeth Colls, *Nell Compton*, Sydney Compton, Jane Connard, *Frederick Cooper*, Violet S. Cooper, Marie Corday, Arthur Corrighan, Ernest H.G. Cox, Peter Creswell, Halstan Crimmins, Oliver Crombie, Maisie Crowley, *Sylvia Crowther-Smith*, Roland Culver, H. Culverwell, Basil Cunard, Philip Cunningham, Neil Curtis, D. Curtis-Hayward,

Julian D'Albie, Gladys Dale, A. Dallas, Bethell Datch, William Daunt, Frances Davie, Hilda Davies*, *Stringer Davis*, Charles Day, John Dean, Dolores Deane, Master Peter Dear, *Norah De Lange*, Ralph De Rohan, Thorold Dickinson, Lamont Dickson, Rosalie Dodsworth, David Donaldson, Sophie Dorival/Damoglou, W.G. Douglas-Hutchinson, Irene Dowson, Francis Drake, Joan Duan, Terence Duff, John Duke, Geoffrey Dunlop, Valentine Dunn, *Phillip Durham*,

Clara Earle, Timothy Eden, James Ellis, *Ernest Elmore*, Vera Ensor, *Peggy Evans*, *Arthur Ewart*, Reginald Eyre,

Victor Fairley, *Charles Fancourt**, *Marion Fawcett*, *Helen Ferrers*, Alexander Field*, *Weston Fields*, Donald Finlay, Gerald Fitzgerald, Stephen Fitzgerald, *Walter Fitzgerald*, M. Fleming, *Wilfred Fletcher*, Stella Florence, Frank Follows, H. Athol Forde, Barbara Forester, M. Forwood, Adela Francis, Beryl Freeman*, Ralph Freeman, *J. Leslie Frith*, *Alex Frizell*,

Marjorie Gabain, Doris Gardiner, Gale Gardner*, *W.V. Garrod*, *Harold Gibson*, Robert Gilbert, Brian Gilmour, *Robert Glennie*, *Philip Godfrey*, Edmund Gordon, Josephine Gordon, Pamela Gordon, Colin A. Gorman, Sandford Gorton, Frank Goulding, Arthur Goullet, *Patrick Gover*, Gore-Graham, Harvey Graham, J. Graham, *A. Corney Grain*, Madeleine Grant, Wilfrid Grantham, Patricia A. Graves, *Rosamund Greenwood*, Dora Gregory, Arthur Grenville, Stanley Groome,

Lilian Hallowes, E. Isaacson Hallows, Arthur Hambling, *Cicely Hamilton**, Dorothy Hamilton, George Hamilton, *Joan Handfield*, Carl Harboard, *R.C. Harcourt**, Cherry Hardy, Zerlina Harrington, Brenda Harvey*, *Daphne Heard*, *Jeanne Heaton*, *Irene Hentschel*, Grace Herringshaw, Charles Herriott, Rachel Hill, Doris Hillier, Henry Hoare, Michael Hogan, *Balliol Holloway*, George Holloway, Rodney Homer, Layton Horniman, Marjorie Horstead, George Howard, Margaret Howard, *S. Wordley Hulse*, Paget Hunter,

Averil Ingram, Frederick Irving, Felix Irwin,

Anatole James, Isabel Jeans, Ross Jefferson, Gerald Jerome, Evan John, Rita John, *Katie Johnson*, *F. Napier Jones*, Ivy Jordan,

Winifred Kaye, Edmund Kennedy, *Barbara Kent*, *Godfrey Kenton*, Jack L. Killick, *John Killner*, Geoffrey King, Malcolm Kirk, Leslie Kyle,

Arthur Lane, *Agnes Lauchlan*, *John Laurie*, Daphne Lea, Eugene Leahy, *Frederick Leister*, *Eileen/Emilie Leslie*, *Hubert Leslie**, Phil Leslie, G.P. Lester, Christine Lindsay, Edward Trevor Lloyd, *Bertha Longmore*, Lucille Lorne, Eric Lugg, *Viola Lyel*, Bettie Lynn,

Frank Macey*, Helen Mack, John MacLean, Frank Macrae, Charles Marford, *Clifford Marle*, J. David (Clifford?) Marquand, Guy Martineau, Edith Martyn, Hilda

Maude, Herbert Maule, Myra Maurel, Alex Mayhew, *Madge McIntosh*, Michael McOwen, Ernest Meade, R. Meadows White, *Frank Mellor*, Harley Merica, John Merry, John Miller, *Algernon Mills*, *John Milner*, Ernest Milton, William Monk, George Morgan, Master Eric Morris, P. Mortell, Joan Mowbray, Frederick Moyes, *Margaret Murray**,

Frank Napier, Ralph Neale, Marjorie Nevile, Leslie New, *Frank D. Newman*, Avril Nicholson, Charles Nicholson, Nora Nicholson, David Noble, Matthew Norgate, *Norman V. Norman*, Phyllis Norman-Parker*, Camelia Norreys,

Cicely Oate, Patrick L. O' Brian, Laurence Olivier, Henry Oscar*, Winifred Oughton,

Walter Page, Elsa Palmer, Victoria Parker, Kathleen Patrick, *Helen Pavey*, *Harold Payton*, H. Pegg Carr, Stanley Pelham, L. Percival-Clarke, W.A. Peterkin, *Mary Phayre*, Edmund S. Phelps, Yvette Pienne*, Mary Pitcher, *Hilda Pocock*, Ruth Povah, Harold Powis, Violet Blyth Pratt, *Nancy Price* CBE,

H. Radleigh, Gypsy Raine, Frank Randell, *Mabel Reece/Rees*, *Kynaston (Philip) Reeves*, Percy Rhodes, Fred Richards, Marie Rignold, Phyllis Rimmer, K. Ritchie-Bennie, Nancy Roberts, *Oswald D. Roberts*, Frank Robertson, Percy Robinson, Ruth Robinson, Gerald Rock, *Dan F. Roe*, Irene Rooke, Oriel Ross, Adah Rothwall, *Queenie Russell*, Tim Ryley,

Doris Sainsbury, Picot Schooling, Daphne Scorer, Lionel Scott, Idina Scott-Gatty, Margaret Scudamore, Marie Sexton, Victor Shaw, Bertram Siems, Christine Silver, Hilda Sims*, *Joan Simson**, Edward Sinclair, Kenneth Skeat, Marie Slade, *Alfred E. Sladen*, *Richard Southern*, Reginald Spink, Jean Stanley, *Kathleen Stanley*, E. Stanley-Goddard, Christopher Steele, Bernard St John,

Phyllis Thomas, Dorinda Thorn, *Diana Tilby*, Elsie Tinker, S. Travers, Paula Trevanion, Kingstone Trollope, Eileen Troughton, *Cecil Trouncer*, Ralph Truman, Richard Turner, Molly Tyson,

Norma Varden, Digby Vernon, Frederick Victor, Douglas Vigors,

Oliver Wakefield, Dundas Walker*, *Hildegard Walker*, *Olive Walter*, *Wilfrid Walter*, Peter Ward, Philip Weathers, *Alan Webb*, Violet A. Wheelhouse, Esther Whitehouse, Madge Whiteman, *Kathleen Wike*, Jackson Wilcox, Edward Wilkinson, Douglas Williams, Elizabeth Williams, Harcourt Williams, Brember Wills, *Beatrice Wilson*, Minna Woodhead*, *Clive Woods*, *H. Worrall-Thompson*, Andrew Wright, Patricia Wyndham,

Duncan Yarrow, Margherita Yorke, Robert Young, Stanley Young.

Bibliography

Manuscript material

Bristol: University of Bristol Theatre Collection: Mander and Mitchenson Collection.

Edinburgh: Scottish Records Office: Carnegie United Kingdom Trust records and minutes

London: BBC Sound Archive Collection.

London: British Library: G.B. Shaw Papers.

London: British Library: Lord Chamberlain's Play Collection.

London: British Library: Maud Arncliffe Sennett Collection, Women's Suffrage in England 1906–36, in 37 vols.

London: Imperial War Museum: Concerts at the Front Scrapbooks in 3 Vols, 1914–1919, Department of Collections Access, Lena Ashwell Collection, 09/771.

London: Public Records Office, London County Council and Greater London Council papers.

London: Royal Academy of Music Archives.

London: Victoria & Albert Museum – Theatre Museum: Lena Ashwell Scrapbooks 1891 to 1914, TM 6055, TM 6056, TM 6063, and Christopher Fry Collection.

Rochester, NY 14627: Lena Ashwell Papers, Department of Rare Books, Special Collections and Preservation, University of Rochester.

St Helens: Hereford & Worcester Record Office: Elgar Society archive.

West Kirby: Moral Re-Armament Archives.

York: Theatre Royal Archives.

Borough, district and county council minutes

Battersea: Local History Library: Public Amenities' Committee, Council of the Metropolitan Borough of Battersea.

Ealing: Local History Library: Ealing Borough Council, Baths' Committee.

Edmonton: Local History Library: Edmonton Urban District Council – Plans, Buildings, Town Hall, Baths, Stores, Housing and Town Planning Committee.

Fulham: Local History Library: Metropolitan Borough of Fulham, Establishment Committee.

Hackney: Local History Library: Hackney Borough Council, Baths' Committee.

Ilford: Local History Library: Ilford Urban District Council.

Lewes, Sussex: County Records Office: Eastbourne Pier Company Management Committee.

London: Public Record Office, London: London County Council – Theatres and Music Halls' Committee.

Shoreditch: Local History Library: Shoreditch Borough Council, Law and Establishment Committee.

Staines: Local History Library: Staines Urban District Council, Town Hall Committee.

Surrey: Local History Library: Sutton Urban District Council, General Purposes Committee.

Newspapers and magazines

London: *Anglo-Russian, Baptist Times, Bioscope, Black & White Magazine, Blackwood's Magazine, British Journal of Nursing, British Weekly, Bystander, Challenge, Christian World, Country Life, Court Circular, Daily Chronicle, Daily Express, Daily Graphic, Daily Herald, Daily Mail, Daily Mirror, Daily News & Leader, Daily Sketch, Daily Telegraph, Drama, East End News & London Shipping Chronicle, Encore, Enfield Gazette & Observer, Englishwoman, Era, Era Annual, Evening News, Express Star, Flair, Fortnightly Review, Freelance, Fulham Chronicle, Gentlewoman, Globe, Hackney & Kingsland Gazette, Hearth & Home, Home Chat, Hospital, Hour Glass, Illustrated Sporting and Dramatic News, Illustrated Sunday Herald, Inquirer, Islington Gazette, Islington & Holloway Press, Kentish Mercury, Kinematograph, Ladies' Field, Lady, Lady's Pictorial, Land and Water, Licensed Victuallers' Gazette, Lloyd's Weekly News, London Opinion, Mammon, M.A.P, Middlesex Chronicle, Morning Advertiser, Morning Leader, Morning Post, Municipal Journal, Musical News, Nation, National News, News of the Week, New Statesman, Nineteenth Century, Nineteenth Century Theatre, Observer, Onlooker, Our Home, Pall Mall Gazette, Pearson's Magazine, Penny Illustrated Paper, People, Performer, Picture Post, Pilot, Play Pictorial, Public Opinion, Queen, Red Triangle, Referee, Reynolds Newspaper, Saturday Review, Sketch, South Western Star, Sporting Times, Sportsman, Stage, Stage Year Book, Standard (Evening Standard), Star, St James's Gazette, Strand Magazine, Streatham News, Suffragette, Sun, Sunday Chronicle, Sunday Evening Telegraph, Sunday Pictorial, Sunday Times, Tatler, Theatre, Time & Tide, Times, Times Literary Supplement, Tit Bits, Today, Topical Times, Tottenham & Edmonton Weekly Herald, Tribune, Truth, Vanity Fair, Vote, Votes for Women, Weekly Dispatch, Weekly Register, West Ham, East Ham and Stratford Express, Westminster Gazette, Windsor Magazine, Woman at Home, Woman's Leader, World, World of Dress.*

British Isles outside London: *Aberdeen Daily Journal, Aldershot News, Bath & Wilts Chronicle, Birkenhead News, Birmingham Daily Mail, Birmingham Post, Blackburn Standard, Blackpool Gazette, Bolton Evening News, Brighton Argus,*

Brighton & Hove Herald, Brighton Society, Brighton Standard, Bristol Daily Mercury, Bristol Evening News, Bristol Times & Mirror, Bristol Western Press, Cork Constitution, Cork Times & Echo, Craven Herald, Dover Express, Dublin Evening Mail, Dublin Evening Telegraph, Eastbourne Chronicle, Echo & Evening Chronicle, Edinburgh Despatch, Glasgow Bulletin, Glasgow Evening Citizen, Glasgow Herald, Glasgow News, Halifax Daily Guardian, Hampshire Chronicle, Huddersfield Weekly Examiner, Ilford Recorder, Irish News, Irish Times, Jersey Evening Post, Leeds Mercury, Leicester Daily Post, Liverpool Courier, Liverpool Daily Post, Liverpool Echo, Liverpool Journal of Commerce, Llanelly Argus, Loughton Advertiser, Manchester Courier, Manchester Dispatch, Manchester Evening News, Manchester Guardian, Manchester Sunday Chronicle, Midland Daily Telegraph, Newcastle Daily Journal, Newcastle Illustrated Chronicle, Northern Star, North Mail, Nottingham Express, Nottingham Guardian, Nottingham Weekly, Rugby Advertiser, Scarborough Evening News, Scarborough Mercury, Scarborough Post & Weekly Pictorial, Scots Pictorial, Sheffield Telegraph, South Wales Daily News, Staines & Egham News, Sunderland Weekly Echo, Surrey County Herald, Sussex Daily News, Sutton Advertiser, Thistle, Western Mail, Western Morning News, West Herts & Watford Observer, West Middlesex Times (West Middlesex Times, Staines Advertiser, Egham Courier & Feltham Observer), Worcester Echo, Yorkshire Evening Press, Yorkshire Post, Yorkshire Telegraph & Star.

USA and Canada: *American, Chicago Chronicle, Chicago Daily Journal, Chicago Daily News, Chicago Post, Chicago Tribune, Cincinnati Post, Gazette Times, Hartford Chronicle, Inter Ocean, New York American, New York Daily News, New York Dramatic Mirror, New York Dramatic News, New York Evening Journal, New York Everybody's Magazine, New York Herald, New York Mail, New York Telegraph, New York Times, Pittsburgh Post, Record Herald, Toronto Daily News, Toronto World, Vancouver Daily Province, Washington Herald, Washington Times.*

Other: *Daily Malta Chronicle, Egyptian Gazette, Malaceine* (Paris).

Published plays and anthologies

Barrie, J.M., *The Plays of J.M. Barrie*, ed. A.E. Wilson (London, 1928).
Bennett, A., *Cupid and Common Sense* (London, 1912).
— *The Great Adventure* (London, 1913).
Berkeley, R., *French Leave* (London 1922).
Besier, R., *Lady Patricia* (London, 1911).
Blow, S. and Hoare, D., *Lord Richard in the Pantry* (London, 1924).
Booth, M.R. (ed.), *English Plays of the Nineteenth Century*, vol. ii: *Dramas, 1850–1900* (Oxford, 1969).
Brieux, E., *Woman on Her Own and Other Plays* (London, 1916).
Broadhurst, G., *Bought and Paid For* (London, 1912).

Byron, H.J., *Our Boys* (London, 1875).

Carr, J.C., *King Arthur* (London, 1895).

Carton, R.C., *Mr Hopkinson* (London, 1908).

— *Mr Preedy and the Countess* (New York and London, 1911).

Cerf, Bennett A. and Cartmell, Van H. (eds), *Sixteen Famous British Plays* (New York, 1941).

Chambers, C.H, *The Tyranny of Tears* (London, 1900).

— *Passers By* (London, 1913).

Chapin, Harold, *The Marriage of Columbine* (London, 1924).

Chesteron, G.K., *Magic* (London, 1913).

Coward, N., *I'll Leave it to You* (London, 1920).

— *Hay Fever* (London, 1927).

Davies, H.H., *Cousin Kate* (London, 1910).

— *The Plays of Hubert Henry Davies*, 2 vols (London, 1921).

Davis, O. and Collins, S., *9.45* (London and New York, 1927).

Deans, H., *Husbands are a Problem* (London, 1923).

De Mille, H.C., and Belasco, D., *Men and Women*, in *America's Lost Plays*, vol. xvii (Bloomington, 1965).

Denny, E., *All of a Sudden Peggy* (London, 1910).

Dickinson, T.H. (ed.), *Chief Contemporary Dramatists* (Boston, 1915).

Drinkwater, J., *Collected Plays*, vol. ii (London, 1925).

Ervine, St John, *Jane Clegg* (London, 1914).

— *The Ship* (London, 1922).

— *Mary, Mary, Quite Contrary* (London, 1923).

— *Selected Plays* (Gerrards Cross, 1988).

Esmond, H.V., *Eliza Comes to Stay* (London, n.d.).

Evans, W. and Pechey, A.T., *Tons of Money* (London, 1927).

Fagan, J.B., *The Earth* (London, 1909).

Fitzsimmons, L. and Gardner, V. (eds), *New Woman Plays* (London, 1991).

Fry, C., *The Dark is Light Enough* (London, 1954).

Galsworthy, J., *Justice and Other Plays* (Leipzig, 1912).

— *The Fugitive* (London, 1913).

— *The Silver Box* (London, 1913).

— *The Skin Game, A Bit o' Love & The Foundations* (London, 1920).

— *A Family Man* (London, 1922).

Gardner, V. (ed.), *Sketches from the Actresses' Franchise League* (Nottingham, n.d.).

Gifford, W. (ed.), *The Works of Ben Jonson*, vol. vii (London, 1875).

Glaspell, S., *Bernice* (London, 1924).

Gordon-Lennox, C., *The Marriage of Kitty* (London, 1909).

Granville-Barker, H., *Waste* (London, 1913).

Grundy, S., *Sowing the Wind* (London, 1901).

Hamilton, Cicely, *Just to Get Married* (London, 1914).

— *Diana of Dobson's* (London, 1925).

— *A Pageant of Great Women* (London, 1948).

Hamilton, Cosmo, *The Blindness of Virtue* (New York, 1913).

Hampden, J. (ed.), *Nine Modern Plays* (London, 1926).

Hankin, St John, *Three Plays with Happy Endings* (London, 1907).

Harcourt, C., *A Pair of Silk Stockings* (London, 1920).

Harwood, H.M., *The Grain of Mustard Seed* (London, 1926).

Hastings, B.M., *Advertisement* (London, 1915).

Hay, I., *Tilly of Bloomsbury* (London, 1922).

— *The Sport of Kings* (London, 1926).

— *A Safety Match* (London, 1927).

Hope, A., *The Adventures of Lady Ursula* (New York, 1910).

Hornung, E.W., and Pressbrey, E., *Raffles, The Amateur Cracksman* (London, 1975).

Houghton, S., *The Younger Generation* (London, 1910).

— *Hindle Wakes* (London, 1988).

Housman, L., and Granville-Barker, H., *Prunella. Or Love in A Dutch Garden*, in *Plays of Today*, vol. ii (London, 1925).

Hudson, E., *The Unfair Sex* (London, 1927).

Ibsen, H., *Lady Inger of Ostraat*, trans. R.F. Sharp, (London, n.d.).

— *The Master Builder and Other Plays*, trans. Una Ellis-Fermor (Harmondsworth, 1958).

— *Ghosts and Other Plays*, trans. P. Watts, (Harmondsworth, 1964).

Jeans, R., *The Kiss Cure* (London, 1925).

Jennings, G.E., *Four One-Act Plays* (London, 1914).

— *The Bathroom Door* (London, 1916).

— *The Young Person in Pink* (London, 1920).

Jerome, J.K., *The Passing of the Third Floor Back* (London, n.d.).

— *Miss Hobbs* (London, 1902).

— *Fanny and the Servant Problem* (London, 1909).

Jesse, F.T. and Harwood, H.M., *The Pelican* (London, 1926).

Jones, H.A., *The Case of Rebellious Susan* (London, 1901).

— *Mrs Dane's Defence* (London, 1908).

— *Mary Goes First* (London, 1913).

Jones, H.A. and Herman, H., *The Silver King* (New York and London, 1907).

Klein, C., *The Lion and the Mouse* (New York, 1906).

Klein, C. and Hornblow, A., *Find the Woman; or, The Third Degree* (London, 1909).

Knoblock, E., *My Lady's Dress*, in *Kismet and Other Plays*, ed. John Vere (London, 1957).

Lonsdale, F., *The Fake* (London, 1926).

— *The Last of Mrs Cheyney* (London, 1929).

Maltby, H.F., *What Might Happen* (London, 1927).

Marriott, J.W. (ed.), *One-Act Plays of Today*, second series (London, 1925).

— (ed.), *One-Act Plays of Today*, fourth series (London, 1928).

— (ed.), *Great Modern British Plays* (London, 1929).

Marshall, R., *His Excellency the Governor* (London, 1901).

Masefield, J., *Good Friday* (London, 1917).

— *Plays*, 2 vols (London, 1937).

Mason, A.E.W., *Witness for the Defence* (London, 1913).

Maugham, W.S., *Mrs Dot* (London, 1912).

— *Caesar's Wife* (London, 1922).

— *Plays*, 2 vols (London, 1931).

McEvoy, C., *The Likes of Her* ['Er] (London, 1923).

McLellan, C.M.S., *Leah Kleschna* (London, 1920).

McNeile, C. 'Sapper', and du Maurier, G., *Bulldog Drummond* (London, 1925).

Milne, A.A., *The Romantic Age* (London, n.d.).

— *Three Plays* (London, 1923).

— *Four Plays* (Harmondsworth, 1939).

Monkhouse, A., *The Education of Mr Surrage* (London, 1913).

Morley, H. (ed.), *Plays from Molière by English Dramatists* (London, 1883).

Morrell, J.M. (ed.), *Four English Comedies* (Harmondsworth, 1950).

Moses, M.J. (ed.), *Representative American Dramas, National and Local* (Boston, 1925).

Murray, D., *The Man from Toronto* (London, 1919).

Noyes, A., *Robin Hood* (London, 1926).

Pakington, M., *The Marble God and Other One-Act Plays* (Oxford, 1926).

Percy, E., *If Four Walls Told* (London, 1928).

Pertwee, R., *Postal Orders* (London, 1916).

Phillips, S., *Paolo & Francesca* (London, 1902).

Pinero, A.W., *Sweet Lavender* (London, 1891).

— *The Magistrate* (London, 1892).

— *The Weaker Sex* (Boston, MA, 1894).

— *The Gay Lord Quex* (London, 1900).

— *His House in Order* (London, 1906).

— *Trelawny of the Wells* (London, 1917).

— *The Enchanted Cottage* (London, 1921).

— *Dandy Dick* (London, 1959).

Pleydell, G., *The Ware Case* (London, 1915).

Pollock, C., *The Sign on the Door* (New York, n.d.).

Robertson, T.W., *Caste* (London, n.d.).

— *David Garrick* (London, n.d)

Robins, E., *Votes for Women* (London, 1907).

Robinson, L., *The Whiteheaded Boy*, in Robinson *et al.*, *My Best Play: An Anthology of Plays Chosen by their Own Authors* (London, 1934).

— *The Lost Leader* (Belfast, 1954).

Rowell, G. (ed.), *Nineteenth Century Plays* (London, 1968).

— (ed.), *Late Victorian Plays, 1890–1914* (London, 1972).

— (ed.), *Plays by A.W. Pinero* (Cambridge, 1986).

Shakespeare, W., *The Complete Works* (London, 1963).

Shaw, G.B., *Plays Pleasant* (Harmondsworth, 1898).

— *Widowers' Houses* (London 1906).

— *The Doctor's Dilemma and Other Plays* (London, 1911).

— *Getting Married* (London, 1913).

— *Misalliance, The Dark Lady of the Sonnets, and Fanny's First Play* (New York, 1914).

— *Press Cuttings: A Topical Sketch* (London, 1924).

— *The Shewing-up of Blanco Posnet: A Sermon in Crude Melodrama* (London, 1927).

— *Pygmalion* (Harmondsworth, 1941).

— *Three Plays for Puritans* (London 1946).

— *Man and Superman* (London, 1956).

— *Selected Short Plays* (Harmondsworth, 1987).

Shay, F. (ed.), *A Treasury of Plays for Women* (New York, 1979).

Sierra, G.M., *The Romantic Young Lady*, trans. H. and H. Granville-Barker (London, 1929).

Sowerby, G., *Rutherford and Son* (London, 1912).

Spender, D. and Hayman, C., *How the Vote Was Won and Other Suffrage Plays* (London, 1985).

Stevenson, R.L., *Works of Robert Louis Stevenson*, vol. xxiv: *Plays* (London, 1924).

Strong, A., *Three Wise Fools* (London, n.d.).

— *The Toymaker of Nuremberg* (London, 1921).

Suderman, H., *Magda*, trans. C.E.A. Winslow (Boston, MA, 1896).

Sutro, A., *John Glayde's Honour* (London, 1907).

— *The Laughing Lady* (London, 1922).

Taylor, G. (ed.), *Trilby and Other Plays* (Oxford, 1996).

Thomas, A.E., *Her Husband's Wife* (London, n.d.).

— *Come Out of the Kitchen* (New York, 1921).

Thornhill, A., *The Forgotten Factor* (Bombay, 1969).

Travers, B., *Rookery Nook*, in *Five Plays* (Harmondsworth, 1979).

Turner, J.H., *The Lilies of the Field* (London, 1925).

Vachell, H.A., *The Case of Lady Camber* (London, n.d.).

Vane, S., *Outward Bound* (London, 1924).

Veiller, B., *The Thirteenth Chair* (London, 1922).

Walter, E., *The Easiest Way* (London, 1911).

Webster, J., *Daddy Long Legs* (Sydney, 1987).

Wharton, A.P., *At the Barn* (London, 1912).

— *Nocturne* (London, 1913).

Wiers-Jenssen, H., *The Witch*, trans. J. Masefield (New York, 1917).

Wilde, O., *The Works of Oscar Wilde*, ed. G.F. Maine (London, 1963).

Worrall, L., *Ann* (London, 1913).

Worrall, L. and Terry, J.E.H., *The Man Who Stayed at Home* (London, 1916).

Wycherley, W., *The Country Wife*, in *Restoration Plays from Dryden to Farquhar* (London, 1912).
Zangwill, I., *Merely Mary Ann* (New York, 1921).

Playscript collections

See Appendix 3 for a complete list of plays performed by the Lena Ashwell Players. Many of the plays included in this appendix are available in:

Author's collection.

London: British Library: Lord Chamberlain's Play Collection.
Sydney: Mitchell Library, State Library of New South Wales: Donald MacPherson Collection of Art and Literature: Twentieth Century British Drama.
Sydney: Sydney University: Fisher Library, research section (former library of the British Drama League in New South Wales).

Other works

Adult Education Board, *British Drama* (London, 1926).
Archer, W. and Granville-Barker, H., *A National Theatre: Scheme & Estimates* (London, 1907).
Ashwell, L., 'With Captains Courageous Somewhere in France', *The Nineteenth Century*, August 1915, 344–52.
— 'Concerts for the Army: Music has a Vocation in Modern Warfare', *Red Triangle*, 15 October 1915.
— 'How Not to Write a Play', *Daily Mail*, 30 October 1915.
— 'A Year's Music at the Front', *Strand Magazine*, February 1916.
— 'The Artistic Growth of the Soldier', *Sunday Evening Telegraph*, 2 March 1919.
— 'Soldiers and the Drama', *Englishwoman*, 129 (September, 1919).
— 'The Theatre and Ruhleben', *Fortnightly Review*, 622 (October, 1919).
— *Modern Troubadours* (London, 1922).
— *Reflections from Shakespeare*, ed. R. Pocock (London, 1926).
— *The Stage* (London, 1929).
— *Myself a Player* (London, 1936).
Atkinson, D., *Suffragettes in the Purple, White & Green, London 1906–14* (London, 1992).
Auerbach, N., *Ellen Terry: Player in Her Time* (London, 1987).
Auster, A., *Actresses and Suffragists* (New York, 1984).
Austin, H.W. (Bunny), *A Mixed Double* (London, 1969).
Barnes, J.H., *Forty Years on the Stage* (London, 1914).
Beerbohm, M., *Around Theatres* (London, 1953).

Benson, C., *Mainly Players: Bensonian Memories* (London, 1926).

Bewsher, P., *The Bombing Of Bruges and Other Poems* (London, 1918).

Blow, S., *Through Stage Doors* (Edinburgh, 1958).

Board of Education, *The Teaching of English in England: Being the Report of the Departmental Committee…* (London, 1921).

Boardman, G., *American Theatre* (Oxford, 1994).

Booth, M.R. and Kaplan, J.H. (eds), *The Edwardian Theatre* (Cambridge, 1996).

Borsa, M., *The English Stage of Today*, trans. S. Brinton (London, 1908).

Bragdon, C., *Old Lamps for New* (New York, 1925).

— *Merely Players* (New York, 1929).

— *The Secret Springs* (London, 1938).

British Drama League, *The British Drama League, 1919–1959* (London, 1959).

Carr, Mrs (Alice) Comyns, *Mrs J. Comyns Carr's Reminiscences*, ed. Eve Adam (London, 1926).

Clarence, O.B., *No Complaints* (London, 1943).

Clarke, I., *Edwardian Drama* (London, 1989).

Cole, M., *Fogie: The life of Elsie Fogerty* (London, 1967).

Collins, L.J., 'The Function of Theatre: Entertainment in the First World War, 1914–1918', PhD thesis, University of London (1994).

— *Theatre at War, 1914–18* (London, 1998).

Craig, G., *Henry Irving* (New York, 1930).

Cran, G., *H. Beerbohm Tree* (London, 1907).

Crane, F., *Just Human* (London, 1920).

Crow, D., *The Edwardian Woman* (London, 1978).

Darroch, S.J., *Ottoline: The Life of Lady Ottoline Morrell* (London, 1976).

Davis, T.C., *Actresses as Working Women* (London, 1991).

Dean, B., *The Theatre at War* (London, 1956).

Dictionary of American Biography, Supplement Four, 1946–1950, eds J.A. Garraty and E.T. James (New York, 1974).

Disher, M.W., *The Last Romantic: The Authorized Biography of Sir John Martin-Harvey* (London, n.d.).

Donaldson, F., *The Actor-Managers* (London, 1970).

Dotterer, R. and Bowers, S. (eds), *Politics, Gender, and the Arts: Women, the Arts, and Society* (Cranbury, NJ, 1992).

Drama (Drama League Annual Report), 3/3 (June 1925).

Dunbar, J., *Mrs G.B.S.: A Biographical Portrait of Charlotte Shaw* (New York, 1963).

Elder, E., *Travelling Players: The Story of the Arts League of Service* (London, 1939).

Ellacott, V., *The First Hundred Years, 1894–1994*, The Theatrical Management Association (London, 1994).

Ellmann, R. (ed.), *Edwardians and Late Victorians* (New York, 1960).

Emmet, A., 'The Long Prehistory of the National Theatre', *Theatre Quarterly*, 6/21 (1976), 55–62.

Ervine, St John, *The Organised Theatre* (London, 1924).

— *The Theatre in My Time* (London, 1933).

— *Bernard Shaw: His Life, Work and Friends* (New York, 1956).

Fagan, E. (ed.), *From the Wings* (London, 1922).

Fawcett, M.G., *Women's Suffrage* (London, 1911).

Fawkes, R., *Fighting for a Laugh* (London, 1978).

Ferguson, J., *The Arts in Britain in World War 1* (London, 1980).

Field, J. and Field, M. (eds), *The Methuen Book of Theatre Verse* (London, 1991).

Forbes-Robertson, Sir J., *A Player Under Three Reigns* (Boston, 1925).

Fowell, F. and Palmer, F., *Censorship in England* (London, 1913).

Fox Smith, C., *Fighting Men* (London, 1916).

Frohman, D., *Memories of a Manager* (New York, 1911).

Fulford, R., *Votes for Women* (London, 1957).

Fuller, J.G., *Troop Morale and Popular Culture in the British and Dominion Armies, 1914–1918* (Oxford, 1990).

Gale, M.B., *West End Women: Women and the London Stage, 1918–1962* (London, 1996).

Gardner, V. and Rutherford, S., *The New Woman and her Sisters: Feminism and Theatre, 1850–1914* (Hemel Hempstead, 1992).

Giddings, R., *The War Poets* (London, 1988).

Gooddie, S., *Annie Horniman: A Pioneer in the Theatre* (London, 1990).

Gourlay, L. (ed.), *Olivier* (London, 1973).

Granville-Barker, H., *A National Theatre* (London, 1930).

Griffin, P., *Arthur Wing Pinero and Henry Arthur Jones* (London, 1991).

Guilbert, Y., *The Song of My Life; My Memories*, trans. Beatrice de Holthoir (London, 1929).

Hamilton, C., *Marriage as a Trade* (London, 1909).

— *Life Errant* (London, 1935).

Hamilton, C. and Baylis, L., *The Old Vic* (London, 1926).

Holden, A., *Olivier* (London, 1988).

Holledge, J., *Innocent Flowers: Women in the Edwardian Theatre* (London, 1981).

Holroyd, M., *Bernard Shaw*, vol. ii: *1898–1918* (London, 1991), and vol. iii: *1918–1950* (London, 1993).

Howard, P., *Frank Buchman's Secret* (London, 1961).

Hudson, L., *The Twentieth-Century Drama* (London, 1946).

Hughes, J.G., *The Greasepaint War* (London, 1976).

Hutchinson, P., *Masquerade* (London, 1936).

Hutchinson, R. and Feist, A., *Amateur Arts in the UK* (London, 1991).

Irving, L., *Henry Irving: The Actor and His World* (London, 1951).

Johnston, J., *The Lord Chamberlain's Blue Pencil* (London, 1990).

Jones, D.A., *Life and Letters of Henry Arthur Jones* (London, 1930).

Jones, H.A., *The Foundations of a National Drama* (New York, 1913, repr. 1967).

Kaplan, J.H. and Stowell, S., *Theatre & Fashion: Oscar Wilde to the Suffragettes* (Cambridge, 1994).

Kennedy, D., *Granville Barker and The Dream of Theatre* (Cambridge, 1985).

Keyserling, Count H., *The Travel Diary of a Philosopher*, trans. J. Holroyd Reece (London, 1925).

Keyssar, H. (ed.), *Feminist Theatre and Theory* (Basingstoke, 1996).

Kiernan, T., *Olivier: The Life of Laurence Olivier* (London, 1981).

Knoblock, E., *Round the Room: An Autobiography* (London, 1939).

Leask, M., 'Lena Ashwell and *The Starlight Express*', *Theatre Notebook*, 63/1 (2009), 34–54.

Loney, G., *20th Century Theatre*, 2 vols (New York, 1983).

Louise, M. (Her Highness Princess), *My Memories of Six Reigns* (London, 1956).

MacCarthy, D., *The Court Theatre 1904–1907: A Commentary and Criticism* (London, 1907).

Mackenzie, M., *Shoulder to Shoulder: A Documentary* (London, 1975).

Macqueen-Pope, W., *Carriages at Eleven* (London, 1947).

Mander, R. and Mitchenson, J., *The Theatres of London* (London, 1961).

— *The Lost Theatres of London* (London, 1968).

Mantle, B. and Sherwood, G.P., *The Best Plays of 1899–1909* (New York, 1944).

— *The Footlights Flickered* (London, 1975).

Marcosson, I.F. and Frohman, D., *Charles Frohman: Manager and Man* (New York, 1916).

Marshall, N., *The Other Theatre* (London, 1947).

Masefield, J., *Sonnets of Good Cheer* (London, 1925).

McCarthy, L., *Myself and My Friends* (New York, 1933).

McLaren, B., *Women of the War* (London, 1917).

Melville, J., *Ellen and Edy* (London, 1987).

Mills, J.P., *Knowledge is the Door* (London, 1937).

Monk, R. (ed.), *Elgar Studies* (London, 1990).

Moore, E., *Exits and Entrances* (London, 1923).

Moore, J.N., *Edward Elgar: A Creative Life* (Oxford, 1984)

— (ed.), *Edward Elgar: The Windflower Letters* (Oxford, 1989).

Morley, E.J. (ed.), *Women Workers in Seven Professions: A Survey of their Economic Conditions and Prospects*, The Studies Committee, Fabian Women's Group (London, 1914).

Mullin, D., *Victorian Actors and Actresses in Review: A Dictionary of Contemporary Views of Representative British and American Actors and Actresses, 1837–1901* (Westport, CT, 1983).

New Encyclopedia Britannica, 15th edn (Chicago, 1998).

Noble, P., *Ivor Novello: Man of the Theatre* (London, 1951).

Olivier, L., *Confessions of An Actor* (London, 1984).

The Oxford Companion to the Theatre, ed. P. Hartnoll (Oxford, 1983).

Palmer, J., *The Censor and the Theatre* (London, 1912).

Parker, J. (compiled and ed.) *Who's Who in the Theatre* (London, 1957).

Pearsall, R., *Edwardian Life and Leisure* (Melbourne, 1973).

Pearson, H., *The Last Actor-Managers* (London, 1950).

— *Beerbohm Tree: His Life and Laughter* (London, 1956).

Peters, M., *Bernard Shaw and the Actresses* (New York, 1980).

— *Mrs Pat: The Life of Mrs Patrick Campbell* (New York, 1984).

Pocock, R., *A Frontiersman* (London, 1904).

— *Chorus to Adventurers* (London, 1931).

Priestley, J.B., *Theatre Outlook* (London, 1947).

— *The Edwardians* (London, 1970).

Redcliffe-Maud, (Lord) J., *Support for the Arts in England and Wales: A Report to the Calouste Gulbenkian Foundation* (London, 1976).

Report from the Joint Select Committee of the House of Lords and the House of Commons on the Stage Plays (Censorship) Together with the Proceedings of the Committee, Minutes of Evidence, and Appendices, Bluebook 214 (London, 1909).

Richards, S., *The Rise of the English Actress* (London, 1993).

Robertson, W., *Welfare in Trust – A History of the Carnegie UK Trust, 1913–1963* (Dunfermline, 1964).

Robertson, W.G., *Time Was* (London, 1981).

Rover, C., *Women's Suffrage and Party Politics in Britain, 1866–1914* (London, 1967).

Rowell, G., *The Victorian Theatre, 1792–1914*, 2nd edn (Cambridge, 1978).

— *Theatre in the Age of Irving* (Oxford, 1981).

Sackville-West, V., *The Edwardians* (London, 1983).

Sanderson, M., *From Irving to Olivier: A Social History of the Acting Profession* (London, 1984).

Schafer, E., *Ms-Directing Shakespeare* (London, 1998).

Scott, C., *The Drama of Yesterday and Today* (London, 1899).

Shaw, G.B., *Shaw on Censorship*, The Shaw Society Shavian Tract no. 3 (London, 1955).

— *Collected Letters*, vol. ii: *1898–1910*, ed. Dan. H. Laurence (London, 1972).

Short, E., *Introducing the Theatre* (London, 1949).

— *Sixty Years of Theatre* (London, 1951).

Simmons, K.E.L., 'Elgar and the Wonderful Stranger: Music for *The Starlight Express*', in *Elgar Studies*, ed. Raymond Monk (Aldershot, 1990).

Spoto, D., *Laurence Oliver: A Biography* (London, 1991).

Stevenson, J., *British Society 1914–1945* (London, 1984).

Still, C., *Shakespeare's Mystery Play* (London, 1921).

St John, C. (ed.), *Ellen Terry and Bernard Shaw: A Correspondence* (London, 1931).

Stowell, S., *A Stage of Their Own: Feminist Playwrights of the Suffrage Era* (Manchester, 1992).

Sutro, A., *Celebrities and Simple Souls* (London, 1933).

Taylor, A.J.P., *English History, 1914–1945* (London, 1970).

Terry, E., *The Story of My Life* (London, 1908).

Thomas, G., *John Masefield* (London, n.d.).

Trewin, J.C., *The English Theatre* (London, 1948).
— *The Theatre Since 1900* (London, 1951).
— *The Edwardian Theatre* (Oxford, 1976).
Trewin, W., *All On Stage: Charles Wyndham and the Alberys* (London, 1980).
— *The Royal General Theatrical Fund* (London, 1989).
Vanbrugh, I., *To Tell My Story* (London, 1948).
Vere, J., 'The Playwright's Progress', intro. to *Kismet and Other Plays*, ed. John Vere (London, 1957).
Vernede, R.E., *War Poems and Other Verses* (London, 1917).
Vernon, F., *The Twentieth Century Theatre* (London, 1924).
Wade, A., *Memories of the London Theatre, 1900–1914*, ed. Alan Andrews (London, 1983).
Walbrook, H.M., *J.M. Barrie and the Theatre* (London, 1922).
Weintraub, S., *Bernard Shaw, 1914–1918: Journey to Heartbreak* (London, 1973).
White, E.W., *The Arts Council of Great Britain* (London, 1975).
Whitelaw, L., *The Life & Rebellious Times of Cicely Hamilton* (London, 1990).
Whitworth, G., *The Theatre of My Heart* (London, 1939).
— *The Making of a National Theatre* (London, 1951).
Who Was Who in the Theatre, 1912–1976, Gale Composite Biographical Dictionary Series, 3 (Detroit, MI, 1978).
Wilson, A.E., *Edwardian Theatre* (London, 1951).

Index

References to titles and illustrations are in *italics*.